Lofoten

Chris Craggs and Thor

Written by Chris Craggs and Thorbjørn Enevold
Editing by Alan James and Chris Craggs
Some text based on original descriptions by Ed Webster
Photography as credited - all uncredited photos by Chris Craggs
Original ROCKFAX design Mick Ryan and Alan James
Printed by Clearpoint Colourprint, Nottingham
Distributed by Cordee (www.cordee.co.uk)

All Rockfax books are printed in the UK. We only use paper made from wood fibre from
sustainable forests and produced according to ISO 14001 environmental standard.

Published by ROCKFAX Ltd. May 2008 © ROCKFAX Ltd. 2008

ISBN 978 1 873341 66 7
www.rockfax.com

This page: Colin Binks on pitch 2 of the magnificent classic of *Bare blåbær* (5-) - *page 116* - in Djupfjord.
Cover: Matt Kilner at the top of pitch 9 (the Slanting Corner) on Lofoten's
most celebrated route *Vestpillaren* (6) - *page 148* - on Presten. Photo: Ali Kennedy

Lofoten Rock

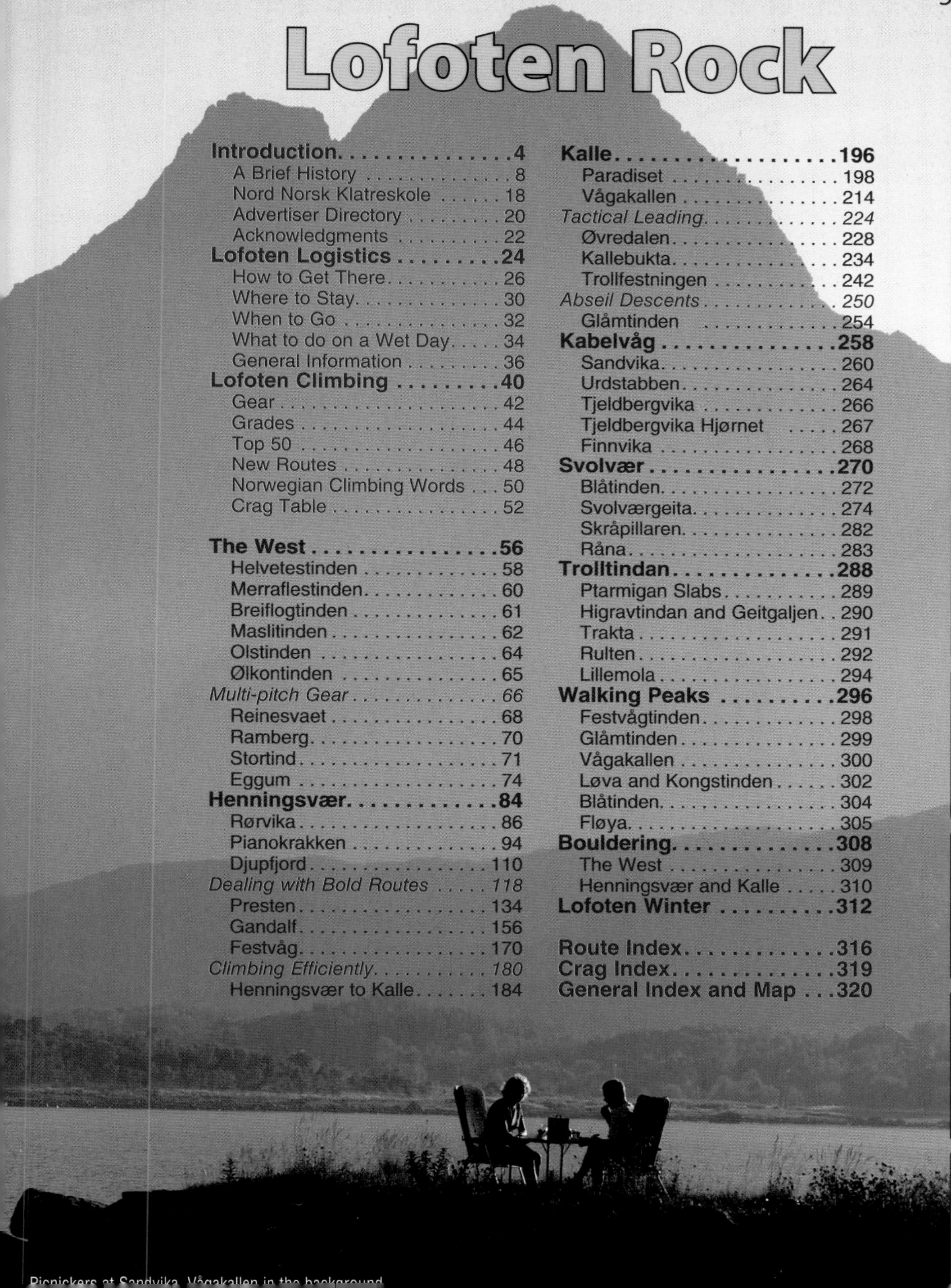

Picnickers at Sandvika, Vågakallen in the background.

The West

Henningsvåg

Kalle

Kabelvåg

Svolvær

Trolltindan

Walking Peaks

Bouldering

Henningsvær, the centre of Lofoten climbing, and its surrounding mountains.

The long rocky chain of islands that makes up Lofoten has an almost mythical status - most Norwegians feel the need to visit the place at least once in their lifetime! For climbers the reputation of Lofoten as home to some great trad climbing has been on the rise in recent years and now the venue is well and truly on the map as one of the most spectacular and beautiful destinations in Europe.

I first heard about these magical islands back in the late 1960s - the story of the first ascent of the *Svolværgeita*, and the terrifying leap between the horns, "*a thousand feet above the graveyard*", fired my youthful imagination. Other venues got in the way as the years rolled by, including the odd visit to southern Norway. Then in 2004 (35 years - some dreams take a lot of chasing) I finally hopped aboard the Skutvik-to-Svolvær ferry on a clear blue day and caught sight of 'The Goat' and the stunning range of peaks that form the backbone of the Lofoten islands.

We hope this guide will showcase this magnificent venue in all its glory, if you have been thinking about making the pilgrimage, perhaps now is the time!

Chris Craggs, April 2008

Dedication

I would like to dedicate this book to Arild Meyer, Odd-Roar Wiik and Thorbjørn Enevold. Without the efforts of these three climbers over the years there would have been precious little to write about.

Arild

Odd-Roar

Thorbjørn

Ten pitches of immaculate rock below you, one above - two climbers come to the end of a great day on the magnificent *Vestpillaren* (6) - *page 148* - on Presten.

The West

Henningsvær

Kalle

Kabelvåg

Svolvær

Trolltindan

Walking Peaks

Bouldering

Arild Meyer doing the leap between the horns of the Svolværgeita in the 1970s.
Photo: Kjell Ove Storvik

The Guidebook History

The first guidebook to climbing in Lofoten, *Rock Climbs in Lofoten, Norway*, was published in 1953. It was written by British Mountaineer Per Prag whilst he worked for the Norwegian Travel Association in London. Rather bizarrely he never actually visited Lofoten but compiled the book by corresponding with both Norwegian and UK climbers who had.

In the early 1990s, American climber Ed Webster visited Lofoten and was involved with a new route goldrush, so it was fitting that he wrote the 1994 *Climbing in the Magic Islands*, which blended Per Prag's earlier work on the extensive mountaineering routes with all the new technical rock climbs put up in the intervening 40 years.

I visited the islands for the first time in 2004, at which point Thorbjørn Enevold was already preparing a reprint of the Webster guide and wondering about a new edition. Conversations ensued and a look at the then recently-published Costa Blanca guide tipped the balance - a new volume was in the offing.

Writing the book in English was traditional, opened it to a larger audience and my only option! We decided to use Norwegian grades throughout for simplicity - conversions to UK/US/ French would only have added a layer of complexity we didn't really need, plus many of the routes had only ever been given Norwegian grades and conversions are an inexact science at the best of times. Three more great summers let me assemble the crag shots, and a selection of actions photos too (apologies for all the pictures of Colin Binks but there aren't many climbers around up there). Much email traffic flowed between the UK, Norway, France, Gran Canaria, Lofoten and an oil rig in the middle of the North Sea and slowly the book emerged.

Feedback

Many of the routes in this book are very thin on information - sometimes they consist of just a rough line on a topo and that's about it. If you climb one of these routes and wish to contribute a description, then please write one and send it to us at **info@rockfax.com**. If we get enough additional information we will assemble it into a MiniGuide for downloading. If you just have brief comments on the information - disagree with a grade, found a description a bit misleading, or just have a strong opinion on a climb - then you can use the Lofoten Route Database on the Rockfax web site - **www.rockfax.com**. This database contains a listing of every route in the book with the possibility for you to lodge comments and vote on grades and star ratings.

Lofoten is not just about long multi-pitch climbs on huge faces, there are plenty of shorter routes on accessible crags with short walk-ins. Here Colin Binks is climbing *Lost in Paradise* (5) - *page 208* - on one of the beautifully situated small crags in the Paradiset area, near Kalle.

The West

Henningsvær

Kalle

Kabelvåg

Svolvær

Trolltindan

Walking Peaks

Bouldering

The Early Days - 1880 to 1950

Climbing in Lofoten is usually recognised as starting with an ascent of Vågakallen in the summer of 1889 when Martin Ekroll and fellow fisherman Angel Johannesen rowed across the sound from the island of Skrova to reach the foot of the mountain. They climbed directly up the *Sydveggen* and reached the summit of this formerly 'unclimbable' peak. They then descended by the same way and rowed back home!

Around the turn of the century, interest in making the first ascents of Lofoten's major peaks became all the rage. Many of these explorations were undertaken by British climbers who took a fancy to exploring Lofoten, particularly the remote and wild Nordre Austvågøy where ascents included Store Trolltindan in 1890 and Higravtinden, Lofoten's highest summit, in 1901. William Cecil Slingsby, the famed British mountaineer, and his partner Prof. J. Norman Collie, brought a new level of enthusiasm to the exploration and wrote prolifically about Lofoten climbing. Slingsby in particular is considered one of the fathers of Norwegian mountaineering - he made 15 climbing trips to Norway before World War I. In 1903 and 1904, camping out for weeks at a time, and travelling by boat between the various islands (in those days the only possible means of transport) Slingsby and Collie made a host of firsts ascents. Especially noteworthy were the first ascents of both summits of 'Lofoten's finest peak', Rulten.

On 1st August 1910 technical rock climbing reached the islands with the arrival of three climbers from Oslo who were part way through an amazing pioneering trip. A few days earlier, Alf Bryn, Carl Wilhelm Rubenson and Ferdinand Schjelderup had managed the unthinkable - the dramatic first ascent of the granite spire of Stetind near Narvik - a goal which had eluded Collie and Slingsby. The irresistible challenge near Svolvær was the Svolværgeita, the twin-horned granite spire jutting out of the steep grassy hillside above the cemetery. After a long day's climbing, which involved several bind alleys, they finally stood cheering atop both horns at 11pm. Today, the *1910 Ruta* is still graded a stiff 4+ and remains an intimidating and gilt-edge classic. The famous jump between the two horns of 'The Goat' was apparently dreamt up by Arne Randers Heen, the well-known Norwegian climbing pioneer based in the Romsdal Valley. He made the notorious leap in about 1930 and had photographs taken to prove that he really did it. Various other firsts have since been performed on the horns, including a radio interview and bivouacs, as well as assorted romantic encounters.

Sjur Nesheim on the 'West Wall Finish' of *Forsida* (5+) - *page 279* - on the Svolværgeita. Photo: Kjell Ove Storvik

Arne Randers Heen, was a strong force in Lofoten climbing in the 1930s and 40s. Working as a tailor, he travelled to Lofoten during the winter cod fishing season to sell his goods. Heen traversed Småkallanryggen in 1933 with his cousin Eirik Heen, and made the first ascents of both *Nordryggen* and *Østryggen* of Vågakallen with Lars Nordby in 1939 and 1940.

In the 1940s, several local climbers came onto the scene. Magnar Pettersen, Emil Olsen, Wilhelm Höyer, Alf Krane and others started out repeating the older classics and eventually began to do new routes of their own. There most impressive first ascent was *Forsida* (5+) on the Svolværgeita, first climbed by Höyer and Krane in 1947, though the crucial *Vestveggen-avslutning* had already been done back in 1928 by Bror Bommen and Bjørn Lyche. They only used a few slings for protection during the first ascent plus they lassoed a rock spike on one of the hard sections. Magnar and his partners were men of exceptional fortitude and courage with a devout love of both their country and the mountains. Occasionally, even during the melee of World War II, they would head off from Svolvær to go climbing, rowing 20km up Raftsundet, and occasionally getting a tow from the milk boat.

The Glory Days - 1950 to 1979

Foreign climbers, and particularly British teams, continued to visit Lofoten in the 1950s as the islands offered quiet surroundings compared with the popular climbing areas of Europe. At the time, local climbers usually made it their aim to climb as many of the Lofoten peaks as possible. Arild Meyer was the driving force of the 1960s Lofoten climbing scene, he learned how to climb in 1965. As Arild explained, "*I asked one of the senior local climbers, Jens Håkon Blix Nielsen, if he could loan us three karab-iners. 'No,' he said pointedly. So Håkon*

A youthful Arild Meyer with some of his 'newfangled' climbing equipment back in the late 1960s. Photo: Kjell Ove Storvik

Størmer and I climbed the Spiralruta up the back side of the Svolværgeita anyway. We climbed up to the old ring pitons, untied the rope from around our waists, threaded the rope end through the ring, then tied back in and kept going. That Christmas, my brother Ulf sent me three brand new Cassin pitons from Norway's only climbing shop in Oslo, but I didn't get my own karabiners until the next summer."

"*There was plenty of competition in my early days of climbing,*" Arild said. "*The goal was to see who could climb the Svolværgeita the greatest number of times. One day I was standing in downtown Svolvær and looked up to see two red dots on The Goat. I immedi-ately dashed home, grabbed my climbing shoes, and ran up the hill to the notch behind The Goat. The two climbers were my regular climbing partners; they were already on the Horns. 'Throw me the rope!' I shouted. 'No!' came the reply. I had climbed The Goat 15 times at that point, and they a few times less.*"

In the 1960s a new generation began to refine the climbing styles of their predecessors and benefited from newly-introduced climbing equipment such as stronger nylon ropes, EB climbing shoes, hard steel pitons and assorted sizes and brands of nuts. Along with Arild Meyer, the local climbers of Kjell Skog, Finn Tore Bjørnstad, Brynjar Tollefsen, Ulf Prytz and Kjell Ove Storvik were active. Also Sjur and Håvard Nesheim from Tromsø were very influ-ential, and with these guys technical rock climbing really took off on Lofoten. *Pianohandler Lunds Rute* (4+) on Pianokrakken was climbed in 1971, *Gandalf* (5) and *Tromsøekspressen* (6) both on Gandalf and climbed in 1978 and 1979 respectively.

The West

Henningsvær

Kalle

Kabelvåg

Svolvær

Trolltindan

Walking Peaks

Bouldering

The Big Walls - 1978 to 1980

The 400m buttress of Presten is a tremendous sweep of rock, and proved an irresistible challenge. Its first ascent via the *Vestpillaren* by Arild Meyer and Brynjar Tollefsen in 1978 was THE modern milestone in the history of rock climbing in north Norway. "*For years I had been twisting my neck looking out of the bus window up at Presten each time I went by it,*" related Arild, "*and the route went almost exactly where I had planned.*" Amazingly, the ascent of the 11 pitch route was done on

Finn Tore Bjørnstad on first ascent of *Storpillaren* (7) - *page 221* - in 1980. Photo: Arild Meyer

their first try, in 14 hours, but ended with an all out struggle in a torrential rainstorm. Today, *Vestpillaren* is Lofoten's most famous and popular long climb.

Arild Meyer followed up his success with the 20 pitch *Storpillaren* (6+/A2 - now free at 7) on Vågakallen. For many years this was Lofoten's biggest big wall climb, which Arild, Kjell Skog and Finn Tore Bjørnstad climbed in an incredible 26 hour tour-de-force in 1980. The climb's long awaited second ascent was finally made in 1993 by Odd-Roar Wiik and Niels Poulsen, in the respectable time of 'only' 13 hours.

A constant friend in the history of Lofoten rock climbing has been the Nord Norsk Klatreskole (or NNKS as it is usually known - see page 18). Many of Lofoten's best local climbers have instructed for the school, and have also done many of the best and hardest new routes listed in this guidebook. One of the school's most talented instructors was the legendary Norwegian climber Hans Christian Doseth who taught at the NNKS during the summer of 1980. Doseth was certainly the most gifted climber of his generation, an expert on grade 7, nut-protected, overhanging finger cracks; winter new routes on Trollveggen in Romsdal; and Himalayan big walls. His finest contribution to Lofoten climbing was the first free ascent of *Vestpillaren* on Presten which he climbed with Håvard Nesheim in 1979. Sadly, Hans Christian was killed along with his partner, Finn Dæhli, in 1984 after making the remarkable first ascent of *The Norwegian Pillar*, one of the hardest big wall climbs in the world, on the Great Trango Tower in Pakistan.

Arild Meyer laybacking his way to glory on the first ascent of *Vestpillaren* (6) - *page 148* - in 1978. Photo: Brynjar Tollefsen

Lo-Profile - Arild Meyer

Arild Meyer goes through his 'Hot Henry' phase - early 1980s. Photo Kjell Ove Storvik

My climbing career began in the era of the bowline - 1965 - with a crawl up the *1910 ruta* on Svolværgeita. We were a group of beginners, isolated from the rest of the climbing world. We sometimes used the hip belay, I'm glad we didn't know then what we were up to; there were scenes of rope handling never witnessed before or since! During a climbing course in early 1970s I learned that there was much more - knifeblades, nuts, sticht plates, sticky rubber and even harnesses. *Vestpillaren* on Presten (1978) was the big break-through for me; we struggled on the upper half in wild conditions with our bongs and bugaboos, unaware of camming devices to come. Presten was a 'Big Wall' to us - today it is a nice crag, covered in climbers on a sunny day. I'm glad we had the thrill of climbing into the unknown, modern speed ascents in less than one hour were unthinkable.

Early climbing memory: I lived twelve years in Tromsø, and my first visit to Lyngen was memorable. A scrambling introduction started at five in the morning and ended late into the night, with one car towing the other the 70 km back to Tromsø. The peaks are almost twice the height of what I was used to with approaches of a 1000m, I soon learnt that apart from climbing it was important to keep the local brewery busy too.

Worst climbing memory: Traversing into the decent gully of Lyngen's highest peak - Jiekkivarri - with Sjur Nesheim after the first winter ascent of the south rib in 1985. Sjur had left his crampons in camp so we had one each. Seracs from the summit glacier were towering over our heads screaming DANGER as we skidded under them. We were so pumped with adrenaline that we kept roped up almost till we crawled back into the tent.

A good climbing memory: The snow and ice from Chamonix up to the top restaurant on Midi during two days in February in 1987. Watching Thorbjørn's face when I told him of the seam failure of our bivi tent as he rolled here and there in the "space-end" of our tiny coffin - he placed some more ice-screws soon afterwards!

As to Lofoten: Well, why do you think I have spent 47 years living here?

Festvåg

Geitvika

Low cloud behind Henningsvær.

Ed Webster making the first ascent of
Gamle rev (6) - *page 163* - in 1993.
Photo: Thorbjørn Enevold

Expansion - 1981 to 1994

One of Lofoten's most popular, long easier routes, *Bare blåbær* (5-) was first climbed by Tim Hansen, an American climber from Colorado, and Ingun Raastad in 1986. The pair also made the first free ascent of an additional major new variation up Presten called *Klokkeren* (7-) originally pioneered by Swedish climber Tommy Nilsson a couple of years earlier.

In 1991 another Colorado climber, Ed Webster, journeyed to Lofoten. He found several new climbs that summer, including two with Thorbjørn Enevold, the director of the NNKS, *Lys og skygge* (5+) on Pianokrakken (also with Trond Solberg) and *The American Tourist* (6), also with Anders Bergwall, a very poorly-protected climb up Reinesvaet, on Moskenesøya.

1992's biggest new climb was the first free ascent of the 11 pitch *Korstoget* (7) which follows cracks and a blank slab towards the left-hand side of Presten's main face. After attempts on the route by other teams in years past had failed, Bengt Flygel Nilsfors and Odd-Roar Wiik added the necessary protection bolts to the crux slab, and finally linked together the first ascent of this difficult and sustained free route - but not until their fifth try.

Several more good free routes were established at Store Festvågvegg - *Den Siste Viking* (6) by Thorbjørn Enevold and Lutta Fagerli, and *Lundeklubben* (6) plus *Skiløperen* (6-), two of Lofoten's best crack climbs, were climbed by Arild Meyer and Thorbjørn Enevold.

1993 was the busiest year to date when approximately 25 new routes were recorded, including numerous classics - *Pan* (7-) on Gullvikasvaet, by Thorbjørn Enevold and Ed Webster; *Månedans* (6+) on Lille Festvågvegg, by Ed Webster and Odd-Roar Wiik; *Solens sønner* (6) on the newly-developed Sjøsvaet, by Webster and Wiik; the sustained arch, *Odins bue* (7) on Trollfestningen by Arild Meyer and Ed Webster; and *Englevinger* (6+) a series of strenuous cracks on the Svolværgeita, by Arild Meyer, Odd-Roar Wiik and Ed Webster. American climber Tom Cosgriff also brought Norwegian grade 8 climbing to Lofoten in 1993 when, with Sjur Nesheim, he climbed *Rasmus ekspressen* (8-) a desperate overhanging crackline on Gandalf. Then Cosgriff and Nesheim added only the fourth full length new route to Presten, *Reisen* (7+) a typical Cosgriff route with several sections of hard and poorly-protected free climbing. Only three days later, Odd-Roar Wiik and Ed Webster added the fifth independent line to Presten, climbing the 12 pitch *Himmel og Helvete* (7) which featured sustained crack climbing and sections of serious face climbing.

Ed Webster's collaboration with the local climbers eventually led to the production of the well-received 1994 guidebook *Climbing in the Magic Islands* which became the Bible for any climber who was headed for Lofoten for the next 14 years.

Mi

Kalle

Kabelvåg

Svolvær

Trolltindan

Walking Peaks

Bouldering

The West

Henningsvær

Kalle

Kabelvåg

Svolvær

Trolltindan

Walking Peaks

Bouldering

Lo-Profile - Thorbjørn Enevold

Thorbjørn lives part time in Henningsvær and Spain with his wife Lutta and their three children. He is an internationally recognised mountain guide and the owner of Nord Norsk Klatreskole.

A passion for climbing and travelling sent him on 15 Himalayan trips between 1984 and 2001.

He came to Lofoten for the first time 30 years ago aiming for The Goat. At the time he did not know that this would lead to 25 seasons of guiding and climbing in Lofoten.

His favourite Lofoten climb is a new route, short or long, with a good friend, finishing just before closing time..

Photo: Jonas Dahlstrup

Colin Binks nearing the top of *Dr. Jekyll* (6) - *page 127* - in Djupfjord. One of Thorbjørn's many first ascents on Lofoten. Although fully bolted, it will keep you on your toes.

Consolidation and New Directions - 1994 to 1999

As is often the case, with the publication of Ed Webster's guidebook in 1994, the pace slackened, though even before the ink was dry Odd-Roar Wiik had put the book out of date with ascents of the devious *Edderkopen* (7-) on Gandalf and the stunning *Vårkåt* (7) the sustained crack that splits the rounded buttress Jomfrupillaren hidden just around the corner from Henningsvær. Also in 1994, Thorbjørn Enevold and Trond Solberg started development of the Upper Walls at Rørvika, though Arild Meyer had opened his account here already with *Sticky Fingers* (7-) on the Lower Tier the year before but he managed to miss the guidebook deadline with his slow reporting.

In 1996, a few bits and pieces were found when Krister Jonsson added *Nøttebus* (6+) to Pianokrakken and *Lille vikke vire* (7-) to Festvåg. 1997 was an altogether more significant year, in June Patrik Fransson and Thorbjørn Enevold added *Himmelen kan vente* (6+) up the right-hand side of Presten on the date of Thorbjørn's mother's cancer operation - the name means 'Heaven can wait'. In July, Holger Jantsch, Ole Klingemann and Eggert Keller spent some time 'out West' and added three major routes to Helvetesinden and Brieflogtinden. Then in August, Håkon Hansen made the first free ascent of the witheringly steep *Butter Arms*. Originally given 9- it was later down-graded to 8+, though it still sees few successful attempts.

Back on more traditional terrain, 1998 saw the addition of *Ørnens brødre* (7) up the attractive sheet of rock up and left for Sjøsvaet by Thorbjørn Enevold and Arild Meyer. The adding of a limited number of bolts to protect blank sections of rock allowed the linking of series of natural features. Also in 1998 the long awaited free ascent of *Odins bue* was made at the surprisingly amenable grade of 7- by, Jonas Tetlie, Andreas Haug Christiansen and Knut Storvik. The most significant ascent of the year was *Freya* (8 A3+) a huge 24 pitch outing up the left-hand side of Vågakallen's Storpillaren by Swiss couple Robert and Daniela Jasper. The ascent took five days and big wall tactics were used throughout - they even filmed the ascent. The route was only recently repeated.

1999 was another busy year, the oft-eyed walls to the right of Gandalf were finally explored by T.Sieger and F.Moell and they produced the impressive outing of *Silmarillion* (7).

Odd-Roar Wiik belaying below Lundeklubben on Festvåg with Henningsvær in the background.
Photo: Mie Kastet

Kilo

Kabelvåg

Svolvær

Trolltindan

Walking Peaks

Bouldering

Lo-Profile - Odd-Roar Wiik

Born in 1973 in Stokmarknes, I grew up in Lofoten and lived there until 1997. I now live in Åndalsnes and work as a rope access supervisor in Linjebygg Offshore AS.

I started climbing as a 12 year old with the help of an informative catalogue from Skandinavisk Høyfjellsutstyr. At the age of 14, I did the *Vestpillaren* on Presten with Leif Håvar Kvande, who spent the summer with his grandparents in the neighbourhood. He was a few years older than me and I didn't lead more than a couple of pitches. *The Direct Finish* was done on jumars,... but the ball had started rolling. Age 16, I got the chance to work as an instructor at NNKS. I stayed for four summers, and it gave me a base for my future climbing career. The fascination with big walls had been there from start, and this motivated me to do *Blåmann Nordvegg* at 17 and my first visit to Yosemite at 18. Ed Webster's visits to Lofoten fuelled my interest in new routes, and I was part of the second golden age in Lofoten. Arild and friends did a lot of stuff in the late 70s and 80s, but then it was fairly quiet until the early 90s. I was lucky it hadn't happened earlier! Since then I've done routes all over the world, both established and new ones (my favourite) - luckily there are still plenty to do in Lofoten. The recent development of sport climbing and bouldering has made Lofoten even better for my summer holidays.

Favourite memory from Lofoten: The winter ascent of *Storpillaren* in 1996 with Magnar Osnes - perfect weather and conditions and a great partner. Five of my best climbing days ever. This was my second attempt on the route in winter and it had also been tried twice by Sjur Nesheim and partners.

Worst memory from Lofoten: Descending the north face of Vågakallen with Arild in bad winter weather. We had climbed the alpine face to the right of *Storpillaren* - a great winter route with loads of moderate snow and ice and one pitch of interesting mixed climbing to the north ridge. But then the weather changed and it was snowing heavily and the spindrift avalanches were bad, with nothing much to abseil from we down-climbed most of the gully

Favourite route: *Vestpillaren*. Not an original choice but great climbing with a short approach is hard to beat. I've done the route many times, with the ascent of the Original West Pillar in 1 hour 8 minutes (or was it 18) with Patrik Fransson, as a high point.

Favourite first ascent: A tricky one but perhaps the first ascent of *Miganpillaren* with Arild. We just did it, the only downside being the fact that we hardly remember anything about it - tricky when trying to help with the new guidebook almost 15 years later. We were climbing a lot together and everything was very quick and efficient - the route was done in a long afternoon.

On Presten, Mark Garthwaite and Mick Fowler forced a series of pitches under the Great Roof then moved right to link grooves and corners to the right of *Vestpillaren's* upper half. The *Codfather* (7) was the product of their labours and much of the ascent was filmed for use in a short UK TV series about climbing destinations around the world. It showed off Lofoten climbing in an excellent light to a huge audience.

1999 was also the year when aid climbing came back into fashion for a short time, with three significant new climbs. On the left-hand side of Trollfestingen the Czech team of Dalibor Mlejnek and Roman Kaspa'rek forced the obvious line of *Cmelak* (A3) taking two days over the ascent. Later the same year the local lads of Jonas Tetlie and Knut Storvik laid seige to the very steep section of rock at the right-hand side of the Gandalf wall producing *Souhaila Andrawes* (A3). Finally to round off the year on the neglected Cornflakesveggen, Fredrik Rapp and Mathias Sjøberg added *Disco Volante* (A3).

Also in 1999 Thorbjørn Enevold and Trond Solberg added two routes to the attractive shoulder of glaciated granite that can clearly be seen from the Djupfjord causeway. The two contrasting styles - one a sport route and the other a trad offering - produced the names of *Dr. Jekyll* (6) and *Mr. Hyde* (6+).

The New Millennium - 2000 onwards

2000 was a year of crack climbs. In March the widening fissure of *Djupfjord sprickan* (7-) was tackled by Simon Thyr. Then in June, Robert Caspersen succeeded on the amazing overhanging crack of *Minnerisset* (9-) - the new 'hardest Trad route' in Lofoten. The name means *Memory Crack* and it was climbed two years to the day since his brother died in an abseiling accident on Presten.

Also significant were Knut Storvik and Jonas Tetlie's two major routes on Merraflestinded out at Reine. *Kor e hammaren Edvard* (6+ A1) and *Borr i Bekkmørtna* (7- A0). Almost 500m high and on superb looking rock they are clear pointers as to what still remains to be done. In 2003 the desperate thin crack of *Huggormen* on Pianokrakken was free climbed at 8- by Petter Restorp and Hanna Mellin and later the same year *Ormen Lange* was also free climbed on Cornflakesveggen at 7+ by Gustaf Leionhuvud and Joachim Vagner. Doubtless the most significant ascent of the year was the five day push on the enormous line of *Storm Pillar* (7+ A3) by Mike and Louise Turner in September. Caught in a two day storm close to the summit, they sat it out before retreating in good order. They were obviously well prepared for all that Lofoten could throw at them.

Since then there has been less of signifi- cance on the trad climbing front, new routes have often been on previously over- looked bits of rock such as the impressive *Jammen, Jammen* (6+) by Øyvind Utley and Andreas Capjon up in the gully behind Store Festvåg and the pair of wild outings of *Daei!* (8- A2) and *Pels of the Fisk* (8) by Robin Thomas and friends high on the edge of the Silmarillion cliff.

With the sport climbing revolution that had been going on across Europe, the younger locals looked for somewhere to develop their own skills. Worried about getting their wrists slapped if they started drilling within earshot of Henningsvær, they hunted out a few bits of rock around Kabelvåg.

Andreas Haug Christiansen showing he doesn't just do hard sport climbing.

Knut Storvik working out on *Aetat* (9-) - page 79 - Eggum

The West

Henningsvær

Kalle

Kabelvåg

Svolvær

Trolltindan

Erik Grunnesjö and Jonas Dahlstrup taking a breather on Storhylla part way through their speed ascent of *Storpillaren* (7) - *page 221* - in 2005. Note: the shot is a montage - they weren't carrying a tripod! Photo(s): each other!

At Sandvika and Urstabben, Knut Storvik and Andreas Haug Christiansen bolted up a clutch of routes back in 2002 including *Revenge of the Niña* (8), *Snykov* (8-), *Ostepopnæva* (8) and *Herman Kraghs vei* (7+).

However the most significantly developments took place on the leaning walls out at Eggum on the north coast. The crag was discovered by Andreas Christiansen in 2002. Together with Knut Storvik he bolted what would become *Gullfaks* in early 2003. However most of the development took place in the summer of 2005 when Knut, along with Andreas, took the place by storm. Such classics as *Gullfaks* (7+/8-), *Full belastning* (8+), *Joker nord* (9-/9) and *Aetat* (9-) will ensure the crag stays very much on the circuit, and there are still some gaps that need plugging.

Also in 2005, and in complete contrast, visiting Americans Beth Rodden, Adam Stack and Tommy Caldwell accompanied by Odd-Roar Wiik, hiked into remote Helvestinden and added two fine free routes to the bit of rock known as the French Pillar, *The Next Best Thing* (6+) and *Norwegian Sheep Ranch* (7). This buttress had originally been climbed back in 1985 by French couple Eric and Anne Lapied. The ascent took almost a week and apparently they filmed the whole thing but details of the precise line became lost.

Another notable ascent in 2005, mirroring similar developments in other parts of the world, was the remarkable 12 hour 'car to car' ascent of *Storpillaren* (7) by Erik Grunnesjö and Jonas Dahlstrup.

So what of the future? There is no doubt the scope for climbing of all styles on Lofoten remains limitless - from bouldering to big walls, from trad to sport and not forgetting winter mountaineering too - there is the feeling that Lofoten's star is very much on the rise. The remoteness of the place adds to the cachet of a visit, though more and more climbers are making the effort to get here and most are well rewarded. So maybe now is the time to experience Presten's peerless granite, the cosy warmth of the Climbing Cafe after a hard day on the rock, the haunting northern twilight and the 'interesting' fishy odour that pervades the islands. One thing for sure, the place will leave its mark on you.

In the early 1970s serious accidents in the mountains of Lofoten had to led to more rescue operations being carried out in difficult terrain. Nils Faarlund, among others, held the first climbing course at Kalle in 1972. The aim of the course was to teach Red Cross members to handle climbing equipment and the terrain. As a result Svolvær Alpine Rescue Group was founded, the first in the whole of Norway.

Arild Meyer, already a dedicated climber, was also one of the instructors. "*We can do this ourselves,*" he thought and the second oldest climbing school in Norway - the Nord Norsk Klatreskole (NNKS) - was founded the following year.

The courses were a great success through the 1970s, with many held through the summer. They were led by the best climbers in the north at that time - Arild Meyer, Finn Tore Bjørnstad, Sjur and Håvard Nesheim and Kjell Skog, to name a few. The instructors were 'hard men', so of course the clients had to be too, ... and from day one! All the courses finished with a climb up *Nordryggen* (4+) on Vågakallen, where they slept under the sky through whatever was left of the night.

Thorbjørn Enevold recalls his first meeting with the NNKS. Seeing an ad in the old Skandinavisk Høyfjellsutstyr catalogue for courses, he joined a weekend winter course in remote Lyngen. "*We started climbing up a snow gully at six o'clock on Friday afternoon. After 1300m though deep snow, we finally reached 'Den himmelske freds plass'. It was time to dig snow caves. At 3am we finally crawled into the sleeping bags. Next day we had*

Rocking the nights away in the Nord Norske Klatreskole Cafe.
Photo: Thorbjørn Enevold

a quick lesson in how to use crampons and ice axes before we went on to climb Store Lakselvtind - eighteen people on one rope. The weekend's lessons were hard, but I never looked back". In Lyngen that weekend Thorbjørn had no idea that he would be running his own climbing courses on Kalle just four years later and eventually that he would take over of the climbing school.

The school was run more or less the same way for several years, but times and climbers change, and the climbing school with them. Novices are no longer expected to start with a 36 hour climb on Rulten anymore.

Then Thorbjørn met Lutta and things started to happen. It wasn't long before they moved out of the rented rorbu at Kalle and into new sea houses in Henningsvær. New to them that is, the houses were already a hundred years old, and had not been used for the last fifty! But what are good friends with carpentery skills really for?

Looking back 18 years on Thorbjørn reminisces, "*Following climbing experiences in the UK and Nepal we were quite determined about how the cafe should look - a mixture of an English climbing pub, a Sherpa tea-house, with the stove in the middle, and a typical Lofoten rorbu. We have no idea how many climbers, bikers, kayak paddlers or 'normal' tourists have had their well-deserved pint, or dried their wet socks on the stove. Or maybe met the love of their life in a weekend dance - there have been a few of those too. One thing we do know, you are all welcome here in the years to come.*"

The West   Henningsvær   Kalle   Kabelvåg   Svolvær   Trolltindan   Walking Peaks   Bouldering

The Nord Norske Klatreskole at its second home, in Henningsvær.

The West

Henningsvær

Kalle

Kabelvåg

Svolvær

Trolltindan

Walking Peaks

Bouldering

Guiding Services

Nord Norsk Klatreskole - Inside front cover
Henningsvær, Lofoten. Tel: +47 90 57 42 08
www.nordnorskklatreskole.no

Gear

Atello - Page 49
Hokksund, Norway. Tel: +47 32 25 21 00
www.atello.no

Beal Norway (Varri) - Page 137
Oslo, Norway. Tel: +47 22 71 92 00
www.varri.no

Berghaus - Inside back cover
Extreme Centre, Sunderland.
Tel: 0191 516 5700
www.berghaus.com

Black Diamond - Outside back cover
Reinach, Switzerland. Tel: +41 61 564 3333
www.blackdiamondequipment.com

Boreal - Page 47
www.e-boreal.com

Haddock - Page 43
Henningsvær. Tel: +47 90 57 42 08
www.haddock.no

Petzl Norway (Varri) - Pages 2 and 23
Oslo, Norway. Tel: +47 22 71 92 00
www.varri.no

Climbing Wall

Awesome Walls - Page 45
The Engine House, Stockport, SK6 2BP.
Tel: 0161 494 9949
www.awesomewalls.co.uk

Shops

Joker - Page 37
The Square, Henningsvær.

Mix - Page 37
Henningsvær.

Accommodation

Anker Brygge - Page 29
Svolvær, Lofoten. Tel: +47 76 06 64 80
www.anker-brygge.no

Henningsvær Booking - Page 31
Tel: +47 95 90 03 91
www.henningsvarbooking.no

Sandvika Camping - Page 260
Kabelvåg, Lofoten. Tel: +47 76 07 81 45
www.sandvika-camping.no

Attractions

Lofoten Opplevelser AS - Opposite
Henningsvær, Lofoten. Tel: +47 76 07 50 01
www.lofoten-opplevelser.no

Galleri Lofotens Hus - Page 31
Henningsvær, Lofoten. Tel: +47 76 07 15 73
www.galleri-lofoten.no

Ocean Sounds - Page 23
Henningsvær, Lofoten. Tel: +47 76 07 18 28
www.ocean-sounds.com

Information

Destination Lofoten - Page 27
Svolvær, Lofoten. Tel: +47 76 06 98 00
www.lofoten.info

The island of Lillemola. The pillar of *Lofoten Panorama* (6+) - *page 294* - is visible just right of centre.

Welcome to beautiful Lofoten

snorkelling trips, sea eagle safari, midnightsun safari, lofoten fishery, Trollfjord
charter trips, conferences, killer whales, northern lights

Ph. (+47) 76 07 50 01

www.lofoten-opplevelser.no

Thanks have to go out to the hard-core of Lofoten climbers without whose vision and abilities there would be far fewer routes here to go at. Pre-eminent amongst these are the trio to the right sharing a beer and trying to sort out the scribblings of all the new routes they had put up in the 12 years since they contributed to Ed Webster's superb guide to the islands, published back in 1994. They are, seated left, Thorbjørn Enevold (Chief Mover and Shaker), with the glasses, Arild Meyer (Grand Master) and right Odd-Roar Wiik (Young Pretender). Also looking on (head down) is Erik Grunnesjö a regular visitor, representing all the Swedish climbers who

have been using Lofoten as their local crag for many years. Thorbjørn deserves a special thanks; he has helped with this project since its inception with his encyclopedic knowledge of Lofoten climbing, translating descriptions, manned the telephone hotline, chased people up for photographs, profiles and first ascent details.

Thanks to all the photographers who have contributed: Ali Kennedy, Kjell Ove Storvik, Eivind Storvik, Arild Meyer, Brynjar Tollefsen, Thorbjørn Enevold, Jonas Dahlstrup, Erik Grunnesjö, Mia Kastet, Odd-Roar Wiik, Ed Webster, Tom Atle-Bordevik, Jamie Moss, Nick Ashton, Sherri Davy, Tim Wilkinson, Nigel Redshaw, Twid Turner, Louise Turner, Lex Pearce, Johanna Wernqvist, Colin Binks, Roger Brown, Mathias Stromquist, Heike I Vester and Andy Hyslop. Also, I am grateful to Graham Hoey and Jonathan Lagoe for their proof reading.

Thanks must also go to Colin Binks who has trekked the thousand odd miles up to Lofoten three years on the trot (and said on his first arrival, "*it felt like coming home*").

As ever there are two other people without whom the guide simply wouldn't have happened. Firstly, Sherri Davy, who knew I had long wanted to visit Lofoten, and so insisted that we made the long drive up there in 2004 and who was so impressed with the place doesn't want to go anywhere else now! And secondly, Alan James, whose magic touch has breathed colour and life into my raw information - cheers to you both.

Chris Craggs, April 2008

First and foremost to Lutta, the love of my life, who is always positive whatever crazy ideas I come up with, and my kids who have always been patient whenever I have had to rush off to answer another email from 'the man'.

To Chris and Sherri, from that first day in the Climbing School we have come a long way together - thanks for all the cow pie too!

To my old friend Arild for taking this project seriously, he started reading AND answering my never-ending stream of emails - it would have been really hard without you. Thanks also to Odd-Roar, always positive on and off the rock and I am glad you found your old diary with details of *Four Pitch Route* in.

Then there is Ed, who blazed the trail we still follow, and Stein, I just hope you can live with the Paradiset chapter!

To Andreas, Knut, Håkon, Kjell Ove, Mathias, Hanna, Erik, Jonas and Sveinung - hope you like the finished product, thanks for all your help.

And last but not least Johan, who put me straight whenever I started to think climbing was all about work - you were right, it wasn't - and thanks for the great days!

Thorbjørn Enevold, April 2008

The West
Henningsvær
Kalle
Kabelvåg
Svolvær
Trolltindan
Walking Peaks
Bouldering

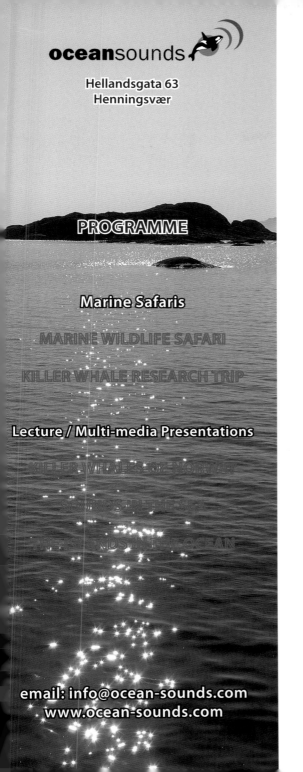

oceansounds

Hellandsgata 63
Henningsvær

PROGRAMME

Marine Safaris

MARINE WILDLIFE SAFARI

KILLER WHALE RESEARCH TRIP

Lecture / Multi-media Presentations

KILLER WHALES OF NORWAY

SECRETS OF THE SEA

LIFE SOUNDS IN THE OCEAN

email: info@ocean-sounds.com
www.ocean-sounds.com

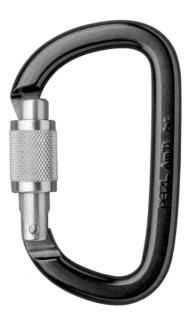

The West

Henningsvær

Kalle

Kabelvåg

Svolvær

Trolltindan

Walking Peaks

Bouldering

Henningsvær in evening light with the distant backdrop of the Austvågøya mountains on the left and Stormolla on the right.

Lofoten Logistics

The West

Henningsvær

Kalle

Kabelvåg

Svolvær

Trolltindan

Walking Peaks

Bouldering

It is a fact that Lofoten is quite a long way from anywhere. On my first visit I was shocked to realise that from Bergen to Skutvik is almost 1600km of which a grand total of only 15km are on a motorway. Factoring in the low speed limits and often rather tortuous roads, means that the driving time for that journey is about 24 hours - though it took us five days that first time! On subsequent trips we have planned more carefully and also tried some of the different options.

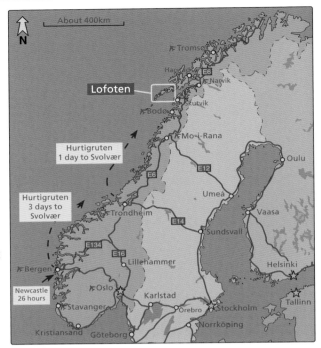

Flying

Flying is far and away the quickest method to get to Lofoten, and often it is also the cheapest. First fly to Oslo, Bergen or Trondheim then take an internal flight to Bodø, before a short hop in a tiny turbo-prop plane over to Leknes, or Svolvær. SAS or Norwegian Air Shuttle fly to Norway then it is Widerøe up-country. There is a 15kg luggage limit on the Norwegian Air Shuttle and this applies on the final short hop anyway, although you can use a ferry for this if you have a lot of gear. The Hurtigbåt - a rapid seacat for foot passengers only - does the Bodø to Svolvær crossing in 2.5 hours. With the opening of the LoFast road, Lofoten was finally connected to the mainland and it is possible that the Evenes (Harstad/Narvik) airport will become a good option for getting to the islands. Currently Norwegian Air Shuttle and Scandinavian Airlines fly there from Oslo. There is an express bus connecting the airport with Lofoten – check Destination Lofoten (opposite) for current prices.
Web sites - www.flysas.com, www.norwegian.no, www.cheapflights.co.uk, www.wideroe.no, plus plenty more.

Train

It is possible to get the train from Oslo to Bodø. This overnight journey takes 17 hours and currently cost about 1200NOK each way. Concessionary fares are available.

Car

If you take a ferry, or drive from Sweden or further afield, then you need to be prepared to spend a lot of time driving north on the E6. Despite this being a quiet road progress is not as fast as you might expect. The speed limit is 80km/h for much of the journey and sneaky speed traps are more common than you might expect, even in the middle of nowhere. The on-the-spot fines are hefty enough to put a real dent in your holiday fund. Although travelling by car is slow and expensive on the ferries, there are plenty of pluses - you can carry lots of gear and plenty of food, it makes getting round the islands easy, and you have somewhere dry to sit when it rains.

The West
Henningsvær
Kalle
Kabelvåg
Svolvær
Trolltindan
Walking Peaks
Bouldering

Deep, placid fjords, jagged, rocky peaks – a historic and geologic masterpiece."

National Geographic 09/07

The West

Henningsvær

Kalle

Kabelvåg

Svolvær

Trolltindan

Walking Peaks

Bouldering

The Hurtigruten Nordkapp heading towards Svolvær - an expensive but classy way to travel. The distant saw-back of Trolltind beckons.

Ferry from the UK

Newcastle to Bergen - From the UK there are two sailings a week with DFDS in the high season (Tuesday/Friday - Monday/Thursday alternate weeks). The crossing takes about 26 hours. Check out **www.dfds.co.uk** for more details and to book. Prices vary with the season, but the cheapest way across in the peak season costs about £450 each way for a car and cabin - travelling in a group of four cuts the cost markedly.

Bergen to Lofoten - From Bergen, drive through the superbly spectacular Fjordland to the E6 and then head north. The shortest ferry crossing to the islands is Skutvik to Svolvær, it takes about two hours and booking is not normally needed. Bodø to Moskenes involves less driving but a longer crossing (three and a half hours) and, in the high season, may need pre-booking and you can't book it the day before crossing.

If money is less of an object, using the magnificently plush *Hurtigruten* (fast route) boat is a spectacular way of getting northwards. There is a daily sailing from Bergen, which takes about three days to get to Svolvær, and they can carry about 40 cars. As to the cost - it is in the 'if you need to ask, you can't afford it' category. The price of meals and beer on board is highly amusing. Driving to Trondheim first and catching the Hurtigruten there speeds things up and cuts the cost as it only involves a single night on board!

The Bodø docking at Moskenes.

The West

Henningsvær

Kalle

Kabelvåg

Svolvær

Trolltindan

Walking Peaks

Bouldering

Lofoten has long been a popular tourist destination and as such is well organised with the
full gamut from swanky hotels to free swamp
camping. Since the arrival of the NNKS at
Henningsvær, the place has been the centre
of Lofoten climbing, and most folks try to stay
somewhere close. The village has a couple of
hotels, the climbing school does nice rooms,
and there are a couple of Rorbuer (fishermens'
huts) - see the sign-board in the main car park.
Web sites - www.henningsvarbooking.no,
www.lofoten.info

A typical Norwegian hut on Moskenesøya

Camping
There are three official campgrounds within easy striking distance (a 10 minute drive) of the
main climbing area. There is Sandvika (see page 260) about halfway between Henningsvær and
Svolvær, and the nearby Ørsvågvær. In the opposite direction there is the Lyngvær Bobilcamp
(camper waggons) ground which also accepts tents. All these are pleasant spots, reasonably well
equipped - small basic kitchen area but little in the way of crockery or utensils, pleasant lounges
plus showers and all pretty cheap by UK standards. A great feature of all Norwegian campgrounds,
are the small camping cabins that every site has. These can be fairly basic - a couple of bunk
beds, a fridge and a cooking ring, all the way up to wooden palaces, with several rooms, shower,
toilet, TV and fridge. Again, the prices can be very reasonable especially if there are four of you
sharing - prices start at about 200NOK. Substantial discounts can be negotiated if you are staying
for several days.
Web sites - www.sandvika-camping.no, eng.lofoten-bobilcamping.no, www.lofoten.info

Free Camping
The area opposite Gandalf (see map on page 85) is the most popular camping spot in the area.
Under the right conditions it is a magnificent place to be - close to the cliffs (no car required),
fantastic views, within walking distance of Henningsvær and with good bouldering nearby. There is
water from the tap set into the Henningsvær water pipe and, of course, it is free - always a consid-
eration for climbers. On the down side, there is nothing to do when the weather is poor and the
headland is exposed to the worst of the weather - bring a decent tent. Also, the area is starting to
suffer a little from overuse. PLEASE keep it clean. Using the sea for a toilet since burying waste is
not a option - the soil is too thin and the area is just too popular.
If you have a car, consider stopping at the free site at Kalle, at least it has a toilet - see page 234.
There are several other excellent and discrete spots nearby, though rather than publicise these,
we will let the adventurer seek them out.

Approaching showers seen from the camping area below Gandalf.

Accommodation in Henningsvær and throughout Lofoten

Rooms, Rorbu, Houses, Cabins
email: hbookings@yahoo.no
Tel: 00 47 95900391

www.henningsvarbooking.no

OPPLEVELSESSENTRET GALLERI LOFOTENS HUS HENNINGSVÆR

Ved opplevelsessentret får du oppleve Norges største private kunstsamling med nordnorske malerier fra forrige århundreskiftet.

I tillegg en stor utstilling av den landskjente og nålevende kunstneren Karl Erik Harr. I tredje etasje er det en stor utstilling av en av Norges mest kjente fotograf A. B. Wilse. Frank A. Jenssens multimediashow får du også oppleve her. Multimediashowet skildrer lofotfisket og lofotnaturen gjennom alle årstidene

Galleriet har åpent alle dager fra 25. Mai til 01. September fra kl.09.00 til kl.19.00

Galleriet åpner også på bestilling hele året

Tel.76 07 15 73
mob.vakt tel.915 95 083
web - www.galleri-lofoten.no
email - post@galleri-lofoten.no

The West

Henningsvær

Kalle

Kabelvåg

Svolvær

Trolltindan

Walking Peaks

Bouldering

When to Go

Situated north of the Arctic Circle, Lofoten has two main seasons - High Summer and Deep Winter (which the locals call simply 'mørketid' - *dark times*) with two periods of rapid transition dividing these contrasting times.

Midnight sun - approximately 27 May to 17 July.
Polar night - approximately 6 December to 6 January.

For rock climbing any time between late May (there will still be plenty of snow around) and August is fine, though by the middle of August many of the Norwegian visitors have gone home and the ferries move over to the winter timetable. As with almost anywhere in Europe, the weather can be a bit of a lottery though most years an Arctic high pressure system exists for weeks at a time and brings prolonged blue skies and settled weather - the tricky part is predicting just when! The averages in the table opposite indicate that May, June and July are the best months for both temperature and least rainfall, but averages are little consolation if you are sat there in the rain waiting for a clear spell.

As a general rule on Lofoten, winds from the north and the east bring settled weather, those from the south and west bring anything from showers to full-on Atlantic storms. A change in the wind direction can be a useful warning.

Temperature °C	Jan	Feb	Mar	Apr	May	Jun	Jul	Aug	Sep	Oct	Nov	Dec
Average monthly high	-1	-1	0	3	7	12	14	14	10	6	3	1
Average monthly low	-3	-3	-2	1	4	8	11	11	7	3	1	-2

Source: www.wunderground.com

Rainfall Days	Jan	Feb	Mar	Apr	May	Jun	Jul	Aug	Sep	Oct	Nov	Dec
Average days > 0.1mm	22	20	18	17	16	14	15	17	20	22	20	22
Average days > 3mm	8	7	6	6	5	4	6	7	8	11	9	10
Average days > 10mm	2	1	1	1	1	1	1	2	2	4	2	2

Source: Meteorologisk institutt - retro.met.no

These average rainfall figures are for Skrøva, which is an island to the south of Svolvær. The precipitation for Svolvær and Henningsvær shows a similar annual total however the mountains of Vestvågøya, and Trolltinden in particular, receive more rain.

Heavy weather on the way!

If you are unlucky enough to have a spell of bad weather, the big question is: what do you do apart from the obvious activity of laying in the tent reading a big fat book, or sitting in the NNKS Cafe and spinning a coffee out for several hours? There is a cinema in Svolvær and a sports centre with a swimming pool in Leknes (50 minutes drive west). Other than that, here are a few ideas for starters.

Colin trying to look happy in the rain.

General Interest

Magic Ice - Ice sculptures/sound and light show (warm clothes provided). Situated by the Hurtigruten quay in Svolvær. Open 12:00-22:00. Entry NOK95.

Lofoten Opplevelser - (*Lofoten Adventures*) Sea safaris from Henningsvær. Call in and book the day before (see page 21). Open 9:00-17:00 Prices from NOK370-600 for trip.

Lofotakvariet - Aquarium and cafe in Storvågen near Kabelvåg. Life in the sea, otter and seal pools, plus cafe. Open 10:00-19:00. Entry NOK80,

Ocean Sounds - Audio visual shows and art exhibitions about life in the ocean (trips when the weather is good) in Henningsvær. Open 10:00-18:00. Entry from NOK50 for shore-based activites and up to NOK700 for a four hour trip (see page 23).

Arts and Crafts

Galleri Lofotens hus - Art galley of Norwegian artists and a multi-media show in Henningsvær (see page 31). Open 9:00-19:00. NOK75.

Galleri Espolin - Art gallery, exhibition, videos and a shop by the E10 between Henningsvær and Kablevåg. Open 10:00-19:00. NOK60.

Engelskmannsbrygga - Pottery, glass workings and photography in the square in Henningsvær. Open 10:00-20:00. Free entry.

Shopping Trips

Before the two elegant bridges were built connecting Henningsvær to the 'mainland' a ferry ran between the central square and the concrete pier that can still be seen at Festvåg. It was said that the children of the town learnt to row before they could walk, such was their reliance on boats.

On occasions the ladies of Henningsvær would commandeer the ferry and take it to Kablevåg to do their shopping, much more efficient than driving there! If visitors wanted to reach the island they would just have to wait!

Museums

Lofotr Viking Museum - Viking museum by the E10, 50km west of Henningsvaer, just past the Eggum turn-off. Open 10:00-19:00. NOK100.

Lofoten Krigsminnemuseum - War memorial museum in Svolvær. Open 10:00-16:00. NOK50.

Museum Nord / Lofotmuseet - General north Norway and Lofoten museum in Storvågan near Kabelvåg. Open 9:00-15:00. NOK60.

.... and for Free ....

Go fishing.
Go for a walk up an easy peak (see page 296) or along the coast.
Search for puffins ......

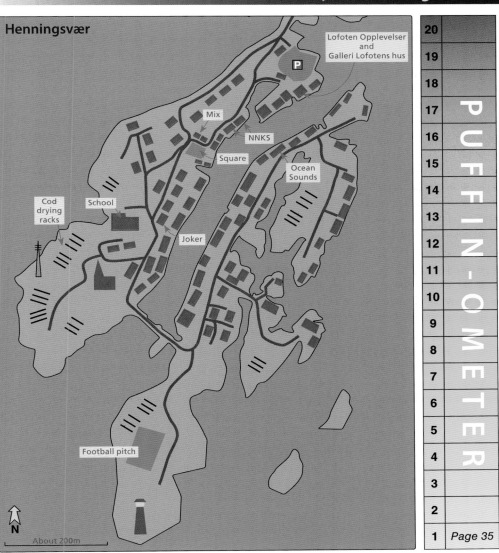

Henningsvær

Lofoten Opplevelser and Galleri Lofotens hus

Mix

NNKS

Square

Ocean Sounds

Cod drying racks

School

Joker

Football pitch

N

About 200m

20
19
18
17
16
15
14
13
12
11
10
9
8
7
6
5
4
3
2
1 | Page 35

PUFFIN-OMETER

The West
Henningsvær
Kalle
Kabelvåg
Svolvær
Trolltindan
Walking Peaks
Bouldering

Find the puffins!

Puffins, puffins, puffins, but where are they all? Well, there are 20 to find hidden away in some secret locations across the island - cracks, beaches and just standing around minding their own business. Some are easy to spot, some hard. To help you get going we have filled in the *puffin-ometer* with the first puffin to the left. See if you can find all his brothers, but you may need a magnifying glass!

1 to 10 - You must have had some great weather
10 to 15 - Good going but you still have a lot of searching to do.
16 to 19 - Excellent, now where is that last one?
20 - The first 10 correct answers to **info@rockfax.com** will get a prize!

Mountain Rescue

In the event of an accident requiring the assistance of Mountain Rescue:

Dial 112 - this connects with the main police command centre.
Ensure you have details of your location and what the incident involves.
This number works on any mobile on a Norwegian network.

Tourist Information

The Destination Lofoten website - www.lofoten.info - (see advert on page 27) offers a huge amount of information on getting to Lofoten, where to stay once you are there and things to do and see in the area. There is also a downloadable PDF available from the web site called *Lofoten Info-Guide* which is well worth a look.

There are Tourist Information Offices in Ramberg and Moskenes but the most useful one is in Svolvær town square - Tel: (+47) 76 06 98 07

Shopping

All the general supplies that you need to survive when camping are available in Henningsvær (see the adverts opposite). For a wider range of goods or to do a major stock-up, there are larger supermarkets in Svolvær including a Co-op and Rimi. Generally prices are higher than in the UK, though the quality of fruit, veg, bread and general produce is normally excellent. Quality meat (and surprisingly fish) is quite hard to come by though the choice of polsen (sausages!) is remarkable. Bringing a fishing rod can be worth the effort - cod and coley can be caught at many places, though I am not telling you our favourites! Later in the year berries, especially bilberries, can be collected to add a little something to the morning muesli. There is an Øl *(beer)* shop in Henningsvær (next door to the Mix), for anything stronger a trip will have to be made to the government run Vinmonopolet 'alcohol outlet' in Svolvær. Beer prices are not too different to UK pub prices though wine and spirits are up to three times as much, and cash is the only acceptable currency.

Tough Puffins

Arild and Thorbjørn made the first ascent of the classic *Lundeklubben* in 1992. About the same time NNKS ordered 5,000 wooden puffins (Lundefugler) from Indonesia to sell in the shop in Henningsvær. They took one with them and jammed it in one of the cracks in the route. It ended up causing a lot of trouble in an alpine rescue training session. Just finishing the training, and in pouring rain, the last man threw down the 200m static rope they had been using, but it never arrived at the cliff base.

"*It's jammed around the neck of that damn bird*", he shouted. It took six men heaving on each end of the rope before there was a mighty crack and the head flew up into the air!

There is still a puffin up there today if you look carefully, but it is a different one.

Svolvær with Fløya and the
Svolværgeita behind.

MIX in the square, Henningsvær.
Basic groceries, Cafe, snacks,
papers and magazines, fancy goods, DVD rental

**For all your grocery needs
in Henningsvær**

The West

Henningsvær

Kalle

Kabelvåg

Svolvær

Trolltindan

Walking Peaks

Bouldering

Money

The currency is the Norwegian Krone. In 2008 this converts at around 8NOK = €1 and 10NOK = £1. Credit Cards are accepted pretty much everywhere for all kinds of payments, though banks and cash points are few and far between. The nearest cash point to Henningsvær is in Kablevåg, for a bank it is necessary to trail the few extra km to Svolvær.

Mobile Phones

Mobile phone coverage is generally good throughout Lofoten (via Telenor), though it may be a bit restricted in the deeper valleys (worth checking before an emergency maybe) but you can certainly get a good signal on top of Vågakallen!

Insurance/Rescue/Medical Advice

Norway has the highest standard of living in the world and a large % of their GDP is spent on healthcare - as you would expect the system is superb. EU residents have a right to emergency healthcare, make sure you bring your documentation to ensure entitlement. If you do require a doctor, check that they have a reimbursement arrangement with the National Insurance Administration - not usually a problem since this includes most medical practitioners. There is a non-refundable standard fee - your Accident/Rescue/Cancellation insurance will cover this (you did remember to take it out before leaving home?).
Chemists are called Apotek. You will have to pay for most prescribed medicines, however, if you are prescribed medication by a doctor on a blue prescription (generally medication for chronic conditions) you will pay only 36% of the costs, up to a maximum of NOK360 per prescription. Charges are payable for specialist hospital consultations and any out-patient treatment. In an emergency, you can get treatment from the nearest public hospital; hospital in-patient treatment, including necessary medication, is free of charge.
You will usually have to pay the full cost of any dental treatment but again your insurance will cover this (second reminder).
In the event of an accident call 112.
The nearest doctor, dentist and chemists are in Svolvær. The nearest hospital is Leknes - local advice is to try and avoid them!

Without a Car

Much of the climbing is centred around Henningsvær and it is possible to manage without a car - though the logistics are tricky; shopping, moving and what to do when it rains being the main problems. There is a regular bus service up and down the spine of the island, taxis and hitchhiking are also possible.

Car Hire

If you have your own car things become more flexible, petrol prices are similar to the UK though petrol stations are often hard to find. Cars can be hired at the airports, or in Svolvær and Leknes - prices start at about £250 a week for a compact model.

Web sites - www.europcar.com, www.tigercarrental.com, www.auto-europe.co.uk, www.easyterra.com, www.avis.co.uk
Speed limits are generally low (50mph/80kph or less) and on-the-spot fines are substantial, whatever your nationality. Drink-driving laws are strictly enforced, legal levels are low enough to be considered zero and 'morning after' checks are not uncommon. If you do get stopped and are over the limit - expect to head straight for jail without passing Go!

Climbing Shops

There is a sports shop in Svolvær that sells general outdoor gear including camping equipment, cycling and fishing stuff, plus plenty of waterproofs. The only specialist climbing shop in the area is the one that is part of the NNKS Cafe complex; this sells ropes, wires, cams, rock shoes, clothing and a good selection of climbing books.

Puffins on Fire

The Indonesian puffins sold well in the shop (see page 36) though when they first arrived there was not enough room to store all of them indoors and 2000 of the birds were damaged by water after standing outside for most of the winter.
All was not lost though, they burnt well and were used to keep the fire in the cafe going when the weather was cold. The look on the faces of the guests who had paid top-dollar to get a puffin from the shop just next door was a sight to see!

Chris and Colin on *Dr. Jekyll* (6) - *page 127* - in Djupfjord. Photo: Sherri Davy

The West
Henningsvær
Kalle
Kabelvåg
Svolvær
Trolltindan
Walking Peaks
Bouldering

The West

Henningsvær

Kalle

Kabelvåg

Svolvær

Trolltindan

Walking Peaks

Bouldering

Øvredalen's cliffs reflected in the quite waters of Kallevatnet.

Lofoten Climbing

The West

Henningsvær

Kalle

Kabelvåg

Svolvær

Trolltindan

Walking Peaks

Bouldering

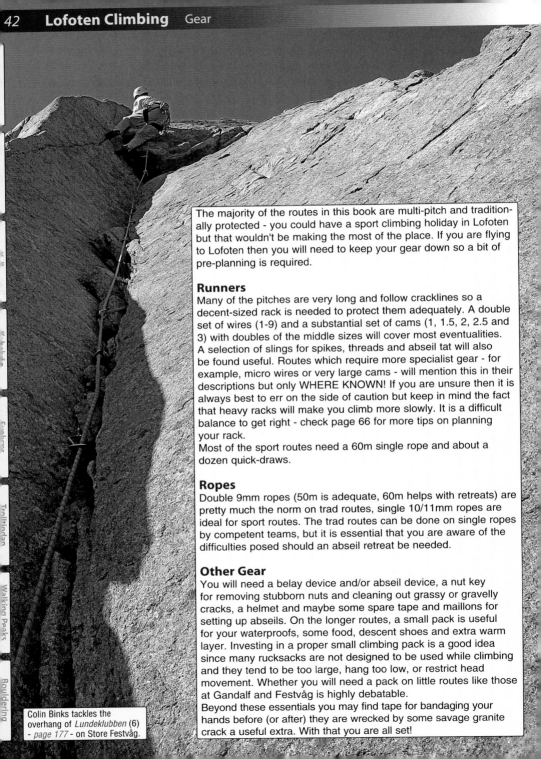

The majority of the routes in this book are multi-pitch and tradition-ally protected - you could have a sport climbing holiday in Lofoten but that wouldn't be making the most of the place. If you are flying to Lofoten then you will need to keep your gear down so a bit of pre-planning is required.

Runners
Many of the pitches are very long and follow cracklines so a decent-sized rack is needed to protect them adequately. A double set of wires (1-9) and a substantial set of cams (1, 1.5, 2, 2.5 and 3) with doubles of the middle sizes will cover most eventualities. A selection of slings for spikes, threads and abseil tat will also be found useful. Routes which require more specialist gear - for example, micro wires or very large cams - will mention this in their descriptions but only WHERE KNOWN! If you are unsure then it is always best to err on the side of caution but keep in mind the fact that heavy racks will make you climb more slowly. It is a difficult balance to get right - check page 66 for more tips on planning your rack.

Most of the sport routes need a 60m single rope and about a dozen quick-draws.

Ropes
Double 9mm ropes (50m is adequate, 60m helps with retreats) are pretty much the norm on trad routes, single 10/11mm ropes are ideal for sport routes. The trad routes can be done on single ropes by competent teams, but it is essential that you are aware of the difficulties posed should an abseil retreat be needed.

Other Gear
You will need a belay device and/or abseil device, a nut key for removing stubborn nuts and cleaning out grassy or gravelly cracks, a helmet and maybe some spare tape and maillons for setting up abseils. On the longer routes, a small pack is useful for your waterproofs, some food, descent shoes and extra warm layer. Investing in a proper small climbing pack is a good idea since many rucksacks are not designed to be used while climbing and they tend to be too large, hang too low, or restrict head movement. Whether you will need a pack on little routes like those at Gandalf and Festvåg is highly debatable.

Beyond these essentials you may find tape for bandaging your hands before (or after) they are wrecked by some savage granite crack a useful extra. With that you are all set!

Colin Binks tackles the overhang of *Lundeklubben* (6) - *page 177* - on Store Festvåg.

Wears Your Head

www.haddock.no

The Norwegian grading system uses a simple numeric open-ended system with + and - to add further gradations. 1 and 2 denote scrambling, with technical climbing starting at about grade 3. The same system is also used for sport climbing grades, with the addition of some split grades (e.g. 7+/8-) to help align the grades with the more common sport grades used pretty much universally elsewhere.

For most Lofoten routes the system works well enough with the minor hitch that the grade takes little heed of the state of the protection on a climb, so a 5+ can be a pleasant well-protected hard move on a jamming crack - or a life threatening smeary move miles from your runners! A look up the pitch should help you decide which. For longer routes with full pitch descriptions, there should be some indication as to the nature of the hardest climbing in the text. Currently the hardest trad route in this book weighs in at 9- (about E7 6c) and the hardest sport route at 9-/9 (about 8a+). For more on grades check **www.rockfax.com**.

Colour Coding

The routes are all given a colour-coded dot corresponding to a grade band and approximate difficulty level. This colour code is designed to indicate a range of grades that a particular climber might be happy attempting.
Green Routes   4+ and under
Good for beginners and those looking for an easy life.
Orange Routes   5- to 6-
General ticking routes for those with more experience including a lot of excellent routes.
Red Routes   6 to 7-
Routes for the experienced and keen climber including many of the area's great classics.
Black Routes   7 and above
A grade band for the talented including some extremely fine challenges.

Sport Routes

Most climbers are happier climbing at a slightly harder level when sport climbing, which is why the colour code for sport grade (and UIAA grade) in the table to the right is set to higher difficulty levels. Climbers used to operating at 'Orange' sport grades should drop their level to the 'Orange' trad grades in the table.

Norwegian Grade Conversion

↓ British Trad Grade

British Trad Grade	USA (Trad)	Sport Grade	UIAA (Sport)
Mod / Moderate	5.1	1	I
Diff / Difficult	5.2	2	II
VDiff / Very Difficult	5.3	2+	III
HVD / Hard Very Difficult	5.4	3-	III+
Sev / Severe	5.5	3	IV
HS / Hard Severe 3c 4b BOLD SAFE	5.6	3+	IV+
VS / Very Severe 4a 5a BOLD SAFE	5.7	4	V-
HVS / Hard Very Severe 4b 5b BOLD SAFE	5.8	4+	V
E1 5a 5c BOLD SAFE	5.9	5	V+
E2 5a 6a BOLD SAFE	5.10a	5+	VI-
E3 5b 6a BOLD SAFE	5.10b	6a	VI
E4 5c 6a BOLD SAFE	5.10c	6a+	VI+
E5 6b 6c BOLD SAFE	5.10d	6b	VII-
E6 6b 6c BOLD SAFE	5.11a	6b+	VII
E7 6c 7a BOLD SAFE	5.11b	6c	VII+
E8 7a 7a BOLD SAFE	5.11c	6c+	VIII-
E9 7a 7b BOLD SAFE	5.11d	7a	VIII
E10 7b 7b BOLD SAFE	5.12a	7a+	VIII+

British grade scale (left margin): 4, 4+, 5-, 5, 5+, 6-, 6, 6+, 7-, 7, 7+, 8-, 8, 8+, 9-, 9, 9+

USA (Trad)	Sport Grade	UIAA (Sport)
5.12b	7b	IX-
5.12c	7b+	IX
5.12d	7c	IX
5.13a	7c+	IX+
5.13b	8a	X-
5.13c	8a+	X
5.13d	8b	X+
5.14a	8b+	XI-
5.14b	8c	XI
5.14c	8c+	XI
5.14d	9a	XI+
5.15a	9a+	

AWESOME WALLS
CLIMBING CENTRE

STOCKPORT

**23.5m lead walls, 400sqm bouldering
no membership fees, loyalty card**

Awesome (adjective) - *so impressive
or overwhelming as to inspire a strong
feeling of admiration or fear.*
(Encarta Dictionary U.K.)

**The Engine House, Pear Mill Ind Est, Lower Bredbury
Stockport, SK6 2BP. TEL 0161 494 9949
www.awesomewalls.co.uk**

Photo: David Simmonite

Top⌐ A Top 50 is a tricky concept with routes varying from 12m clip-ups by the road to remote 20 pitch
L50 trad offerings. With so many brilliant routes in Lofoten that have had very few ascents we can't really
claim that the following selection is actually 'the fifty best routes', but it is 50 routes that are popular and
worthwhile and we think you will be impressed. We have also added a UK grade to the Norwegian one to
help those looking for some conversion between the two systems, although don't take it too seriously.

Tick	Route	Crag	Grade	Trad/Sport	Page
☐	Minnerisset	Sørfjellet	9-	E7 6c	97
☐	Joker nord	Eggum	9-/9	8a+	79
☐	Freya	Vågakallen	8 A3+	E6 6a/A3+	217
☐	Aetat	Eggum	9-	8a	79
☐	Storm Pillar	Vågakallen	7+ A3	E5 6a/A3	217
☐	Butter Arms	Paradiset	8+	7c+	206
☐	Full belastning	Eggum	8+	7c+	79
☐	Gullfaks	Eggum	7+/8-	7a+	81
☐	Reisen	Presten	7+	E5 6b	147
☐	Storpillaren	Vågakallen	7	E5 6a	221
☐	Vårkåt	Jomfru Pillaren	7	E4 5c	186
☐	Odins bue	Trollfestningen	7	E4 6a	247
☐	Ninjarisset	Tjeldbergvika	7	E4 6a	266
☐	Korstoget	Presten	7	E4 6a	143
☐	Dosethrisset	Paradiset	7	E3 6a	200
☐	Tapir	Pianokrakken	7-	E3 6a	102
☐	Vågarisset	Paradiset	6+	E3 5c	212
☐	Månedans	Festvåg	6+	E3 5c	172
☐	Himmelen kan vente	Presten	6+	E3 5c	150
☐	Svenske diedret	Paradiset	6+	E3 5c	204
☐	Englevinger	Svolværgeita	6+	E3 5c	279
☐	The American Tourist	Reine Slab	6	E3 5b	68
☐	Solens sønner	Sjøsvaet	6	E3 5c	129
☐	Vestpillaren (Presten)	Presten	6	E2 5b	148
☐	Drømmen om Michaela	Finnvika	6	6b	268
☐	Pizzatyven	Maurpillaren	6	E2 5c	100
☐	Månens døtre	Sjøsvaet	6	E2 5c	129
☐	Gaukerisset	Festvåg	6	E1 5b	174
☐	Lundeklubben	Festvåg	6	E1 5b	177
☐	Tromsø ekspressen	Gandalf	6	E1 5b	163
☐	Gamle rev	Gandalf	6	E1 5b	163
☐	Colibrien	Trollfestningen	6-	E1 5b	244
☐	Automatic for the People	Rock and Roll Wall	6-	6a	90
☐	Fingerrisset	Trollfestningen	6-	HVS 5a	247
☐	Guns 'n' Roses	Gandalf	6-	HVS 5a	165
☐	Skiløperen	Festvåg	6-	HVS 5a	178
☐	Rom and Cola	Alkoholveggen	5+	E1 5a	230
☐	Puffrisset	Cornflakesveggen	5+	HVS 5a	237
☐	Lys og skygge	Pianokrakken	5+	HVS 5a	105
☐	Applecake Arete	Pianokrakken	5+	VS 5a	105
☐	Forsida	Svolværgeita	5+	VS 5a	279
☐	Sea Breeze	Reine Slab	5	HVS 4c	69
☐	Gandalf	Gandalf	5	VS 4c	163
☐	Living in Paradise	Paradiset	5	VS 4b	208
☐	Gollum	Gandalf	5	VS 4c	163
☐	Bare blåbær	Bare blåbær	5-	VS 4b	116
☐	1910 ruta	Svolværgeita	4+	HS 4b	277
☐	Pianohandler Lunds rute	Pianokrakken	4+	HS 4c	103
☐	Nordryggen	Vågakallen	4+	S 4a	226
☐	By the Dashboard Light	Paradiset	4	S 4a	206

Espen Samuelsen on a nice 7b+ in Brenna

There is a lot of superb quality unclimbed rock in the area covered by this guide, and I mean a LOT! For anyone keen on new routing Lofoten should be an essential destination - a few minutes spent spotting some of huge and impressive unclimbed faces visible in this book will leave you in no doubt, and these are only the ones we photographed! If you are keen to do a new route then doing a bit of research is a good idea. Is the cliff accessible? Has someone else tried and failed on the line? Is there a reasonable descent? The answer to most of these questions can probably be gleaned from the Climbing Cafe in Henningsvær either by talking to one of the locals, or by checking the new routes book.

The New Routes Book

This legendary document is kept behind the counter in the Climbing Cafe in Henningsvær and it makes a fascinating read for those interested in the history of the routes on Lofoten. The original entries for many of the area's most famous routes can be found and it is a great way to while away the hours if it is raining.

Recording a New Route

If you are fortunate enough to put a new route then the New Routes Book is the place to record it. Please try and make the entry readable and let us know EXACTLY where the route goes - a decent diagram will do, though a digital photograph with a line would be better. The information should include which cliff the route is on, full details about the approach and descent, full pitch descriptions with grades and lengths in metres, plus any other information like specialist gear, and an email contact address would be great too. Bizarrely, often the most difficult thing to read in any entry in the New Routes Book is the signature of whoever first did the climb - you may know who you are, but what about the rest of us? We are also happy to receive reports of new routes via email to **info@rockfax.com**

As good as new route information gets - a decent diagram, grades, descriptions, pitch lengths, who did it, when and all in a readable format -10/10.

Abseil	rapell (nedfirning)
Aid climbing	teknisk klatring
Anchor/Belay	anker/standplass
Arete	*same word used*
Belay	standplass
Belay device	taubrems
Bolt	borrebolt
Bouldering	*same word used*
Broddler/Nut Key	nøttepirker
Bucket/Jug	jug
Chalk	kalk
Chimney	kamin
Chockstone	klemblokk
Clean climb	*same word used*
Corner/Groove	hjørne/diedre (innvendig hjørne)
Crack	riss
Crash Pad/Mat	*same word used*
Crimp	*same word used*
Crux	*same word used*
Daisy Chain/Cow's Tail	*same word used*
Deck out	bakkefall
Descender	åtter/taubrems
Dihedral (US) / Groove (UK)	diedre
Down climb	nedklatring
Dynamic rope	dynamisk tau
Dyno	catching
Edge	kant
Edging	kanting
Exposure	luftig
Face climbing	vegg klatring
Fall	*same word used*
Figure of Eight	rapellåtter
Finger board	*same word used*
First ascent	første bestigning
Fist jam	knytneve jam
Fixed rope	fast tau
Flake	flak
Flash	*same word used*
Follow/Second	andremann
Free climbing	fri bestigning
Grade	grad
Gully	renne
Hand Traverse	*same word used*
Hanging Belay	hengende standplass
Harness	sele
Haul bag	heisesekk
Headwall	hoved vegg
Helmet	hjelm
Hexcentric	hex
Jamming	*same word used*
Jumar	*same word used*
Karabiner	*same word used*
Knots	knute
Layback	*same word used*
Lead climbing	lede
Loose	løst
Mantelshelf	mantle hylle
Multi-pitch climbing	flere taulengder
Nut	nøtt
Off-width	*same word used* (or risskamin)
On-sight	*same word used*
Overhang	*same word used*
Pitch	taulengde

Climbers on *Puffrisset* (5+) - *page 237* - dwarfed by Vågakallen. Photo Sherri Davy

The West · Henningsvær · Kalle · Kabelvåg · Svolvær · Trolltindan · Walking Peaks · Bouldering

Peg/Piton	.bolt
Protection	sikring
Prusik	*same word used*
Quickdraw	kortslynge
Redpoint	*same word used*
Rock (as in falling)	stein
Roof	tak
Rope	tau
Route	rute
Runner	mellomforankring
Runout	*same word used*
Scrambling	klyving
Scree	ur
Second	andremann
Sidepull	sidetak
Slab	sva
Sling	slynge
Smearing	smøring
Solo climbing	solo klatring
Sport climbing	sportsklatring
Stopper	*same word used*
Tape/Webbing	slynge
Top rope	top tau
Traverse	*same word used*
Undercut/Undercling	*same word used*

The West · Henningsvær · Kalle · Kabelvåg · Svolvær · Trolltindan · Walking Peaks · Bouldering

	Routes	up to 4+	5- to 6-	6 to 7-	7 and up
The West					
The West	18	- ✗	6 ✓	10 ✓✓	2 ✓
Eggum	41	- ✗	1 ✗	3 ✗	27 ✓✓✓
Henningsvær					
Rørvika	25	1 ✓	7 ✓	5 ✓	1 ✗
Pianokrakken	40	3 ✓	9 ✓✓	16 ✓✓	12 ✓✓
Djupfjord	21	1 ✗	8 ✓✓✓	10 ✓✓✓	2 ✓
Presten	21	- ✗	4 ✓	7 ✓✓✓	10 ✓✓✓
Gandalf	27	- ✗	6 ✓✓✓	9 ✓✓✓	12 ✓✓✓
Festvåg	30	- ✗	11 ✓✓✓	15 ✓✓✓	4 ✓✓
Henningsvær to Kalle	11	- ✗	7 ✓	4 ✓✓	1 ✓
Kalle					
Paradiset	62	12 ✓✓	30 ✓✓✓	15 ✓✓	5 ✓
Vågakallen	8	1 ✓	1 ✓	2 ✓✓	4 ✓✓✓
Øvredalen	8	1 ✓	2 ✓	4 ✓✓	1 ✓
Kallebukta	7	- ✗	1 ✓	4 ✓	2 ✓
Trollfestningen	13	1 ✗	3 ✓✓✓	5 ✓✓✓	4 ✓✓✓
Glåmtinden	3	- ✗	3 ✓	- ✗	- ✗
Kabelvåg	56	1 ✗	10 ✓✓	22 ✓✓✓	23 ✓✓✓
Svolvær	12	1 ✓✓	5 ✓✓✓	4 ✓✓	2 ✓✓
Trolltindan	14	11 ✓✓	1 ✓	2 ✓	- ✗

Quality and range of routes in different grade bands: ✓✓✓ - Excellent ✓✓ - Good ✓ - Okay ✗ - Not worth a visit

The West · Henningsvær · Kalle · Kabelvåg · Svolvær · Trolltindan · Walking Peaks · Bouldering

Approach	Sun	Sport	Multi-pitch	Shelter	Mountain Weather	Summary	Page
Various approaches Roadside to 90 min	Sun and shade		Multi-pitch		Bad weather	Major routes on some very impressive (and inaccessible) cliffs, plus the extended roadside fun on the Reinesvaet.	56
5 min	Not much sun	Bolts		Sheltered		Lofoten's best sport climbing venue, accessible and with routes that are ever-dry. The downside - most of them are pretty tough.	74
10-20 min	Lots of sun		Multi-pitch		Bad weather	A few routes scattered amongst a lot of rock - rising above the E10. The Rock and Roll Wall is worth a visit for somewhere different.	86
2-15 min	Lots of sun	Bolts	Multi-pitch			One of Lofoten's most popular cliffs with a fine set of short multi-pitch routes. Accessible and quick drying, queues are not unknown.	94
15-90 min	Afternoon		Multi-pitch		Bad weather	A fine set of cliffs along the side of Djupfjord, composed of great rock. Despite the quality, only a small selection of the routes see action.	110
10-30 min	Afternoon		Multi-pitch		Bad weather	The area's pre-eminent crag, with some great routes on magnificent rock and up to 10 pitches long. *Vestpillaren* is the MUST DO!	134
5-10 min	Lots of sun		Multi-pitch	Sheltered		Popular and with good reason, the Orange Spot routes in particular see a lot of action. A five minute walk from the free camping helps.	156
20 min	Lots of sun		Multi-pitch			About the closest cliff to Henningsvær and with a great collection of crack and groove climbs. Quite sheltered and popular too.	170
15-30 min	Morning		Multi-pitch		Bad weather	A remote section of extensive cliffs with only a few routes. Could well be the next Gold Rush venue.	184
10-20 min	Lots of sun			Sheltered		Great rock, lovely setting and a long-time favourite. Nowadays you even get some descriptions, so should be more popular than ever.	198
15-90 min	Morning		Multi-pitch		Bad weather	A great contrast to Paradiset - very big, north-facing routes and a fair hike-in too. No queues up here to worry about.	214
20-60 min	From mid morning		Multi-pitch			A sunny slab in a spectacular position opposite Vågakallen. Good multi-pitch routes too - the hour walk-in keeps the crowds away.	228
5-10 min	Lots of sun		Multi-pitch	Sheltered		Only a small set of climbs, but in a lovely setting - the beach is superb. Can easily be combined with a visit to Paradiset.	234
30 min	Not much sun		Multi-pitch			A fine cliff, big and sombre, almost always in the shade and with damp streaks too. Despite the negatives the routes are memorable.	242
60 min	Lots of sun		Multi-pitch		Bad weather	Only really two routes and just one of those gets done. The rock is a bit crumbly but the setting makes up for it.	254
3-10 min	Sun and shade	Bolts		Sheltered		Sporty climbing (with the odd trad route) on a small collection of cliffs that are easy to access and with a sunny aspect.	260
20-40 min	Lots of sun		Multi-pitch			The Svolværgeita is Lofoten's most sought-after and enigmatic summit. Fortunately it has some great routes too.	272
60+ min	Sun and shade		Multi-pitch		Bad weather	Remote routes on remote peaks in remote settings - you get the message, self-reliance is the name of the game here.	288

The West

Henningsvær

Kalle

Kabelvåg

Svolvær

Trolltindan

Walking Peaks

Bouldering

The West

Henningsvær

Kalle

Kabelvåg

Svolvær

Trolltindan

Walking Peaks

Bouldering

The West

The West

Henningsvær

Kalle

Kabelvåg

Svolvær

Trolltindan

Walking Peaks

Bouldering

The amazing pyramidal peak of Olstinden seen from Reine.
Sørvest pillaren - page 64 - is the left-hand skyline.

Late in the evening on the beach at Ramberg.

Lofoten's western island of Moskenesøya is well known for its superb scenery of magnificent jagged granite peaks. Despite this the amount of climbing that has been done is very limited and in reality Moskenesøya is a better destination for mountaineers and hillwalkers than rock climbers. The are a few exceptions; the big roadside slab found on Reinesvaet, (the Reine Slab) and a small collection of major routes scattered around the spectacular peaks of Kjerkfjord. In general the rock isn't quite as good as elsewhere and the stubborn vegetation can be a bit of a nuisance though doubtless there are many more high quality routes and venues waiting to be discovered.

Although the island chains run southwest/northeast the old-time fishermen always referred simply to travelling west or east and this tradition has stuck throughout Lofoten.

The tiny ferry - MS Fjordskyss (30 places) - operates daily from Reine to Kjerkfjorden (also spelt 'Kirkefjord') and Vindstad (also spelt 'Vinstad'). In the peak season (late June to mid August) there are normally three sailings a day, with an extra late evening sailing on Fridays.

Peak Timetable late June to mid August

	Mon-Fri	Mon/ Tue/Fri	Wed/ Sat/Sun	Thurs	Fri	Daily
Depart Reine	07.00	10.00	11.00	09.45	21.30	15.00
Kjerkfjorden	07.20	10.20	11.20	10.05	*Request*	15.20
Vindstad	07.35	10.25	11.35	10.20	*Request*	15.35
Arrive Reine	08.00	11.00	12.00	10.45	22.30	16.00

Off-peak Timetable mid August to late June

	Mon	Wed	Thu	Fri	Fri	Daily*
Depart Reine	07.00	11.00	09.45	07.00	21.30	15.00
Kjerkfjorden	07.20	11.20	10.05	07.20	*Request*	15.20
Vindstad	07.35	11.25	10.20	07.35	*Request*	15.35
Arrive Reine	08.00	12.00	10.45	08.00	22.30	16.00

*This return only runs on alternate Sundays in the Off-peak season
Ferry stops at Rostad on request - ask the skipper.

The West

Henningsvær

Kalle

Kabelvåg

Svolvær

Trolltindan

Walking Peaks

Bouldering

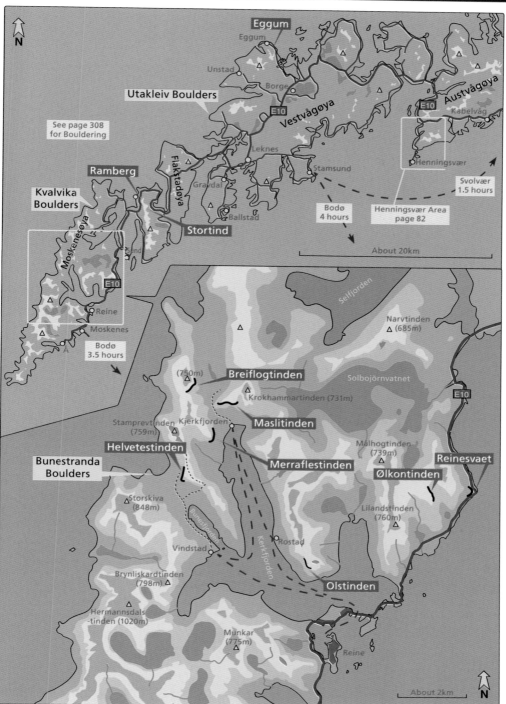

The West

Henningsvær

Kalle

Kabelvåg

Svolvær

Trolltindan

Walking Peaks

Bouldering

N

Eggum

Unstad

Borge

E10

Vestvågøya

Utakleiv Boulders

Austvågøya

Kabelvåg

See page 308
for Bouldering

Leknes

Henningsvær

Svolvær
1.5 hours

Ramberg

Flakstadøya

Stamsund

Kvalvika
Boulders

Gravdal

Bodø
4 hours

Henningsvær Area
page 82

Moskenesøya

Ballstad

Stortind

About 20km

E10

Reine

Moskenes

Å

Bodø
3.5 hours

Selfjorden

Narvtinden
△ (685m)

(750m)

Breiflogtinden

Solbojörnvatnet

E10

△ Krokhammartinden (731m)

Stamprevtinden
(759m) △

Kjerkfjorden

Maslitinden

Målhogtinden
(739m)
△

Helvetestinden

Merraflestinden

Reinesvaet

Bunestranda
Boulders

Ølkontinden

Storskiva
(848m) △

Lilandstinden
(760m)
△

Vindstad

Rostad

Brynliskardtinden
(798m) △

Olstinden

Hermannsdals-
-tinden (1020m) △

Munkar
(775m)
△

Reine

About 2km

N

The West

Henningsvær

Kalle

Kabelvåg

Svolvær

Trolltindan

Helvetestinden

(The Hell Peak) This pointed peak north of Bunesfjorden has a huge west-facing slabby wall that looks over the Bunestranda and out into the Norwegian Sea, and heaps more rock on the Kjerkfjord side too.

Approach - Take the ferry from Reine to Vindstad at the entrance to Bunesfjorden. Walk alongside the fjord on a gravel road for 2km towards the low pass of Einangen. Go past the beautiful Vindstad graveyard, then northwest up sheep trails to the pass (80m - hardly a pass really) before descending to the enormous Bunestranda, the beach, below Helvetstinden's West Face - 60 to 90 minutes from the ferry.

Helvetestinden (606m)

Descent

Descent for all routes except Helvetesveggen
From the top of the climbs it is possible to scramble up and right for about 200m to the join the south ridge. Turning left, a short extension reaches the summit of the mountain. From here descend down *Sør ryggen*, which involves some scrambling. Follow the ridge all the way down to the col of Brunaksla then descend the gully (some scrambling) as it drops westwards towards the approach path.

Photo: Odd-Roar Wiik

Helvetestinden (606m)

Stamprevtinden (606m)

West Face (behind ridge)

Merraflestinden

Breiflogtinden

Maslitinden

Kjerkfjorden

The West / Henningsvær / Kalle / Kabelvåg / Svolvær / Trolltindan / Walking Peaks / Bouldering

❶ Left Approximation . . . . [   ] **6-**
About 600m. This route has about 18 pitches and leads up the left-hand edge of the face, bounded by grass slopes to the left. Start right of these and cross the right-hand side of a curving overlap (**5-**) then trend left up slabs for four or five pitches (**4**) to reach a prominent steep groove. Above this, some huge loose flakes have to be crossed to reach three left-trending overlaps. Cross the first one and belay under the second, before following it leftwards to a grassy ledge. Head round the right-hand side of a roof and climb flake-cracks up and right to poorly-protected friction moves (**6-**) leading to the base of a basalt dyke/gully. From here there are three choices:
1) Abseil down the route (no fixed anchors?).
2) Trend left across slabs to reach a col on the ridge.
3) Follow the dyke for seven more pitches, crossing a roof (**5**), and arriving on the north ridge one pitch below the summit.
FA. Ole Klingeman, Eggert Keller 7.1997

❷ Helvetesveggen . . . . [   ] **5+** *A1*
About 500m. *(Hell's Wall)* This 11 pitch route, which was never completed, tackles most of the centre of Helvetestinden's huge west face, rising above the superb Bunestranda. Start below a large grooveline in the centre of the wall. The first three pitches head towards this groove to several large ledges, then move left of the groove and climb flake systems back to the right until you are above the groove. There are 5 bolts for protection and belay anchors above the big ledge at the top of pitch 3. The highest bolt marks the point of retreat.
FA. Arild Meyer, Finn Jensen 8.1984. They climbed 11 pitches up the wall before being forced to retreat by steady rain and darkness with only 2 more pitches to go. The first few pitches were good, the rest had much loose rock, flakes and grass.

The attractive pillar on the right-hand side of the wall is known as the French Pillar after the first route up it. The next two routes were put up in 2005 and they doubtless cover some of the same ground as the original French Pillar route. The climbing is generally on good rock following shallow crack systems. Although it might be seen as a bit of historical vandalism to describe these rather than the original, since details of the French Pillar have been impossible to find, it is probably the best solution.

❸ The Next Best Thing . . . . . . ⚐ [   ] **6+**
300m. The slightly easier climb of the pair is seven pitches long, starting on the left and crossing to the nose of the pillar higher up.
FA. Odd-Roar Wiik, Adam Stack 2005

❹ Norwegian Sheep Ranch ⚐ ✍ [   ] **7**
300m. The more difficult of the two climbs, with pitches 1, 3 and 4 being close to 60m long. The route is described as *"being sustained and on good rock".*
FA. Tommy Caldwell, Beth Rodden 2005

❺ Den Franske pillaren . . . . . . ⚐ [   ] **?**
300m. *(The French Pillar)* Little is known about the original line, except it is about 6 pitches long.
FA. A French climbing and film team led by Eric and Anne Lapied, made the first ascent of the route between 15 - 20.6.1983. They filmed the entire ascent.

Sør ryggen
(South Ridge) The descent route is also the main way up the mountain and makes an excellent scramble. It is gained via the large gully on the right shortly before the top of the col of Einangen is reached. The easy-angled gully leads to the col of Brunaksla on the ridge (views over the other side to Kjerkfjord), then turn left and scramble up the ridge to the top - 2 to 3 hours.

The West

Henningsvær

Kalle

Kabelvåg

Svolvær

Trolltindan

Walking Peaks

Bouldering

Merraflestinden

The conspicuous flat-topped peak dominates the northwest side of the head of Kjerkfjorden and is only a short walk from the pier. Currently the crag only has two recorded routes for which limited information is known.

❻ Kor e hammaren Edvard . . . 🔲 **6+** *A1*
485m. The route is 14 pitches long with grades up to **6+** and a little aid (*A1*) on pitch 4. Named after a well-known traditional Lofoten song.
FA. Jonas Tetlie, Knut Storvik 2002

❼ Borr i Bekkmørtna . . . . 🔲 **7-** *A0*
470m. This route shares the same start for two pitches before taking a direct line up the centre of the pillar. Named after a renown Norwegian wanderer. Around 12 pitches.
FA. Jonas Tetlie, Knut Storvik 2002

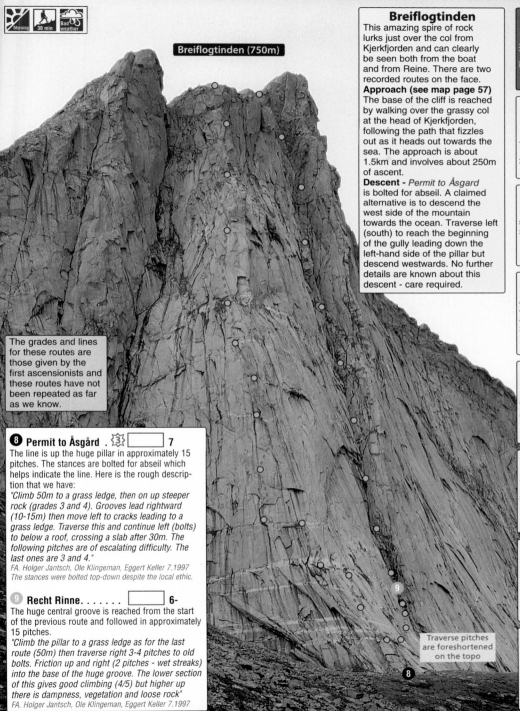

Breiflogtinden (750m)

Breiflogtinden

This amazing spire of rock lurks just over the col from Kjerkfjorden and can clearly be seen both from the boat and from Reine. There are two recorded routes on the face.

Approach (see map page 57)

The base of the cliff is reached by walking over the grassy col at the head of Kjerkfjorden, following the path that fizzles out as it heads out towards the sea. The approach is about 1.5km and involves about 250m of ascent.

Descent - *Permit to Åsgard* is bolted for abseil. A claimed alternative is to descend the west side of the mountain towards the ocean. Traverse left (south) to reach the beginning of the gully leading down the left-hand side of the pillar but descend westwards. No further details are known about this descent - care required.

The grades and lines for these routes are those given by the first ascensionists and these routes have not been repeated as far as we know.

8 Permit to Åsgård . 〔3〕 ☐ 7

The line is up the huge pillar in approximately 15 pitches. The stances are bolted for abseil which helps indicate the line. Here is the rough description that we have:

"Climb 50m to a grass ledge, then on up steeper rock (grades 3 and 4). Grooves lead rightward (10-15m) then move left to cracks leading to a grass ledge. Traverse this and continue left (bolts) to below a roof, crossing a slab after 30m. The following pitches are of escalating difficulty. The last ones are 3 and 4."

FA. Holger Jantsch, Ole Klingeman, Eggert Keller 7.1997
The stances were bolted top-down despite the local ethic.

9 Recht Rinne . . . . ☐ 6-

The huge central groove is reached from the start of the previous route and followed in approximately 15 pitches.

"Climb the pillar to a grass ledge as for the last route (50m) then traverse right 3-4 pitches to old bolts. Friction up and right (2 pitches - wet streaks) into the base of the huge groove. The lower section of this gives good climbing (4/5) but higher up there is dampness, vegetation and loose rock"

FA. Holger Jantsch, Ole Klingeman, Eggert Keller 7.1997

Traverse pitches are foreshortened on the topo

The West
Henningsvær
Kalle
Kabelvåg
Svolvær
Trolltindan
Walking Peaks
Bouldering

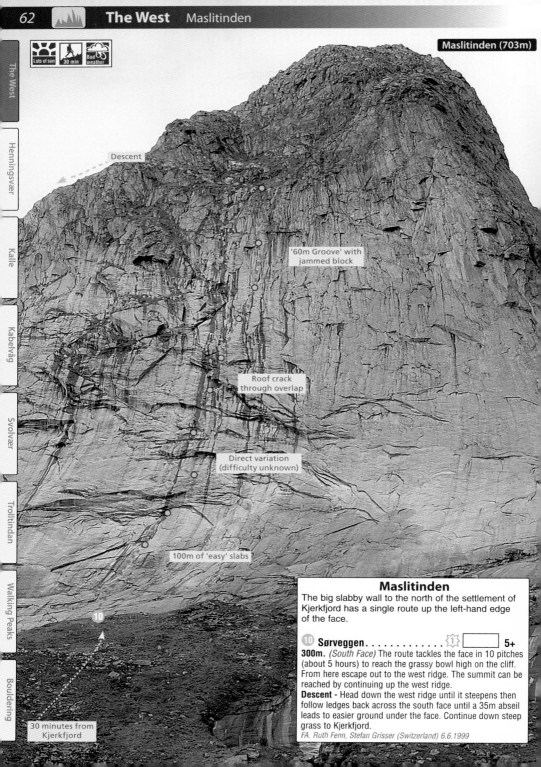

Maslitinden (703m)

Descent

'60m Groove' with jammed block

Roof crack through overlap

Direct variation (difficulty unknown)

100m of 'easy' slabs

10

30 minutes from Kjerkfjord

Maslitinden

The big slabby wall to the north of the settlement of Kjerkfjord has a single route up the left-hand edge of the face.

⑩ Sørveggen . . . . **5+**

300m. *(South Face)* The route tackles the face in 10 pitches (about 5 hours) to reach the grassy bowl high on the cliff. From here escape out to the west ridge. The summit can be reached by continuing up the west ridge.

Descent - Head down the west ridge until it steepens then follow ledges back across the south face until a 35m abseil leads to easier ground under the face. Continue down steep grass to Kjerkfjord.

FA. Ruth Fenn, Stefan Grisser (Switzerland) 6.6.1999

The West

Henningsvær

Kalle

Kabelvåg

Svolvær

Trolltindan

Walking Peaks

Bouldering

63

The West

Henningsvær

Kalle

Kabelvåg

Svolvær

Trolltindan

Walking Peaks

Bouldering

The superb deserted beach at Kvalvika and the peak of Ryten 543m and its unclimbed cliffs. The bay is one of several on the north and west coasts of Lofoten that were inhabited until relatively recently - a harsh existence on the edge of the world was guaranteed.

Olstinden

The huge slabs overlooking Kjerkfjord have a solitary route.

Approach (see map on page 57) - Take a boat from Reine disembarking at Rostad - ask the skipper and he will let you off - then scramble south along the coast for almost a kilometre before heading up and right to the wide grassy terrace at the foot of the slabs.

Descent - Scramble up and right then left to the highest grass terrace then head towards the summit to intersect the north ridge. Continue down this until a wide grassy gully (snow early in the season) leads all the way down to the sea.

---

⑪ Sørvest pillaren . . . . 2 ⬜ **5+**

300m. From a start on the left of the slabs, traverse right to the cracks that lead to a big grass ledge. Traverse right again and climb cracks and grooves and traverse right, heading to a stance below a big overhang. Climb left of this up grassy grooves and exit right to the terraces above the cliff. Around 10 pitches.

FA. Trond Seem, Haakon Christiansen 7.7.1994

The West
Henningsvær
Kalle
Kabelvåg
Svolvær
Trolltindan
Walking Peaks
Bouldering

Ølkontinden (735m)

12

13

Ølkontinden

This peak lies to the north of the village of Hamnøy (which is 3km northeast of Reine). There are a couple of steep long groove and corner lines here, although neither is likely to prove popular.

Approach (see map on page 57) - About 3km north of Hamnøy, there is a small parking area on the left (travelling north). From this, follow a small river to the lake of Ølkona (at 81m). From the lake follow the valley by bushwhacking and hiking up slabs to the base of the wall. About 2 hours in total.

Descent - Follow the ridge southwards until it is possible to get down into the valley to the east and join the approach route.

⓬ It's All About the Numbers .. ☆ [ ] **6+**
250m. The striking long groove that splits the highest part of the face. Sadly the line involves wide cracks and quite a lot of grass climbing and is a less attractive prospect than first appearance might suggest. It has six pitches and the first ascensionists described it as adventurous!
FA. Odd-Roar Wiik, Adam Stack 7.7.2005

⓭ Looks can be Deceiving. . . . . . [ ] **6**
200m. The right-hand line follows the steep imposing corner with two harder pitches and some easier climbing. Again grass, some of it vertical, was a problem. Above the climbing, 500m of scrambling leads to the top. The first ascensionists commented that the route was unlikely to become a classic.
FA. Tommy Caldwell, Beth Rodden 7.7.2005

Adam Stack following the 2nd pitch on the first ascent of *It's All About the Numbers* (6+), Ølkontinden. Photo: Odd-Roar Wiik

The West / Henningsvær / Kalle / Kabelvåg / Svolvær / Trolltindan / Walking Peaks / Bouldering

The West

Henningsvær

Kalle

Kabelvåg

Svolvær

Trolltindan

Walking Peaks

Bouldering

Multi-pitch Gear

While a standard rack may work well for most routes, when you're contemplating a long multi-pitch route you should question very carefully what you carry with you. Taking too much gear has three negative effects: firstly it weighs you down, making everything more strenuous than it needs to be; secondly, it makes you feel encumbered; and thirdly, the more gear you have, the harder it can be to locate the piece you want.

Looking at the route, the first thing you need to work out is what sort of gear is likely to be crucial for the key pitches. If you know the route has some wide cracks then you are naturally going to want to take some big gear. Alternatively, if your route is a thin slab with hairline cracks, you'd be better off taking plenty of small wires and micro-cams. Take a reasonable range of this important gear.

Once you've decided what sort of gear is crucial, you need to work out roughly how much other stuff to take to complete your rack. Take the length of the hardest pitch and the distance at which you'll be happy (or forced) to run it out, and divide the former by the latter to know how many placements you are likely to be using. So if your pitch is 30m, and you are expecting to place a piece every 2m, that's 15 pieces. Of course there will be instances where you run it out on easy ground, or stop and place several pieces together, but on average you should be expecting to be able to place 15. Now consider the grade of the longest pitch and do a similar calculation only this time you may be prepared to run it out a bit more if the pitch is relatively easy for you. Using these rough guidelines you should be able to work out roughly how many pieces of gear you need. Keeping in mind the gear you need for the crucial sections, choose a wide range that covers most eventualities and make sure you have enough quickdraws and karabiners to clip them all.

There are some good tricks to optimising your rack so you don't carry unnecessary gear. Consider using gear for multiple jobs; short slings can be wrapped up to turn them into extendable quick-draws with three different lengths (slingdraws); holding your chalk bag up using your prusik loops ensures you've always got prusiks with you without taking up valuable harness space; and carrying your nut key on a solid screw-gate means that you have an extra screw gate for the belays.

Reducing the clutter on your harness makes it easier to find the items you're looking for. While on slabby, low grade routes you can stand around for ages looking for things, when you're hanging off your arms you need to be able to locate the right piece as quickly as possible. Whichever way you rack, consider placing size-critical pieces at the front of your harness where you can see them, and non size-critical pieces at the back (such as quickdraws), put other gear such as your belay device, screw-gates (with nut key) at the back of your harness out of the way.

Wires are best racked according to size since this will help you quickly identify them when in extremis. You might have one karabiner with small wires, one with medium, and one with large. Oval karabiners seem best for racking wires but use full-strength karabiners for racking gear as you will probably find yourself wanting to clip it one day.

Too much gear? If, after optimising your rack, you still find your harness struggling to fit all your gear, you can make a lot of space by Yosemite racking your quickdraws - simply clip the first to your gear loop then clip subsequent identical quickdraws to the top karabiner of the first. Lastly, consider an over-the-shoulder bandolier to keep your quickdraws out of the way.

Based on text from the **Tactics** chapter of **Trad Climbing+**
by Adrian Berry and John Arran, published by Rockfax 2007 - see back cover flap

The West

Henningsvær

Kalle

Kabelvåg

Svolvær

Trolltindan

Walking Peaks

Bouldering

Matt Kilner finishing pitch 11 of
Vestpillaren (6) - *page 148* - on Presten.
Photo: Ali Kennedy

Thorbjørn Enevold setting sail into the unknown on the first ascent of *The American Tourist* (6) Reine Slab. Photo: Ed Webster

The West

Henningsvær

Kalle

Kabelvåg

Svolvær

Trolltindan

Walking Peaks

Bouldering

⑭ The American Tourist . . 50 🖤   **6**

315m. Fine but very bold climbing up the left-hand side of the slab - one for the committed. Though both this and *Sea Breeze* have only a grade between them, this one in particular is a serious undertaking, with minimal protection and some indifferent belays. Skyhooks may be found useful as runners, or as a means of escape if things get too much! Start 100m left of the flake at the toe of the slab, where there is a small grass ledge amongst the ferns.

1) 5-, 30m. Trend right via friction and the occasional flake to a stance in the base of a shallow groove. Scary!

2) 5, 45m. Move left then climb the face before trending right to a stance at the base of a huge flake laid on the slab. Scary!!

3) 5+, 50m. Climb the flake to its end then trend left across the slab before climbing to the base of a thin crack. Scary!!!

4) 5+, 45m. Climb straight up the slab (effectively unprotected) to a poor stance at a down-pointing flake. Very scary!!!!

5) 5, 50m. Trend right via the occasional flake (poor protection again) to a stance at the base of a long curving overlap. Scary!

6) 5, 45m. Move right to the second overlap and follow the crack (runners - yippee!) to a stance.

7) 3+, 50m. Easy climbing leads to the ledges above the slab.

FA. Thorbjørn Enevold, Andreas Bergwall, Ed Webster 4.8.1991

Descent - There is a line of bolt anchors (old and in poor condition) that roughly follows the line of *Sea Breeze*. Alternatively, a more sensible option is to traverse left across a terrace into a vegetated gully (not the one that bounds the slab, but the next one). Down-climb and abseil from trees (look for slings - 4 x 50m) down the gully and over small cliffs back down to the jungle of ferns growing at the cliff base.

Reinesvaet (The Reine Slab)

A huge barrel-shaped buttress right above the road, just north of the small town of Reine. Those who arrive on the ferry to Moskenes will drive past it on their way north. The slab only has two routes (instead of the twenty-odd it would have anywhere else in Europe) and both are poorly protected and have lines that are tricky to follow. Despite this, if you are in the area ......

Approach (see map on page 57) - Park on the right and cross the road.

⑮ Sea Breeze 5

355m. The natural line of the slab is bold and has a rather scrappy upper section, though there is also plenty of good climbing. Start at the toe of the buttress on top of a fallen flake. A much more amenable outing than its near neighbour.

1) 4+, 35m. Climb direct via scoops and grooves to a stance in a shallow corner - old bolt and nut belays.

2) 4+, 35m. Keep in the same line to a loose flake then traverse left to a belay at the base of a crack up the right-hand side of a huge flake.

3) 5-, 50m. Climb the crack, past an old bolt, to its end then continue in the same line to a stance at the base of The Webster Arch - a large left-trending overlap.

4) 5, 45m. Climb the slab on the right to a stance. Alternately layback the flake (worth **5+** and watch the rope-work) then move right at its top to a stance.

5) 5-, 40m. Follow flakes and grooves (some grass) rightwards to a stance.

6) 4, 45m. Continue in the same line to a small stance at a white flake.

7) 4+, 45m. A friction slab leads to an overlap and above this things ease. Continue to ledges.

8) 3, 50m. Easy climbing leads up a dyke to the ledges above the slab.

FA. (to top of pitch 3) Thorbjørn Enevold, Lutta Fageri 5.1991. FA. (full route) Ed Webster, Thorbjørn Enevold 8.1991

The West · Henningsvær · Kalle · Kabelvåg · Svolvær · Trolltindan · Walking Peaks · Bouldering

Nubben (240m)

Descent

16

Ramberg

Just to the south of the lovely little town of Ramberg, and its superb beaches, is a fine and steep crag on the peak of Nubben, just a few minutes scramble from the road. Currently there is just one route here, although the scope for more is obvious and being easy of access and steeper than many other crags, expect new developments. The summit of Nubben is a popular short (and steep) walk from Ramberg.

To the east of Ramberg is the impressive peak of Stortind which currently has two routes, although one is a bit of an unknown quantity.

Approach - See map on page 57.

⑯ **Midtgardsormen** . . . 〔3〕 🖊 🗺 ☐ **6+**

140m. Named after a mythical monster that protects the human race from the outside world. Start under a left-facing series of flakes to the left of a vertically cracked wall.

1) 6+, 35m. Climb the flakes for 10m then swing right across the wall (bold) and head into the left-facing groove. At its top, where things blank out, pull out right then up to belay at the base of a huge left-facing groove.

2) 6+, 25m. A tricky start gains the groove which is climbed to a belay on the right, at the left-hand end of a long grass ledge.

3) 6+, 20m. Step into the groove and jam up to the overhang. Pull left around this (exposed) to reach a thin crack. Up this to a stance in a bay.

4) 3, 60m. Climb out of the bay via its left-hand corner, then scramble diagonally rightwards to a belay on a large block.

Descent - Head out to the right and descend grass slopes back to the base of the cliff.

FA. Andy Perkins, date unknown.

There is another route on this cliff - **Moanshine, 5+**. *Unfortunately no-one, including the first ascensionist, knows where it goes. The only thing we do know about it is that it stopped where the crag got steep (FA. Nick Ashton, Linn Yttervik, Vidar Kolstad 2000).*

Stortind seen across Flakstadpollen. Øst pillaren (6) is marked with the approach and descent.

17

Descent

Stortind (866m)

18

17

P

Stortind

Stortind *(Big Peak)* is the impressive pointed peak which stands to the west of the Flakstadpollen, the shallow inlet that cuts south into the western coast of Flaksadøya, 3km east of Ramberg.

Approach (see map on page 57) - The approach from roadside parking is obvious.

17 Øst pillaren . . . . 🚶 ▢ **6**
(East buttress) This route tackles the huge slab which is reached by a loop left then right at the bottom to gain the grass ledges below the face. It involves nine pitches; the lower section is easier and grassy, the upper slab provides better climbing.
Pitches - 1) 3, 2) 4, 3) 4+, 4) 4, 5) 6-, 6) 6-, 7) 6, 8) 6, 9) 5.
Descent - From the top of the climbing, trend left to a grassy ramp that leads to the ridge. Follow this south until gullies lead leftwards (east) down to the valley and back towards the road.
FA. Arild Meyer, Jonas Tetli 1997

18 Slovakiaruta . . . . 🚶 ▢ **7-** *A?*
The rambling west face to the south of Ramberg is said to have a solitary route, 1200m (24 pitches) long. Despite attempts, no-one has actually managed to locate the bit of rock this route is on yet. For completeness, here are the words of the first ascensionists: *"the lower section, as far as a large terrace was rather grassy and easy, it led to a gully. The upper part was cleaner, steeper and significantly harder. The rock was good throughout and a full rack was used including pegs and birdbeaks. The ascent took 12 hours."*
FA. Miro Mrava, Brano Turcek 10.8.2005

The West

Henningsvær

Kalle

Kabelvåg

Svolvær

Trolltindan

Walking Peaks

Bouldering

The West

Henningsvær

Kalle

Kabelvåg

Svolvær

Trolltindan

Walking Peaks

Bouldering

Eggum

The West

Henningsvær

Kalle

Kabelvåg

Svolvær

Trolltindan

Walking Peaks

Bouldering

Some old English guy on *Alkotest* (7+) - *page 81* - Eggum.
Photo: some other old English guy.

A rarity on Lofoten, a selection of hard and ever-dry sport routes, tucked away on the northeast coast of Vestvågøya, far enough from the trad climbing heartlands not to cause too much of a fuss.

The crag was discovered by Andreas Haug Christiansen in 2002. Together with Knut Storvik he bolted what would become *Gullfaks* in early 2003. In February (well there is a little daylight) *Eggulf* became the first completed route on the cliff, though most of the development took place in the summer of 2005 when Knut, along with Andreas and Odd-Roar Wiik took the place by storm.

The locals have made two very reasonable requests:
1) No chipping on existing or new climbs
2) If you find quick-draws in place on a route, please leave them there.

Conditions

The crag faces almost north though of course, this is the Arctic, so you can clip bolts at midnight bathed in full sunshine - how weird is that! The crag is steep enough to stay dry at all times, but there is a little seepage. The rock is not too hard on the hands.

Sindre Sætre taking a hands-off rest on *Joker nord* (9-/9) - *page 79* - at Eggum. Photo: Eivind Storvik

Approach   See map on page 57

From Henningsvær, follow the E10 southwest for approximately 45km. When you reach Bøstad, turn right following signs for Eggum on ever-narrower roads. Park on the right side of the road 7.2 km after leaving the E10, just after a causeway, and by a right turn to a 'sjøhus'. Continue along the road for 130m, keeping an eye for a narrow path branching off to the left between the two sets of twinned electricity poles. Follow this to the crag in a little over five minutes. Be careful not to cross the local farmer's field as this might jeopardise access to this nice weatherproof crag.

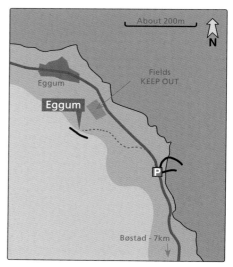

Side tabs: The West / Henningsvær / Kalle / Kabelvåg / Svolvær / Trollfjorden / Walking Peaks

The West

Henningsvær

Kalle

Kabelvåg

Svolvær

Trolltindan

Walking Peaks

Bouldering

Mie Kastet on *Ildvann* (7-) - *page 81* - on the right-hand side of the main cliff at Eggum. Photo: Odd-Roar Wiik

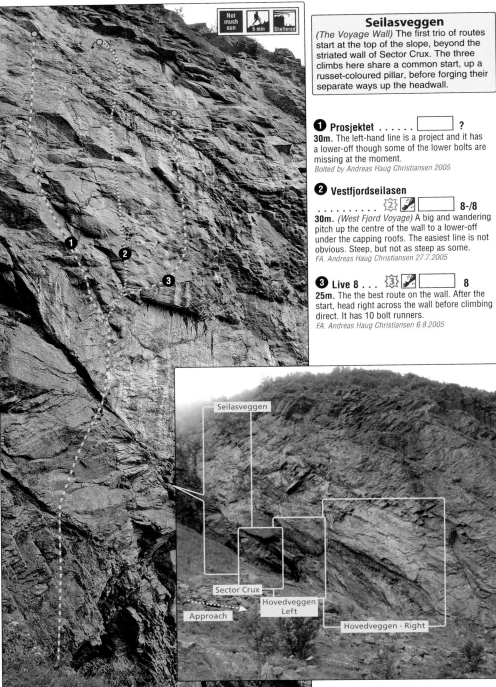

Not much sun | 5 min | Sheltered

Seilasveggen

(The Voyage Wall) The first trio of routes start at the top of the slope, beyond the striated wall of Sector Crux. The three climbs here share a common start, up a russet-coloured pillar, before forging their separate ways up the headwall.

❶ Prosjektet . . . . . . ▭ ?
30m. The left-hand line is a project and it has a lower-off though some of the lower bolts are missing at the moment.
Bolted by Andreas Haug Christiansen 2005

❷ Vestfjordseilasen
. . . . 🌟 ▭ 8-/8
30m. *(West Fjord Voyage)* A big and wandering pitch up the centre of the wall to a lower-off under the capping roofs. The easiest line is not obvious. Steep, but not as steep as some.
FA. Andreas Haug Christiansen 27.7.2005

❸ Live 8 . . . 🌟 ▭ 8
25m. The the best route on the wall. After the start, head right across the wall before climbing direct. It has 10 bolt runners.
FA. Andreas Haug Christiansen 6.8.2005

Seilasveggen

Sector Crux

Hovedveggen Left

Approach

Hovedveggen - Right

Two views of climbing *Gullfaks* (7+/8-) - *page 81* - one of the classics of the crag at Eggum. Main photo: Tom Atle-Bordevik
Inset: Eivind Storvik climbing. Photo: Eivind Storvik collection

The West, Henningsvær, Kalle, Kabelvåg, Svolvær, Trolltindan, Walking Peaks, Bouldering

Sector Crux

Tucked under the biggest roof is the Sector Crux, easily recognised by the series of near horizontal overlaps cutting across is right-hand side. The routes here are 'cruxy' and action packed but a little shorter than on the walls on either side.

4 Crux-Judas . . . . . . [icons] 7-

18m. Climb the lower wall to some awkward shelving rock. The bolts of *Rutger Hauer* head into desperate territory above, instead continue along the flakes leftwards then hand traverse smartly back rightwards to the lower-off of *Rutger Hauer*. Not very popular and regarded as the cliff's worst route.
FA. Knut Storvik 7.4.2005

5 Rutger Hauer . . . . . [icons] 8-/8

14m. From the shelving rock on *Crux-Judas* tackle the short leaning wall to a lower-off on the rim.
FA. Knut Storvik 16.4.2005

6 Mølje kalas . . . . [icons] 8-

12m. Four bolts protect a line up the leaning wall directly above the sloping rock at the start. Awkward climbing through bulges.
FA. Andreas Haug Christiansen 11.4.2005. Named after a typical north Norwegian dish (the whole fish).

7 Svart magi . . . . . . [icons] 9-

12m. *(Black Magic)* Five bolt runners protect this arduous outing up the wall then rightwards along the diagonal break. Very bouldery moves.
FA. Sindre Sæther 25.5.2005

8 Lukket prosjekt . . . . [icon]

12m. Destined to be a hard direct finish where *Svart magi* sneaks off right. The name indicates that is a 'closed' (as opposed to an 'open') project.
Bolted by Odd-Roar Wiik 2005

9 Lille vakre Anna . . . . . . [icons] 7-

12m. *(Little Beautiful Anna* - a traditional song). The right-hand line has four bolt runners leading to the lower-off dangling from the lip, and a hard last move.
FA. Eivind Storvik 14.10.2004

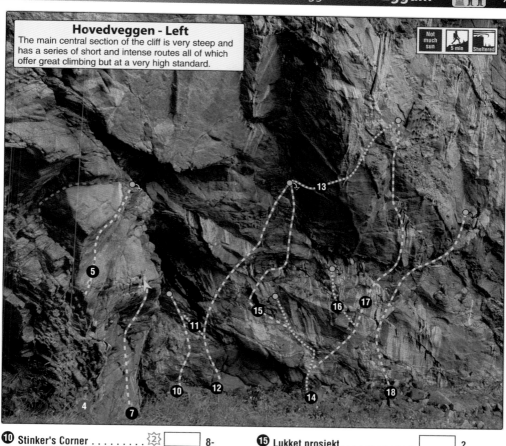

Hovedveggen - Left

The main central section of the cliff is very steep and has a series of short and intense routes all of which offer great climbing but at a very high standard.

⑩ Stinker's Corner . . . . 〔⚡〕 〔　　〕 8-
10m. The right-hand wall of the black recess is escapable towards the end. Straight up at the last bolt earns the 8- tick. Despite appearances, the route is not normally spoilt by seepage.
FA. Andreas Haug Christiansen 1.8.2004

⑪ Hoppalong Knut . . . 〔⚡〕 🔧 🔺 〔　　〕 8-
10m. Follow *Full belastning* for four bolts then go diagonally into *Stinker's Corner*. Again it needs to be done direct past the last bolt for the true 8- tick. Easier than the last climb.
FA. Knut Hatteland Sømme 1.8.2004

⑫ Full belastning . . . . 〔Top 50〕 🔧 🔺 〔　　〕 8+
16m. *(Full Power)* Steep and juggy. Climb rightwards through the roofs to a lower off in the huge groove. The route often seeps between the roofs but all the crucial holds tend to stay dry. 10 bolts.
FA. Andreas Haug Christiansen 5.7.2005

⑬ Attaca con tufa . . . . 〔⚡〕 🔧 ◀ 〔　　〕 9-/9
26m. A granite tufa - sort of. The roof above the lower-off used by the last two routes is one of the best and hardest here.
FA. Eirik Birkelund Olsen 28.5.2007

⑭ Ellinor's vise . . . . 〔⚡〕 🔩 〔　　〕 8-
8m. *(Ellinor's Song)* Short, with a single bolt anchor. Start as for *Commando* but trend left and bale out at the earliest opportunity.
FA. Andreas Haug Christiansen 25.6.2005

⑮ Lukket prosjekt . . . . 〔　　〕 ?
16m. Starting as for *Ellinor's vise*, and heading for the lower-off on *Full belastning*, is a 'closed' project (so keep off).
Bolted by Andreas Haug Christiansen 2005

⑯ Commando . . . . 〔⚡〕 🔧 〔　　〕 8
12m. Short and 'ard right from the ground! Start along *Joker nord* but then trend left to a lower-off under the (even) steeper rock.
FA. Knut Storvik 2005

⑰ Joker nord . . . . . . 〔Top 50〕 ◀ 🔺 〔　　〕 9-/9
25m. The two previous routes are just appetizers for this one, another mega-offering. Trend right eventually doing battle with the hanging shark-fin feature. Continue up the overhanging groove.
Photo page 74.
FA. Sindre Sæther 24.6.2005

⑱ Aetat . . . . 〔Top 50〕 ◀ 🔧 🔺 〔　　〕 9-
20m. *(Job Center)* Start directly below *Joker nord's* shark's fin, head rightwards along the diagonal white strip of rock that cuts across the crag, to a lower-off in a groove. The initial groove is often wet. *Photo on page 16.*
FA. Knut Storvik 7.7.2005

Midnight Sun

We have used the "not much sun" box here as the cliff faces north. Despite this, if you are here between 26 May and 17 July your ascent may be bathed in the rays of the sun as it dips towards the horizon but never actually sets.

Hovedveggen - Right
The tall right-hand side of the cliff has some superb long pitches with a couple of easier offerings just sneaking in at the right-hand edge.

The next routes are 20m down the slope, past the steepest, smoothest and as yet undeveloped part of the wall.

⑲ Uvørn sjænking 9-/9
24m. (*Careless Drinking*) The left-hand line trends left following the rib continuing in the same line until it is possible to get rightwards round the roof. A tricky start needs an alert belayer.
FA. Knut Storvik 6.8.2005

⑳ Heimlich maneuver. 8
22m. Starts in the same place as the last route but takes a more direct line to and through the big bulge. Give yourself a hug!
FA. Andreas Haug Christiansen 2004

㉑ Åpent prosjekt .... ?
24m. Linking the two previous routes (or currently not linking them) is the left-slanting line of an open project.

㉒ Reidar Sjuse .... 8/8+
20m. A popular line which crosses the centre of the bulge.
FA. Knut Storvik 28.7.2004

㉓ Gullfaks. .... 7+/8-
20m. (*A North Sea sector*) One of the best here, a great pitch taking the easiest line up the central part of the wall. Follow the rib then head to the bulges and follow the jugs leftwards until it is possible to pull through final roof. *Photos on page 77.*
FA. Knut Storvik, Andreas Haug Christiansen 2003

㉔ Gullpils .... 8+
35m. (*Golden Beer* - a Norwegian beer) The rightwards extension from just below the lower-off on *Gullfaks* is a big one. Long quick-draws on the *Gullfaks* lower-off reduce drag.
FA. Knut Storvik 8.2007

㉕ Polakken .... 8/8+
15m. (*A Polish guy*) A short tough offering goes left through the biggest bulge. Awkward and harder than it looks.
FA. Knut Storvik 29.7.2005

㉖ Alopølsa 8-/8
15m. The same start but continue direct using the pølsa (sausage) and some superb pockets higher up.
FA. Andreas Haug Christiansen 15.7.2005

㉗ Alopils .... 8/8+
32m. A harder extension to the last climb gives a massive pitch.
FA. Knut Storvik 2007

㉘ Alkotest. .... 7+
16m. (*Breathalyser*) A short groove (tricky second clip for the short) leads to the roof which is passed with difficulty - there are at least five ways of doing it - all are **7+**. The wall above is easier.
Photo page 72.
FA. Odd-Roar Wiik 9.7.2005

LoProfile - Andreas Haug Christiansen
My name is Andreas Christansen. I was born in 1978 and I work as a Landmåler (making maps). I live in Bergen but was raised in Lofoten and will keep on coming back whenever I get the chance.

My Lofoten: Midnight sun and the whole island is still nice and quiet with just about enough people. The rock climbing is fantastic and you can climb from March until October. On Eggum you can even climb dry rock on Christmas Eve.

Favourite routes: *Vestpillaren* of course, like everybody else, but also *Ostepopnæva*, *Ninjarisset* and *Gullfaks*. Not to mention the fantastic layback on the second pitch of *Odins bue* – when it's dry that is.

My story: After a long working day I and Jonas Tetlie went to climb *Vestpillaren*. At the time we had not done very much climbing, so we ended up aiding most of it. Nowadays we know that climbing aid, the second will normally follow on jumars, but then we didn't, so the second was aiding too. This took 20 hours of course, but we still had a great time.

㉙ Ildvann 7-
15m. (*Fire Water*) A short pitch with some hard moves on poor holds. The warm-up for the area. *Photo on page 75.*
FA. Odd-Roar Wiik 12.7.2005

㉚ Sankthansormen... 7+
28m. (*The Glowworm*) The extension from the lower-off makes *Ildvann* into a three star outing. Sustained and a little devious.
FA. Eivind Storvik 2.7.2005

㉛ Eggulf .... 5+
15m. The last (and first, geographically and historically) route on the cliff is a nice taster. Steep moves on jugs lead to a tricky move onto a ramp. Move left to a belay.
FA. Knut Storvik 2003

Presten

Storhylla

Lille Presten

A superb view of Presten bathed in midnight sun. Photo: Thorbjørn Enevold

Henningsvær

Festvågtinden (541m)

Harley Davidson Wall

The West

Henningsvær

Kalle

Kabelvåg

Svolvær

Trolltindan

Walking Peaks

Bouldering

Henningsvær harbour with a backdrop of Festvågtinden
on the left, and Vågakallen on the right.

The tiny fishing village of Henningsvær, on its scattered rocky archipelago, has long been rightly considered as the spiritual home of Lofoten climbing. The Nord Norske Klatreskole and cafe moved here from Kalle back in the 1980s, and pretty much brought 'the scene' with it. The last edition of the guide actually measured the distance to the cliffs from the Cafe, and described them in increasing distance from Henningsvær.

The cliffs in this area are the most popular and well developed on the island. They cover the full range; from the tiny Svenskeveggen; to the ever-popular Pianokrakken, Gandalf and Festvåg with their short multipitch routes on great rock; and on to the magnificent Presten with its major undertakings. Also added into the mix are the fine climbs along the shores of Djupfjord, and then there are the extensive and as yet mostly undeveloped cliffs running along the coast towards Paradiset. It seems likely that this area will long remain at the heart of Lofoten rock climbing.

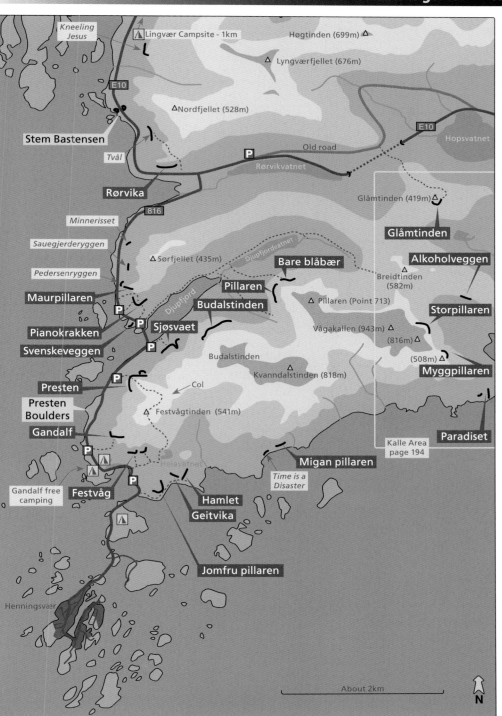

Kneeling Jesus

Høgtinden (699m) △

Lingvær Campsite - 1km

Lyngværfjellet (676m) △

E10

△ Nordfjellet (528m)

Stem Bastensen

E10

Hopsvatnet

Tvål

P

Old road

Rørvikvatnet

Rørvika

Glåmtinden (419m) △

816

Glåmtinden

Minnerisset

Sauegjerderyggen

△ Sørfjellet (435m)

Djupfjordvatnet

Bare blåbær

Alkoholveggen

Breidtinden
(582m) △

Pedersenryggen

Pillaren

Djupfjord

Maurpillaren

Budalstinden

△ Pillaren (Point 713)

Storpillaren

P

Pianokrakken

P **Sjøsvaet**

Vågakallen (943m) △

Svenskeveggen

P

(816m) △

Budalstinden

(508m) △

Presten

P

Kvanndalstinden (818m) △

Myggpillaren

**Presten
Boulders**

Col

△ Festvågtinden (541m)

Gandalf

Paradiset

Kalle Area
page 194

P

Migan pillaren

Helavatnet

*Time is a
Disaster*

Gandalf free
camping

Festvåg

Hamlet

Geitvika

Henningsvær

Jomfru pillaren

About 2km

N

Kalle Area page 194

The West

Henningsvær

Kalle

Kabelvåg

Svolvær

Trolltindan

Walking Peaks

Bouldering

The West

Henningsvær

Kalle

Kabelvåg

Svolvær

Trolltindan

Walking Peaks

Bouldering

Rørvika

A small collection of routes in a dramatic situation dominated by the prominent *Rock and Roll Ridge*. Just to the north of this are a few less popular routes at Lyngvær (see next page for details of approach and conditions) but the main areas of interest for most climbers are the tiered walls at Rørvika overlooking the beach.

Approach   See map on page 85
The Rørvika crags are visible high above the road just to the south of the popular sandy bay of Rørvika. From roadside parking the Lower Wall is reached by following the grassy slope to the left of the large blocks and boulders of the scree - 5 to 10 minutes. The Upper Wall is reached by scrambling up the lower section of the *Rock and Roll Ridge* for about fifteen minutes then moving out right to the sloping terrace under the face.
An interesting way to get back down from the wall (and earning an extra tick) is to continue up the *Rock and Roll Ridge*, over the top and down the steep grass slopes on the right-hand (south) side of the ridge.

Conditions
The hillside faces south and gets the sun until late afternoon. It doesn't take much drainage and is rapid drying, making it a good bet after rain. The ledge under the face is sloping and a little awkward for gearing up - not a prime picnic spot.

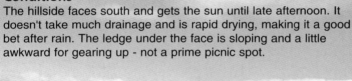

Rock and Roll Ridge - page 90

Lyngvær - 3 mins drive

P P

Rørvika beach

Rørvika Upper Wall

Rørvika Lower Wall

P

The West

Henningsvær

Kalle

Kabelvåg

Svolvær

Trolltindan

Walking Peaks

Bouldering

Rørvika and the Rock and Roll Wall. Photo: Sherri Davy

The West
Henningsvær
Kalle
Kabelvåg
Svolvær
Trolltindan
Walking Peaks
Bouldering

Lyngvær

To the north of Rørvika the road is squeezed in between the hills and the sea. There is a stack of impressive rock here, but apart from the bouldering (see page 310) there are only a few routes at the moment.

The crags face west and their mossy nature means they are a little slow to dry.

The scope for new routes is immense, and although some of the rock is a little flaky and mossy in places, there is little doubt that plenty remains to be done.

Approach - Follow the E10 west and north from Rørvika for a couple of minutes until the crags appear on the right. Both buttresses can be clearly seen from the road and are approached by steep and rather rough scrambles from appropriate roadside parking.

Descent

Approach - round to the left of the lower red wall and up under the base of the upper one

The West

Henningsvær

Kalle

Kabelvåg

Svolvær

Trolltindan

Walking Peaks

Bouldering

❶ **Kneeling Jesus**. . . . . . . 🔲 👤🔲 **6+**
95m. About 1km south of the Lyngvær caravan campsite is a huge cliff with two steep reddish walls. Above the lower one, and to the right of the upper one, is a grey slab forming the arete of the cliff. Aim for this by scrambling round to the left of the lower cliff then up the right-trending ramp that runs under the base of the upper cliff. Start at the top of the ramp under the grey slab.
1) 5-, 15m. Climb the crackline heading leftward to a belay on a good ledge - trickier than it looks.
2) 6+, 35m. Climb the good crack by sustained jamming with moves rightwards at half height. Good well-protected climbing (big cams) but rather mossy in places.
3) 6+, 45m. Take the easiest way to the top by moving round to the left of the arete or more difficult, follow the short steep crack on the right.
Descent - Go over the top of the buttress then head down to the right via an unlikely looking grass ledge at the start which leads back round to the base of the route and the top of the approach ramp.
FA. Gustaf Leijonhovud, Jens Åstrøm, Nils J. Vagner 3.8.2003

❷ **Kom igjen for Helvete** . . 🔲 🔲🔲 **6+**
An eight pitch route up the highest section of the cliff. No precise details are known.
FA. Jonas Tetlie, Kurt Kristiansen c2000

The second buttress is a white slab conspicuous above the road, just north of the Stem Bastensen boulders, and situated roughly mid-way between the Rock and Roll Wall and Lyngvær camping ground.

❸ **Tvål** . . . . 🔲 🔲🔲 **5+**
The name is the Swedish for soap - whether this refers to the look or the feel of the rock was never made clear. The route is four pitches long and has an overall grade of **5+**. Individual pitch lengths and grades are unknown.
Descent - Head rightwards across the hillside aiming for the col above the *Rock and Roll Ridge*. Descend the steep grass slopes (small path) on the south side of this.
FA. Patrick Fransson, Odd-Roar Wiik early 1990s

Upper Wall

A fine place to climb with a superb outlook down towards the beach far below.

Approach - The walls are approached by scrambling up the *Rock and Roll Ridge* which leads to the left-hand end of the ledge below the wall. This is a nice scramble in its own right.

Descent - Scramble back down the *Rock and Roll Ridge* (abseil for the timid) or walk over the top and head down the wide grassy gully to the right (south). It is also possible to abseil and scramble down rightwards to reach the Lower Wall, though this is loose and awkward and not recommended.

❹ The Rock and Roll Ridge . . . ☆ [   ] 3
200m. More of a scramble than a climb, the clean-cut arete is the easiest way of getting to the Upper Wall. It is also worth doing in its own right, especially the upper section which has nice exposed moves and easier options - the timid may require a rope in places.
Descent - Cross the summit ridge then descend the steep open slopes to the right. See the page 86 for the lower part of the line.

❺ Happy Campers . . . . [   ] 6-
25m. The left-hand line on the wall up the slanting crack until a right-trending crack can be followed to a steeper finish.
FA. Thorbjørn Enevold, Trond Solberg 1994

❻ Moody Blue . . . . ☆ [🧗] [   ] 6-
40m. Gain the crack from the left to avoid the wide loose section then follow it (a bit scruffy) until a crack leads up and right - tricky to start - leading to a groove. Climb up this then move right again to where easy rock gains the top.
FA. Thorbjørn Enevold, Trond Solberg 1994

❼ Tom Jones . . . . ☆☆ [🧗] [   ] 6-
45m. A fine diagonal line swaggering up the centre of the wall. From the base of the crack tackled by *Moody Blue*, climb up and right to access the right-trending flake that cuts across the centre of the face. Follow this (stay low for the first section) and then follow it all the way to an easier groove, before breaking out left to finish up a short crack. There is a possible stance at the end of the overlap section.
FA. Thorbjørn Enevold, Trond Solberg 1995

❽ Automatic for the People [Top 50] [🧗] [   ] 6-
45m. A fine fully-bolted line up the tallest part of the face offering sustained, interesting and devious climbing.
FA. Thorbjørn Enevold, Ken Pettersen 2000. The first fully bolted pitch in Lofoten - Thorbjørn sees what is coming and gets in first.

❾ BB King was Wrong (the Thrill isn't Gone)
. . . . ☆ [🧗] [   ] 6
50m. The long groove bounding the right side of the face gives a two pitch outing with a mid-height stance. Awkward belays.
FA. Thorbjørn Enevold, Johan Sandberg 1994

❿ Fugledansen . . . . ☆ [   ] 6
80m. *(The Birdie Song).* This is a three pitch outing up the long white face at the right-hand side of the wall. Start up a right-trending flake-crack and climb the face in two long pitches and one short one.
FA. Patrick Fransson, Thorbjørn Enevold 1994

⓫ Venus Passagen . . . . ☆ [   ] 5+
110m. The broad buttress at the right-hand side of the face is climbed - some route-finding skills may help. Named after a classic album from the Swedish rock band *Reeperbahn*.
FA. Thorbjørn Enevold, Johan Sandberg 7.2007

The West

Henningsvær

Kalle

Kabelvåg

Svolvær

Trolltindan

Walking Peaks

Bouldering

Otto Romfo strutting his stuff as he picks his way across *Tom Jones* (6-). Photo: Thorbjørn Enevold

Lower Wall

Tucked amongst the mass of rock that towers above the beach and bay at Rørvika is a fine pillar with a trio of worthwhile routes that follow cracklines up the face.
Approach - The buttress is reached by a short scramble up from the road and is tucked in the back of the widest gully (see page 86).
Descent - Abseil back down the face from slings on a tree. Despite its proximity it is not possible to scramble up and left to reach the Upper Walls.

12 Jerry Lee . . . . 1️⃣   **5+**
40m. Scramble up the grassy ramp on the left to gain the left-hand crack. Move right into the base of the crack and follow it through a steeper section to reach a belay on the terraces above.
FA. Thorbjørn Enevold, Trond Solberg 1994

13 Sticky Fingers . . . . 2️⃣   **7-**
40m. From the base of the grassy ramp, move out right into the crack that splits the centre of the slab. Follow this by good sustained climbing to the terraces.
FA. Arild Meyer, Odd-Roar Wiik 1993

14 Elvis . . . . 2️⃣   **7**
40m. Start under the right-hand arete of the buttress and weave through the bugle to reach the base of the crack that splits the face just left of the arete. Follow this with sustained interest.
FA. Jimmy Halvardsson, Thorbjørn Enevold 1996

The West

Henningsvær

Kalle

Kabelvåg

Svolvær

Trolltindan

Walking Peaks

Bouldering

Evening action on the ever-popular *Pianohandler Lunds rute*
(4+) - *page 103* - Pianokrakken. The leader is approaching
the base of the steep crack on pitch 3.

Pianokrakken

93

The West

Henningsvær

Kalle

Kabelvåg

Svolvær

Trolltindan

Walking Peaks

Bouldering

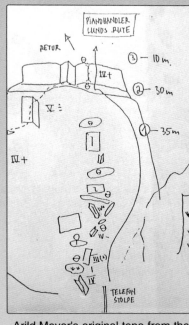

Arild Meyer's original topo from the
pamphlet guide to Lofoten that he
produced in the early 1980s.

Pianokrakken *(the Piano Stool)* is one of the most popular cliffs in the guide; easy accessibility, great outward views, a good spread of grades, quality rock and some excellent lines - it isn't surprising that many folks make their first contact with Lofoten rock here. The routes are multi-pitch but generally the stances are good, as is the protection, hence the place is popular for instruction.

Towering above is peak of Sørfjellet which throws a pillar down towards the sea. The south face of this is known as Maurpillaren *(Ants' Pillar)* - a tall steep slab rising above a cracked base. There are a few scattered routes to the north of the pillar, including the desperately hard crack of *Minnerisset* (9-).

Also covered in this section is the single pitch crag Svenskeveggen with its mixture of sport and trad routes - see page 106 for full details.

Approaches   See map on page 110

The crags are located just north of where the road heads into a rocky cutting and then crosses Djupfjord. There is roadside parking in one of several lay-bys from which steep approaches can be made to Maurpillaren and Pianokrakken. Svenskeveggen is situated on the opposite side of the road. For the crags on the northern slopes of Sørfjellet, continue on the road northwards. See the individual crags for more detailed approach descriptions.

Conditions

Pianokrakken faces south on the right and west further to the left. It does take some drainage though the rock is clean and most of the routes are quick to dry. Maurpillaren faces south and Svenskeveggen faces southeast. The rock is clean and rapid drying though some of the lower cracks seep after rain.

95

The West

Henningsvær

Kalle

Kabelvåg

Svolvær

Trolltindan

Walking Peaks

Bouldering

Colin Binks and Chris Craggs
enjoying the great rock architecture
of *Lys og skygge* (5+) - *page 104* -
on Pianokrakken. Photo: Sherri Davy

The West

Henningsvær

Kalle

Kabelvåg

Svolvær

Trolltindan

Walking Peaks

Bouldering

Robert Caspersen catches superb late evening light while ticking the first ascent of *Minnerisset* (9-). Photo: Odd-Roar Wiik

Minnerisset

As the Henningsvær road heads round the bend from Rørvika it passes a series of ribs and buttresses that fall from the crest of Sørfjellet far above. The first is home to the awe-inspiring roof crack of one of Lofoten's hardest routes. The route is clearly visible from the road and is easily approached from the roadside parking.

❶ Minnerisset . . . . . . [Top 50] 🪝🥾 ⬜ **9-**

28m. *(Memory Crack)* The hardest trad route on Lofoten - this fearsome overhanging roof crack makes Yosemite's famous *Separate Reality* look a bit feeble. The climbing is safe with enough cams but it will tax the strongest of climbers, and unless you are a really proficient jammer, then you might as well forget it. Start at the right end of the ledge with blocks and flakes under the roof and climb up to reach the crack. Follow it past a little niche and past a flake to a crucial thin section, beyond which the crack becomes vertical and a ledge can be reached. Getting onto the belay ledge is all part of the fun. Recovering the gear is another problem!
FA. Robert Caspersen 10.6.2002. The route was named in memory of Robert's brother Pål Espen who died in an abseiling accident on Presten on 10.6.2000.

The West

Henningsvær

Kalle

Kabelvåg

Svolvær

Trolltindan

Walking Peaks

Bouldering

Luke Skywalker

Ladies Jigsaw . . . . 4+

135m. A route up the lower section of the ridge. Scramble to the base of the pillar and start at a crack behind the trees at the lowest point of the cliff.

1) 4+, 20m. Climb the crack to a belay ledge with a small bush at its right-hand end.

2) 4+, 40m. Step onto the slab and traverse right (poor protection) to reach a black vein. Climb this a to a ledge with spikes then traverse right along ledges to a stance on a ledge beneath a short cracked wall.

3) 4+, 25m. Move left and climb cracks to a big ledge. Move left up a groove then left again onto a short slab leading to a large ledge. Flake belays.

4) 3, 25m. Trend left up a rising crack onto an easy slab and head up this to a large grassy ledge - nut belay.

5) 3, 25m. Following a rising traverse, heading for a large spike at the left edge of the buttress. Drop down and right (facing out) to a small grassy bay and a belay.

Descent - Abseil off a square spike (occasionally a sling in place) 40m into the gully and descend this, cutting back under the face to the starting place.

FA. Pauline Bird, Donna Thompson 24.7.2000

Sauegjerderyggen

Rising above Route 816, well to the left of Maurpillaren and Pianokrakken are two long, rocky ridges. The left-hand ridge has two routes at present. Neither are very popular, although *Ladies Jigsaw* is worth seeking out since it offers a 5 pitch route at a friendly grade.

Approach - Both routes are reached direct by walking up the hillside from roadside parking.

Sauegjerderyggen 5-

(The Sheep Fence Ridge) This route tackles the full height of the ridge all the way to one of the Sørfjellet summits. The lower pitches are mostly grade **3** and **4** but there is one harder pitch near the top up a 5m slab above a block, **5-**.

Descent - From the top of the route, or the escape routes, traverse south across the hillside to reach the col at the top of *Pedersenryggen* (page 100) then descend the grass slopes on the other side of this to join the Piannokrakken descent.

FA. Ulf Prytz, Arild Meyer and some NNKS climbing students, early 1970s.

The West · Henningsvær · Kalle · Kabelvåg · Svolvær · Trolltindan · Walking Peaks · Bouldering

Luke Skywalker

An isolated route on a good clean slab of rock which has potential for new routes. The slab is quite tricky to spot from below, but is located to the north of the *Pedersenryggen*, which is the long rocky ridge with huge caves on its right-hand side, to the north of Maurpillaren and Pianokrakken.

Approach - From roadside parking, flog up the wide gully to reach the base of the slab, 40 minutes.

Descent - Walk/scramble off rightwards and skirt around the edge of the slab and back to the base.

4 Luke Skywalker . . . . ☆ 5+

65m. Tackles the highest part of the cliff, start on a grass ledge.
1) 5, 35m. Follow various crack systems to a stance at a ledge.
2) 5+, 30m. Continue up following the crack, then move right to the diagonal overlap and make hard moves to easier ground.
2a) 5, 30m. An easier left-hand finish. Continue straight up the crack in the same line until the angle eases.

FA. (Original) Johan Sandberg, Truls Seines Summer 1993
FA. (Left-hand finish) Thorbjørn Enevold, Johan Sandberg, summer 1993

Maurpillaren

(Ant's Pillar) This is the tall slabby pillar rising above a lower face seamed with cracks, up and left of Pianokrakken. There are several worthwhile routes here.

Approach - Start up the Pianokrakken descent and cross the boulder-field, (care needed) to ledges below the face, a 15 minute approach.

Descent - From the highest ledge above the wall, follow a grassy ramp which leads down and left (facing out) to join the approach track leading to the boulders and the road.

Labels on photo: Pianokrakken, Maurpillaren, P

---

❶ Pedersenryggen . . . . [ ] 4

About 300m. *(The Pedersen Ridge)* This is the borken ridge which leads up to the southernmost summit of the Sørfjellet ridge. At the base of the ridge is a prominent cave, start left of this and climb the ridge in as many pitches as required.

Descent - Drop down the grassy gully southwards and descend steeply under the Maurpillaren face.

FA. Tom Pedersen and some NNKS climbing students in the mid 1970s.

❷ Kjærlighetens kjøtere . . [ ] [ ] [ ] 6

90m. *(Love Dogs - a Norwegian film)* A line up the blocky left arete of the face, then on up the cleaner rock above.

1) **5-, 25m.** Start just to the right of big bushes, climb a nice crack up to the big ledge then move left and belay below the blocky groove that splits the arete.

2) **6, 35m.** Start up a loose corner, then climb a continuation corner to reach a belay on the left.

3) **6-, 30m.** Climb the groove then trend left up slabs and cracks until easy scrambling leads to the top.

FA. Odd-Roar Wiik, Arild Meyer 9.1996

❸ Ingen sommerferie . . . . [ ] [ ] [ ] 6+

90m. *(No Summer Holiday)* A worthwhile route that follows a left-to-right diagonal up the face and has a tough finale.

1) **5-, 30m.** Start as for *Ingen sommerferie* but walk left to a belay below the undercut left-hand corner of the slab.

2) **6-, 25m.** Weave between the overhangs to access the bottom left corner of the slab then climb cracks up to its top right corner before moving over left to a bolt belay. A good pitch.

3) **6, 25m.** Climb the groove to the bulge then pass this and gain the crack on the right. Up this to a square overhang then move right to a good stance.

4) **6+, 10m.** Climb the overhanging crack with difficulty then move left to another crack that leads to easy ground.

FA. Odd-Roar Wiik, Niels Paulsen 12.8.1995

❹ Pizzatyven . . . . . . [Top][ ][ ][ ] 6

85m. *(The Pizza Thief)* The route follows a series of cracks and corners which start on the steep slab at the cliff's base. Originally an aid climb done in the depths of winter, it is still used for aid training on occasions, but hammer-less only please.

1) **5-, 30m.** Climb the near-parallel finger-cracks to the big ledge then walk left across the grassy ledge to a belay under the right arete of the big slab.

2) **5-, 25m.** Start up the crack system on the right side of the bottom slab then traverse left to a small stance and bolt belay.

3) **6, 10m.** Climb up a steep corner (as for *Ingen sommerferie*), then traverse left, climbing through an overhang to a belay on a good ledge.

4) **6, 10m.** From the right end of the ledge climb the left-facing corner to reach the comfort of a large ledge.

5) **5+, 10m.** At the back of the ledge, climb the steep groove, then after a few metres, switch to the crack on the right. Finish up easy slabs.

FA. Odd-Roar Wiik (solo) 11.1993 as Teknisk Trening (Aid Practice).
FFA. Odd-Roar Wiik, Thorbjørn Enevold 6.1995

❺ Ant Line. . . . . [ ] [ ] 5+

85m. Makes the most of the right-hand side of the cliff.

1) **5- 30m.** Climb the near-parallel finger-cracks as for *Pizzatyven* to the big ledge then walk left across the grassy ledge to a belay under the right arete of the big slab.

2) **5-, 40m.** Start up the crack system on the right side of the bottom slab (still the same as *Pizzatyven*) and continue until the chimney on the right can be gained. Follow this chimney for 20m, passing some overhangs to reach a small ledge.

3) **5+, 15m.** A short steep groove with a leftwards exit completes the route.

FA. Haakon Christiansen and Niels Poulsen climbed the first pitch in 7.1988. A few days later, Kjell Ove Storvik and Niels Poulsen completed the route.

Lots of sun

15 min

Descent

The West

Henningsvær

Kalle

Kabelvåg

Svolvær

Trolltindan

Walking Peaks

Bouldering

4

5

2 3

West Face

A good places for starters as there is a classic easy route plus a few other interesting offerings. It is minutes from the road.

Approach - For *Pianohandler Lunds rute*, or any of the climbs on the left, the best approach is via a good path from the road just north of the cutting.

Descent - Scramble up and left to the upper end of a steep gully, descend this with care. It is steep and loose.

❶ Huggormen   8-
26m. *(The Adder)* On the far left, right of the descent gully, are two thin vertical cracks in the north-facing wall. This is the left-hand crack system, splitting a large roof low down. Approach from below and climb the bulge and sustained zig-zagging crack to ledges. Abseil off. It is also possible to start further to the left and miss out the crux - *Håkon Magnus*, **6+**, joining *Huggormen* at 10m, though the start is hard and bold.
FA. Odd-Roar Wiik, Neils Poulsen (some aid and called Kaos) 1990s
FFA. Petter Restorp and Hanna Melin

❷ Tapir . . . .   Top   7-
22m. The right-hand crack system is excellent when it is dry. Climb the sustained crack up to a bolt which protects a hard move to the finish. Lower-off from paired bolts.
FA. Odd-Roar Wiik had aid soloed the first ascent in the winter of 1990/91
FFA. Odd-Roar Wiik, Anders Bergwall 8.1991

❸ Nøttebus . . . .   6+
45m. *(Quiz Fun)* A good route up the crack and groove to the left of the arete. Start by the tree and climb the crack to stance on the right. A variation start (**5+**) goes up the fine slanting groove on the right. Follow the long elegant groove to a stance on the crest of the pillar, then finish up the slab and crack above.
Descent - Abseil from the trees or finish up *Dagens rett*.
FA. Krister Jonsson, Hanna Falkestrøm 1996

❹ Svaclownen   6
30m. *(Slab Clown)* From the foot of *Dagens rett*, climb the fine slab on the left and thin cracks to reach the 2nd stance on *Nøttebus*. Finish up this.
FA. Fredrik Rapp, Martin Jakobsson 1990s

❺ Dagens rett   6-
70m. *(Speciality of the Day)* A worthwhile climb without much of a line but with three nice pitches. Start below a shrubby groove.
1) 6-, 30m. Scramble up the groove for 8m, then climb the finger-crack on the left wall with hard moves to a ledge.
2) 5+, 28m. Continue up the cracked arete, then traverse right across the groove on to the right wall. Move up on suspect flakes then continue to the overhang, which is passed steeply on the right. Up the groove to a belay on the terrace.
3) 6-, 12m. Up and right is a short rounded arete. Climb up onto this from the left or the right, then step right and jam a thin finger-crack to the top. A sweet finish!
FA. (Pitch 1) Niels Poulsen, Haakon Christiansen 1989. Thorbjørn Enevold and NNKS climbing students climbed the top finger-crack around the same time. Ed Webster and Arild Meyer linked the pitches together on 18.5.1994

Descent

South Face

The West · Henningsvær · Kalle · Kabelvåg · Svolvær · Trolltindan · Walking Peaks · Bouldering

6 Pianohandler Lunds drøm . . 🌙 ☐ 5+
80m. *(Piano Dealer Lund's Dream)* Not as popular an outing as *Pianohandler Lunds rute*, but with some worthwhile and interesting climbing. Start on a ledge at the top of a steep approach trail about 50m to the left of the two telephone poles.
1) 5+, 35m. Climb a grassy V-groove/corner up to below the slanting overhang at the top of the corner. Step right into a thin crack in the wall (or step right earlier) and move up awkwardly (**5+**) onto a sloping ledge. Belay here (25m), or continue up steep cracks on the right (**5**), step right again, and head up another short crack to a belay ledge on the prow of the buttress. A more direct version is loose and not recommended.
2) 5+, 25m. Traverse right across a slab and climb a short awkward groove to a good ledge. A short crack and corner reaches another spacious ledge.
3) 2, 20m. Climb easy cracks to the top.
FA. Sjur Nesheim, Kjell Ove Storvik 7.1979

7 Sterk, Naken og Biltyvene
. . . . 🌙 ✒️ ☐ 7
45m. *(Strong, Naken and Car Thieves - a Norwegian rock band)* A steep line up the groove in the crest of the buttress to the right of the hanging shield. The entry is devious but the groove itself presents even more problems.
FA. Neils Poulsen, Odd-Roar Wiik (some aid) 1994
FFA. Bjarte Bø, Anne Grete Nebell 29.7.1997

8 Pianohandler Lunds rute . . . Top☐ L50 ☐ 4+
100m. Nice climbing with commodious stances. Start by the twin telegraph poles, below the prominent left-slanting corner.
Photo page 92.
1) 4, 35m. Climb the corner then slabs and a short steepening to a big ledge on the right.
2) 4+, 20m. Climb up cracks on the right then smear up a slab to reach the right end of the hand-traverse. Up this to another big ledge with assorted belays.
3) 4+, 20m. Traverse right along a fault and climb through a bulge to gain a steep groove. Go up this and a short jamming crack above to a good ledge. A great pitch.
4) 4, 10m. Climb the short awkward crack (at least **5** if you can't jam) to a big ledge system below the final tier.
5) 4+, 20m. Climb the centre of the face to bulges then head up and left to thin cracks which give a good finale. The awkward finger and hand-crack on the left gives an alternative finish - **4+**.
FA. Arild Meyer, Kjell Skog, Ulf Prytz made the first ascent of Lofoten's most popular easy route in 1971 whilst looking for routes for students from the Nord Norsk Klatreskole. The route name, suggested by one of the students, honours a popular comic character from an early 70s radio show.

9 Pianisten . . . . 🌙 ✒️ ☐ 6
90m. *(The Piano Player)* A good direct finish to *Pianohandler Lunds rute* up cracks, above an old direct start.
1) 6, 35m. The steep cracks lead to the normal route.
2) 4+, 20m. As for *Pianohandler Lunds rute*.
3) 6, 35m. Climb the strenuous leaning jamming crack to the easier groove, then up this to a terrace. A short crack in the next wall is the best way on. You can also climb directly through the A-shaped overhang at about the same grade.
4) 2, 20m. As for *Pianohandler Lunds drøm*.
FA. Kjell Skog and partner 7.1979. FA. (Pitch 1) Knut Storvik, Andreas Christiansen 1999. FA. (Pitch 3 direct) Knut Storvik, Andreas Christiansen 1999

South Face

A good collection of climbs on this fine face which overlooks the causeway across the seaward end of Djupfjord. It has a quick and easy approach, gets plenty of sun and is always popular. It is worth checking from the road to see how busy the crag is to save a walk up if your intended route is occupied.

Approach - Follow a path along the north shore of Djupfjorden for 100m then head directly up to the crag on a good path through the billberries.

Descent - Either make a spectacular free-hanging abseil (50m) off the fixed chain straight over the huge roof (don't be tempted to try and abseil down the arete on the left - a big scary rope-knackering swing will ensue). Alternatively, walk over the ridge (to the left looking at the cliff) and descend the gully as for the West Face routes - see page 102.

Lots of sun | 5 min | Sheltered

Descent as for West Face

Sørfjellet southern minor summit

Abseil Chain

Routes 18 and 19

⑩ Kangshungrisset... 6+
60m. *(The Kangshung Crack)* The vertical crack system just to the left of the big black chimney. Steep sport, especially the top finger-crack. Start on ledges up and left of *Applecake Arete.*
1) 6-, 30m. Scramble up grassy ledges then traverse 3m left to the base of a shallow vertical black groove that runs up to the right end of a roof. Pass the overhang on the right then continue up a groove to a belay on the right.
2) 6+, 30m. Strenuous finger jamming leads up a slightly overhanging section, then an easier finish up the final crack.
FA. Ed Webster, Knut Fausa Storvik 12.5.1994. The 6th anniversary of Webster's near summit day on Mt. Everest's Kangshung Face.

⑪ Sorte Orm 6
60m. *(Black Adder)* The big forbidding groove that bounds the left side of the main section of the face gives an atmospheric outing.
1) 5, 30m. Start up the arete but move out left and climb past an overlap onto a small stance below the upper chimney.
2) 6, 30m. Climb right of the crack then move left into the awkward leaning groove. Up this as it widens awkwardly until the finger-crack in the slab can be reached for a pleasanter finish.
FA. Thorbjørn Enevold, Trond Solberg 1992. They finished leftwards via a loose crack - not recommended.
FA. (Finish as described) Mathias and Eirik Andersen 1992

⑫ Applecake Arete ...... Top 50 5+
60m. Start at the foot of the arete under the tree-filled corner.
1) 4+, 40m. Climb onto the arete proper and follow it through a couple of bulges to a small stance below the upper crack.
2) 5+, 20m. Climb the finger-crack to the top - quite testing at half height and then again just below the crest.
FA. Odd-Roar Wiik, Ed Webster, Thorbjørn Enevold, Lutta Fagerli 13.8.1991

⑬ Lys og skygge ...... Top 50 5+
60m. *(Light and Shade)* Start at the foot of a right-trending grassy ramp. *Photo on page 95.*
1) 5+, 25m. Climb the ramp then the steep fingery wall on the left, and thin cracks, to a belay on the left below a roof.
2) 4+, 35m. Step left and climb the wall then the arete for 12m until a step right can be made into a groove. Up this to the chain. A more direct version of the upper section of this pitch is the exposed **Solformørkelsen,** 6-.
FA. (P1) Ed Webster, Trond Solberg 2.8.1991
FA. (P2) Ed Webster, Thorbjørn Enevold 3.8.1991

⑭ Soria Moria ...... 7+
65m. *(A castle in a Norwegian fairytale)* A difficult climb up the prominent right-trending groove. Originally a hard aid route and now a harder free one.
1) 7, 30m. As for *Lys og skygge,* but continue for 10m to a small stance - poor bolt belay, a decent nut belay below.
2) 7+, 35m. Sustained and hard climbing follows the thin cracks up the large right-leaning groove all the way to the top.
FA. Odd-Roar Wiik, Niels Poulsen (aid) 3.1993
FFA. Linus Kullstad late 1990s

Above the stance on Soria Moria are two overhanging cracks - both give aid routes at A2, the left-hand one was the work of Odd-Roar Wiik and the right-hand one of Patrik Fransson.

⑮ Nye tider A3
40m. *(New Times)* A serious aid route taking the only line up the big slab under *Soria Moria.* Bring birdbeaks, copperheads and knife-blades. Climb the groove then move left to get through the overlap and continue up the face to join *Soria Moria.* Finish up this - free *(7+)* or on clean aid, no hammered gear please.
FA. Odd-Roar Wiik, early 1990s

⑯ Kongens hjørne 6
45m. *(The King's Arete)* A serious lead, with ground-fall potential. Start at the top of the grassy ramp. Climb slightly left, then up and right to a block, before continuing up the face above just to the left of an arete (minimal protection) until you reach easier climbing just below the top.
FA. Odd-Roar Wiik 8.1991. The day that King Harald was visiting Henningsvær. He stopped his car to watch Odd-Roar finish the pitch.

⑰ Dream of White Whales.... 5+
28m. The thin dyke on the diagonal buttress below and right of the rest of the cliff. Gain and follow the dyke up and right until it meets a vertical crack/groove. Up this to a belay at the top of the ramp. Descend this, or finish up *Kongens Hjorne.*
FA. Thorbjørn Enevold, Lutta Fagerli 1992. The route is as long as a whale.

There are three outlying routes.

⑱ Djupfjord sprickan . 7-
18m. *(Djupfjord Crack)* A smart vertical crackline in a clean sheet of rock round and right of *Lys og skygge.* It can be seen from the road. The crack starts nice and narrow, but sadly it becomes off-width in the end. Requires good jamming skills. Abseil descent.
FA. Simon Thyr 5.2000

⑲ Jørn Roger. A2
45m. An aid route starting from loose blocks and following a groove to a stance *(A1, 15m)* then up the thin cracks in the face above *(A2, 30m).* Abseil from a tree on the right to descend.
FA. Andreas Christiansen, Jonas Tetlie, Easter 1997

⑳ Slemgutt risset......... 5+
10m. *(Bad Boy's Crack)* The crack in the small outcrop above the cliff.
FA. Kjell Ove Storvik, Kjell Skog 6.1976

Approach *Djupfjord sprickan* from further along the path that runs beside the fjord and scrambling up to the face

The West
Henningsvær
Kalle
Kabelvåg
Svolvær
Trolltindan
Walking Peaks
Bouldering

❶ Frøken Sverige . . . . . . 🗒️📷☐ **6**
14m. *(Miss Sweden)* The steep cracks on the far left.
FA. Simond Thyr 1990s

❷ Du gamla du fria. . . 🗒️📷📷☐ **7**
14m. *(The Old and the Free - The Swedish National Anthem)*
Trend right to the horizontal break then sprint direct.
FA. Geir-Rune Holm 1990s

❸ Madelene . . . . 🗒️📷📷☐ **7-**
14m. The left-hand of the right-trending cracks and wall above.
FA. Simond Thyr 1990s

❹ Blåklokka. . . . . 🗒️📷☐ **6-**
14m. *(Bluebell)* A steep right-trending crack leads to a finish up a
groove. There is a harder **Direct Start** just to the right.
FA. Niels Poulsen, Odd-Roar Wiik 1989

❺ Blåhval superstar . . . . . 📷📷☐ **7**
14m. *(Blue Whale Superstar)* Start as for *Blåklokka* but finish up
the bold arete.
FA. Petter Restorp 1990s

The rest of the routes are on the right-hand side of the wall.

❻ Jammerfest . . . . . . 🗒️📷📷☐ **6+**
14m. *(Jamming Party)* The evil looking roof crack is a must for
homesick gritstoners. Take some big gear.
FA. Jimmy Halvardsson 1990s

❼ Steepstone. . . . . 🗒️📷📷☐ **8-**
14m. The right wall of the crack and precarious ramp above.
FA. Jimmy Halvardsson 1990s

Descent - walk off the back

The West

Henningsvær

Kalle

Kabelvåg

Svolvær

Trolltindan

Svenskeveggen

This small steep roadside crag has some bolted routes and trad crack climbs and is good for a short day. It looks a bit small from a distance but it is actually bigger than it appears courtesy of the hidden starts. Although not great these routes do offer an easily accessible workout and are usually quite sheltered.

Approach (see map on page 110) - It is situated on the south side of a knoll, on the opposite side of the road from Pianokrakken, and is reached by a short scramble.

⑧ Project? . . . . 🔆 ☐ ?
14m. The centre of the wall above the left-hand crack is an unknown quantity/project.

⑨ Arbetsskygg . . . . 🔆 ☐ 7
14m. *(Work Shy)* Gain the steep upper flake-crack by a tough start up the left-hand crack in the lower wall.
FA. Peter Restorp 1990s

⑩ Snickar glädje . . . . 🔆 ☐ 7-
14m. *(Carpenter's Pleasure)* A classic crack with a steep start and pumpy finish.
FA. Climbed by unknown Swedes in 1995 - or at least their entry in the New Routes' Book was unreadable.

⑪ Reisefeber . . . . 🔆 ☐ 8
14m. *(Travel Fever)* The desperate wall just right of the flake-crack.
FA. Petter Restorp

⑫ I rampelyset . . . . 🔆 ☐ 8
14m. *(In the Limelight)* The right-hand crack leads to the bolted headwall.
FA. Robert Caspersen 1990s. Bolted and climbed with an audience from a NNKS course to show how sport climbing actually works. He stopped between moves to explain what he was doing!

⑬ I rampelyset direkte . . . 🔆 ☐ 8
14m. An independent start up the wall just to the right.
FA. Knut Storvik 1990s

Djupfjord

The West

Henningsvær

Kalle

Kabelvåg

Svolvær

Trolltindan

Walking Peaks

Bouldering

Bare blåbær

Djupfjordvatnet
(hidden)

Terminal moraine

Pillaren/Point 713m

Descent

Vågakallen/
Kvandalstinden col

Pillaren

Budalstinden

Djupfjord

The West

Henningsvær

Kalle

Kabelvåg

Svolvær

Trolltindan

Walking Peaks

Bouldering

The road to Henningsvær crosses the narrow neck of Djupfjord on a causeway, and a quick 'eyes-left' will reveal a mountain-side of high quality granite running along the eastern side of the fjord. These are the flanks of Budalstinden. Beyond the end of the fjord, and rising above the freshwater lake of Djupfjordvatnet (hidden from the road) is the great spur that forms the northwest buttress of Vågakallen which terminates in Point 713m, and is known to climbers simply as 'Pillaren' (the Pillar), it is home to one of the most sought-after routes on Lofoten; the great classic of *Bare blåbær*.

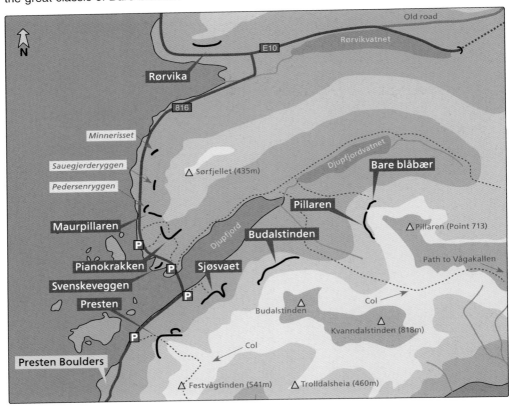

Approaches

Bare blåbær and the routes on Pillaren and the eastern side of Budalstinden are approached by following the path along the northwestern shore of Djupford to the terminal moraine that cuts right across the valley - allow about an hour. The Two Faces Face and Sjøsvaet (the Sea Slab) are reached from parking by the bend on the Henningsvær side of the causeway. Individual approaches are described with each cliff.

Conditions

The hillside faces northwest and so gets the sun from mid afternoon onwards. In high summer it is illuminated until the sun finally dips behind Sørfjellet, late in the evening. The hillside takes drainage - a couple of days of decent weather are needed to bring the routes into condition, although *Bare blåbær* suffers from little drainage and dries quickly.

"*Arild Meyer had told us there was probably a good new climb up there,*" remembered Tim Hansen. "*Ingun and I had come up to Lofoten so that she could teach a climbing course for the Nord Norsk Klatreskole.*" Well, Arild was certainly right! Tim Hansen and Ingun Raastad made the first ascent of the classic route *Bare blåbær* in the summer of 1986.

The West

Henningsvær

Kalle

Kabelvåg

Svolvær

Trolltindan

Walking Peaks

Bouldering

The second pitch of *Bare blåbær* (5-) - *page 116* - on Pillaren. Probably the most popular route of its grade on Lofoten and, despite the approach, most good summer days see a team or two at work.

The West

Henningsvær

Kalle

Kabelvåg

Svolvær

Trolltindan

Walking Peaks

Bouldering

Pianokrakken

P

To Pillaren

To Vågakallen
Nordryggen

To *Bare blåbær*

The view from the base of *Bare blåbær*.

Tim Wilkinson and Ali Kennedy seconding Jamie Moss while he takes a photo on the classic *Bare blåbær* (5-) - *page 116*. Meanwhile, across the valley, Chris Craggs coincidentally captures the same moment on his long lens (backdrop).

Bare blåbær

A fine, granite slab beyond the head of Djupfjorden is home to one of Lofoten's most popular, long routes, *Bare blåbær (Only Bilberries)*, a Norwegian expression meaning an easy task.
Approach - Park just north of the causeway across Djupfjorden. Follow the Djupfjorden path along the northern shore of the fjord to the terminal moraine that separates the upper freshwater lake and the fjord. Keep left, heading for the grove of pine trees, and follow the path until just short of the freshwater lake of Djupfjordvatnet, at which point a path dives rightwards into the wood. Cross the small stream and head for the open gully between the two slabby outcrops. Scramble up this then head out left onto the spur, continue leftwards under an easy-angled slab which leads to the base of the main slab - 1 hour from the road.

Pillaren

Bare blåbær

Vågakallen/
Kvandalstinden col

The West

Henningsvær

Kalle

Kabelvåg

Svolvær

Trolltindan

Walking Peaks

Bouldering

Coley Smoke

Left of Bare blåbær buttress is a smaller triangular buttress. This one is generally slabby but has some steep roofs in its mid-section.

Approach - See page 112.

Descent - For routes 1 and 2, traverse left round rocky ribs for 50m and descend a steep crack to a rock spur. A 50m abseil (slings in place) leads back to the ground. Alternatively continue up *Very Expensive Ticket*.

Bare blåbær

Glen Henry on pitch 4 of *Coley Smoke* (5) on the first ascent. Photo: Nick Ashton

The West

Henningsvær

Kalle

Kabelvåg

Svolvær

Trolltindan

Walking Peaks

Bouldering

① Coley Smoke . . . . 🔲 **5**
120m. A line up the cracks and grooves in the centre of the buttress. Start below and left of the prominent straight crack that splits three offset overhangs.
1) 4, 30m. A wandering pitch up the slabs, trending leftwards to a belay at the foot of the attractive open groove.
2) 5, 30m. Climb the groove to a stance on the left at its top.
3) 5-, 30m. Climb up and right, then leftwards to a short steep crack splitting the overlap. Continue up the cracks above then move right to a constricted belay in the chimney on the right, at the top of the prominent corner system.
4) 5-, 30m. Climb the chimney past the jammed boulder and follow the groove until the delightful finger-crack in the slab to the left can be reached. Belay well back on a good ledge by a block and tree.
FA. Nick Ashton, Glenn Henry, Dave Musgrove 11.8.1998

② Child's Play . . . . 🔲 **5+**
125m. A route that covers some of the same ground as *Coley Smoke* albeit in a more direct version. Start at a large finger-shaped boulder at ground level, below a scooped boulder with three grooves in its top half.
1) 5, 25m. Climb the centre of the scoop and exit via the middle one of the three grooves. Continue up easy slabs to a spike belay below the main crack.
2) 5, 30m. Climb steeply up the jagged crack then, when the angle eases, step right into a left-slanting groove. Up this as it steepens into a blind layback crack then, where this ends, step right and belay a little higher below some loose blocks.
3) 5+, 40m. Move left for 5m over the loose blocks (care needed) to gain the main corner. Follow this past a roof to where it steepens. Pass the steepening with difficulty then belay in the base of the chimney above.
4) 5-, 30m. As for *Coley Smoke*.
FA. Michael Hayes, Graham Weston 8.8.2001

③ Very Expensive Ticket . . 🔲 **7**
220m. The crest of the broad pillar to the left of the central chimney system, initially up the huge left-facing groove, then up the rounded crest of the buttress.
1) 4+, 40m. From blocks, climb easy slabs, grooves and cracks to a stance below and left of the huge left-facing corner system.
2) 7, 30m. Gain the corner and climb it with increasing difficulty, - poor protection. The final section may be done with a bit of aid at **6+** *A2*. Above the roof, belay on a good flake.
3) 6+, 30m. Bold! Climb the slabs to a small flake (gear) then continue climbing in the same line to the sanctuary of the crack systems. Up these to the grass ledge.
4) 5, 50m. Climb the left-facing grooves to a stance on a ledge with blocks.
5) 3, 20m. Easy slabs lead to top of the central gully.
6) 4+, 50m. Follow the groove and then easy slabs all the way rightwards to the belay at the top of *Bare blåbær*.
Descent - Abseil down *Bare blåbær*, taking care that the ropes don't jam on the second abseil, and avoiding annoying those who are having their own epics on the way up.
FA. Pawel Grenda, Bartek Malinowski, Marcin Szymelfenig (Poland) 16.6.2005

③a Rännesnärja. . . . . 🔲 **5**
220m. The thin crack in the slab right of *Very Expensive Ticket*. At the top join *Ticket* and follow it to the descent down *Bare blåbær*. A last minute addition to the guide - the line and pitch locations have not been confirmed, treat the information with care.
FA. Fredrik Rapp 2007

As a scary alternative finish to any of these routes, traverse the grassy break rightwards into the wide gully.

④ Whale Meet Again . . . . 🔲 **7-**
40m. A very bold traverse from the central chimney to the bolt belays above the fourth pitch of *Bare blåbær*, passing a solitary runner. Equally serious for leader and second.
FA. Nick Ashton, Glenn Henry, David Musgrove 11.8.1998

Bare blåbær

One of Lofoten's most popular favourites, this superb climb may be the most sought-after route on the islands - well protected and not too steep. it is an excellent expedition.

Approach - See page 112.

Descent - Abseil back down the line of *Bare blåbær*, or alternatively, abseil down to the left (facing out) down the Black Arch.

> Take care when abseiling - this wide crack eats ropes!

5 **Bare blåbær.** . . . . [Top 50] ☐ **5-**

236m. *(Only Bilberries)* A pure classic and, despite its distance from the road, it is hugely popular. The name is Norwegian for a task of no great difficulty, obviously it refers to the actual climb and not the walk in. *Photos on pages 1, 111, 112, 224 and 250.*

1) 4, 26m. Start up a small slab and move up to a shallow left-facing corner. Up this, or climb a thin finger-crack on the right, to reach a good ledge at the base of a main crack.

2) 5-, 34m. Finger and hand jam up the fantastic crack above to a small belay stance where the angle of the rock lessens. Cams helpful at the belay.

3) 5-, 32m. Continue up the V-groove, which steepens and becomes increasingly awkward. When the crack inside the groove becomes too thin, step out right around the arete into another crack. Climb up this to a good belay at flakes and a ledge.

4) 5-, 28m. Layback the flake wedged inside the V-groove above until you reach several loose chockstones. Now step delicately to the right around the corner into a hidden crack and climb this to more flakes and another good stance.

5) 5-, 40m. Continue up the single, sustained crack system splitting the upper slab - elegant finger and hand jamming up perfect rock. When the crack finally thins, climb to the right to a bolt and chain belay to the left of a huge flake.

6) 5-, 40m. An unlikely looking pitch with excellent climbing. Climb up and move left to pass a small roof. Step back right and follow a shallow groove and crack system more or less straight up the upper slab to a small belay stance with a two bolt belay.

7) 4-, 36m. One last pitch leads up the easier slab to reach a belay at the base of the cliff's steeper headwall. Beware of loose rock on this final pitch and the fact there will be climbers below.

FA. Tim Hansen, Ingun Raastad 1986

The West
Henningsvær
Kalle
Kabelvåg
Svolvær
Trolltindan
Walking Peaks
Bouldering

Ali Kennedy follows the crucial 2nd pitch *Thiras Mirith* (6). Photo: Jamie Moss

The West

Henningsvær

Kalle

Kabelvåg

Svolvær

Trolltindan

Walking Peaks

Bouldering

❻ Thiras Mirith . . . . 🕸 🦎 ▭ 6

240m. This is the parallel crack system between *Bare blåbær* and the Black Arch. It features some excellent hand-jamming, but there is also a difficult thin crack, plus a long unprotected off-width pitch. Carry tiny wires and a good selection of cams. *Photos this page and 118.*

1) 4, 26m. Climb the first short pitch of *Bare blåbær*.

2) 6, 44m. Jam up the finger-crack at the start of *Bare blåbær* pitch 2, then traverse right across the face into a thin crack. Climb this then make a hard traverse into the perfect crack on the right. Take a semi-hanging belay here.

3) 6, 50m. Continue up the superb crack system which starts as a hand-crack then slowly becomes thinner until it narrows to just a thin seam just above the Black Arch. Make off-balance jamming moves up the thin crack to the bolted belay at the top of pitch 4 of *Bare blåbær*, or in the cracks just below this.

4) 4+, 45m. A long and unprotected off-width leads up the left side of the huge detached flake above. Belay at the top of the flake. Abseil from the bolts over to the left or:

5) and 6) Finish up *Bare blåbær*.

FA. (Middle section - the traverse and hand-crack) Odd-Roar Wiik, Jørgen Sundby, Borghild Hansen 7.1989. FA. (as described) Thorbjørn Enevold, Per Kylner, Jenny Gustavsson 8.7.1993

The West

Henningsvær

Kalle

Kabelvåg

Svolvær

Trolltindan

Walking Peaks

Bouldering

Dealing with bold routes

There are many routes on Lofoten where the protection is spaced, poor, or even non-existent. While some climbers shy away from bold routes, others thrive on the excitement of the ultimate test of their ability as climbers. Experiences overcoming bold sections of climbing are often the most memorable, and treasured of all climbing memories. Over time, what may start off as something you try to avoid may turn out to be an unstoppable addiction.

To climb bold routes requires a real sense of determination and the ability to focus technically on the climbing without being distracted by the risk. These two factors result in what we usually refer to as 'boldness'. No matter if you consider yourself a bold climber or not, there are a few ways that you can improve your chances of success on a pitch.

While we like to think that we always choose to succeed with what we are trying, when pushing our limits on a bold route, success always comes at a price: feeling scared, being painfully pumped, bleeding from your fingers each time your push your tips into a thin crack, not having an epic story to tell in the pub and so on. Often, we will fail in our attempt not because we didn't have 'it' in us to succeed, but because we choose not to. This is often the case when we're pushing ourselves to our very limit, though sometimes we find other reasons for our failure rather than accepting that, at a subconscious level, our failure was our own choice.

Choosing to succeed can simply be a matter of accepting the price that has to be paid and asserting to yourself that this time around - you are choosing to succeed. Reliving past glories is a good way of convincing ourselves that the price is worth paying.

Other benefits can be gained from the way we approach the gear. Climbing protection has two roles to play - physically, it is there to stop our falls, but it also provides psychological support in spurring us on. An attempt is more likely to end because we aren't happy with the protection than because we physically can't do the next move. Often, it is psychologically advantageous to place more protection than is strictly needed in order to boost our mental morale, whether the physical cost of placing the extra protection is worth paying is a matter of judgement.

Anyone who has climbed with marginal protection will testify that what seems crazy from the comfort of flat earth, may make complete sense when you're runout on the lead. Placing protection that is barely able to support the weight of the quickdraw you have clipped to it clearly isn't a good idea from a 'fall arrest' perspective, but often, the mere act of having a rope leading upwards rather than downwards, and the visual impact of having something clipped is enough to get you through a bold section and out of trouble. Needless to say, 'psychological protection' is something that requires a calculated approach, though once in a while, it actually holds.

The better your technique, the 'bolder' you can afford to be, simply because you know you are less likely to fall. Bold climbing requires technique with a wide margin for error, this can involve making moves using more strength than neces-sary, but remaining in better control.

Based on text from the *The Mind* chapter of *Trad Climbing+* by Adrian Berry and John Arran, published by Rockfax 2007 - see back cover flap

The West

Henningsvær

Kalle

Kabelvåg

Svolvær

Trolltindan

Walking Peaks

Bouldering

Tim Wilkinson running it out on the 2nd pitch of *Thiras Mirith* (6) - *page 117*. Photo: Ali Kennedy

Pillaren (Point 713m)

Facing down the valley is the impressive bastion that terminates the northwest ridge of Vågakallen. There are currently only three long routes here for which limited details are known.

Approach - See page 112

Descent - Long and arduous. From the summit of Pillaren, Descent - follow the ridge, ledges and gullies (quite complicated) to the col between Vågakallen and Kvandalstinden, then descend the steep trail back down to Djupfjorden - about 2 hours.

Pillaren/Point 713m

Descent

Arild Meyer on pitch 3 of *Høstgull* (7-) on the first ascent. Photo: Thorbjørn Enevold

❶ Haakon's Restless Crack . . . 4+
50m. A fine long crack away on the left, and about 100m right of *Bare blåbær*, leads to a fixed sling belay/abseil point.
FA. Haakon Christiansen, Nils Paulsen 1.8.2004. Rather than join the queue for 'Bilberries' the team decide to go off and do a new route.

❷ Celebrian. 6-
About 400m. A twelve pitch climb up the centre of Pillaren's massive buttress, that forms the main angle of the mountain between the tall rambling face to the right and the clean slab of the main slabby section and *Bare blåbær* down to the left. A good quality long route with an Alpine feel and not too difficult. Some large gear will be found useful for the wider cracks. Route finding can be difficult, though in general stay just to the left of the grassy section in the middle of the buttress. Once the steeper rock of the summit wall is reached (above the large ledge system) climb a high quality crack and groove system up the middle of the headwall.
FA. Odd-Roar Wiik, Niels Poulsen 9.1990

❸ Høstgull 7-
About 400m. *(Autumn Gold)* A very fine climb with some bold slabs requiring good route finding skills. This route has 9 pitches then the top 3 of *Celebrian*. Approach as for *Celebrian*, but head 100m further to the right to start at an area of attractive slabs. Follow very nice slabs and cracks for 8 pitches, to gain the huge ledge system, then move left to the headwall section of *Celebrian* - a suitably grand finale.
FA. Thorbjørn Enevold, Arild Meyer 9.1995

❹ Elgfesten 6
About 400m. *(The Elk Party)* On the far right-hand side of Pillaren, up on the side of a steep pillar, is a prominent left-facing groove system. About 8 good pitches up these grooves lead to a scrambling finish, trending right to easier ground.
FA. Odd-Roar Wiik, Niels Poulsen 9.1992

Descent along ridge to col

The West
Henningsvær
Kalle
Kabelvåg
Svolvær
Trolltindan
Walking Peaks
Bouldering

Budalstinden

The southeast shore of Djupfjord is basically a huge cliff face, much of it composed of quality granite. It gets the afternoon and evening sun but sections of it are rather slow to dry after rain.

Approach - The easiest way to reach the face is to follow the track along the northern shore of Djupfjord then head across the boulders and round to the face. Approaching along the eastern shore looks shorter but is much more arduous.

❶ Budalspillaren . . . . 〖2〗 ⬜ **6+**

The fine pillar on the left-hand side of the face. The route starts up a thin crack in the left-hand wall of the biggest groove.

1) 6+. Climb the long thin crack in the left wall of the long groove, then move left to a stance.

2) 6+. Traverse left, then climb the crack in the compact slab, up to a good ledge.

3) 6. The pillar, edge and cracks up to big ledge.

4) 5+. Climb cracks, trending rightwards. Beware of a loose block on this pitch.

5) 6. A short pitch leads over a steep bulge.

6) 3. Traverse left over grass, then climb a crack.

Descent - Abseil back down the route. 2 x 60m ropes required.

FA. Frøydis Ravlo, Robert Caspersen 2.6.2002

The West

Henningsvær

Kalle

Kabelvåg

Svolvær

Trolltindan

Walking Peaks

Bouldering

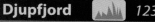

❷ Skvis . . . . ⛰ [____] **6**
(Squeeze) A right-hand variation on the last route has some good climbing. A little aid was used on the first ascent because of wet rock but it should go free at a reasonable grade in the dry.
1) 6+. As for *Budalspillaren*.
2) 6. Start as for *Budalspillaren* but move out right then climb left through a roof and up to a big ledge.
3) 6. Climb to the top of the beautiful groove.
4 and 5) 4+. A bit of crumbly and loose rock rather spoils the adventure.
Descent - Abseil down *Budalspillaren*.
FA. Jan Helge Furnesvik, Odd-Roar Wiik 2.6.2002

❸ Kjære frøken Johansson . . . ⛰ [____] **6+** *AO*
(Dear Miss Johanson - a Swedish song) 4 pitches. This is the fine looking pillar right of *Budalspillaren*.
Descent - Abseil back down the line.
FA. Odd-Roar Wiik, Arild Meyer 6.1995

❹ Bibel hjørnet . . . . ⛰ [____] **5+**
(Bible Corner) Scramble across grass ledges to reach the prominent tall corner groove and climb it in two pitches.
Descent - Head down the grassy ramp on the right and, either loop back to the base of the route, or continue scrambling down the ramp to arrive above the Two Faces Face.
FA. Thorbjørn Enevold, Trond Solberg 7.1995

124

The West

Henningsvær

Kalle

Kabelvåg

Svolvær

Trolltindan

Walking Peaks

Bouldering

The West

Henningsvær

Kalle

Kabelvåg

Svolvær

Trolltindan

Walking Peaks

Bouldering

Two shots showing the beautiful slabs of Djupfjord.
Left: Colin Binks and Chris Craggs enjoying the second
pitch of *Mr. Hyde* (6+) - *page 127* - on the Two Faces Face.
Photo: Sherri Davy.
Right: Two unknown climbers on *Solens sonner* (6) - *page
129* - on Sjøsvæt. Photo: Chris Craggs

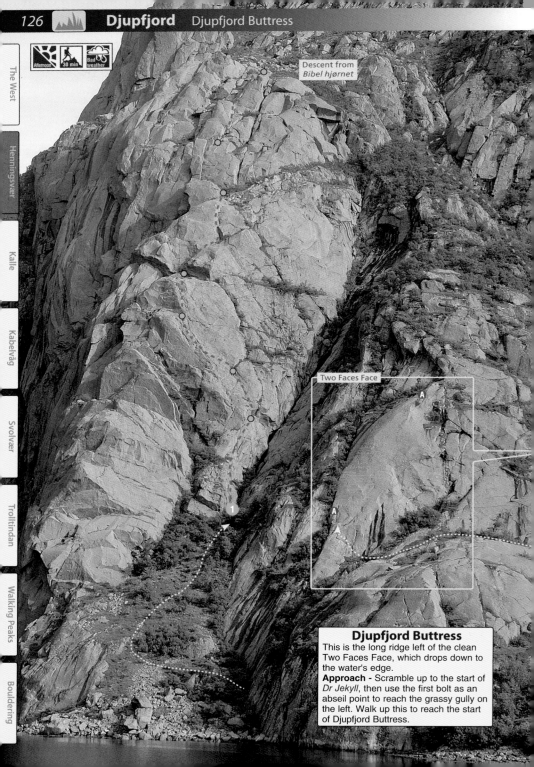

Descent from
Bibel hjørnet

Two Faces Face

A

A

Djupfjord Buttress

This is the long ridge left of the clean
Two Faces Face, which drops down to
the water's edge.
Approach - Scramble up to the start of
Dr Jekyll, then use the first bolt as an
abseil point to reach the grassy gully on
the left. Walk up this to reach the start
of Djupfjord Buttress.

The West

Henningsvær

Kalle

Kabelvåg

Svolvær

Trolltindan

Walking Peaks

Bouldering

To Djupfjord
Buttress

Easy scramble

The Two Faces Face
Clearly visible from the causeway across
Djupfjord is this clean buttress of excellent
granite. It looks quite small from the road, but
is over 60m tall and has a pair of excellent
climbs.
Approach - Boulder hop along the beach for
ten minutes then scramble up the open gully
to the right of the buttress to reach the ledges
below the face - 15-20 minutes from the road.
Descent - Abseil from the belay bolts. Two
60m ropes will just get you back to the start of
Mr Hyde on the stretch.

1 Djupfjord Buttress . . . . 5+
The right-hand side of the long ridge in about 7 pitches - great
rock and gradually easing as height is gained. Stances can be
taken at many places along the way.
Descent - Head down the grassy ramp on the right, to arrive
above the Two Faces Face and continue in the same line.
*FA. Thorbjørn Enevold, Lutta Fagerli 1995. A nice piece of rock that may have
been climbed earlier and not recorded.*

2 Dr. Jekyll 6
52m. A line of 7 bolts runs up the smoothest part of the slab
- naughty but nice. Scramble up and left to a nut belay in a flake
then head up the slab, following the line of bolts. More a sporting
climb than sport climbing, the run-outs and slightly lichenous
rock combine to concentrate the mind wonderfully. Double-bolt
belay, abseil descent. *Photo on pages 13 and 38.*
FA. Thorbjørn Enevold, Trond Solberg 1999

3 Mr Hyde . . . . 6+
70m. The right-hand line is the trad side of the face - altogether a
more memorable and scary experience. *Photo on page 124.*
1) 6, 35m. Start just left of the black streaks and climb flakes to
a large lump of quartz. Head up and right, following the seeping
crack, to easier ground and a belay (large wires) on a sloping
ledge further right.
2) 6+, 35m. Climb the groove on the left then make hard moves
to and past the bolt, heading right to gain the base of the thin
flake-cracks. These give sustained climbing with poor and spaced
protection (tiny wires and a small cam) until things ease and the
belay of the previous route can be reached. Abseil descent.
FA. Thorbjørn Enevold, Trond Solberg 1999

Sjøsvaet

(The Sea Slab) This glaciated granite slab is located high up above the entrance of Djupfjorden. The best climb here is *Solens sønner* - a broad slab split by a series of finger-cracks. The sister route of *Månens døtre* is also well worth the effort.

Descent - Abseil back down the routes (twin 50m ropes are a minimum) from the belay anchors. The abseil point in the bushes is an extra one, off the line of the route.

Approach - Park at a lay-by on the Henningsvær side of the causeway and boulder-hop along the beach until just short of the first telegraph pole. Turn right up the hillside, following a very vague path through a fern jungle and up an open gully. A tricky (especially when wet) rock section can be avoided on the right, and leads to a small ledge - gearing up is awkward.

The West · Henningsvær · Kalle · Kabelvåg · Svolvær · Trolltindan · Walking Peaks · Bouldering

❶ Ørnens brødre 7

195m. *(The Eagle's Brothers)* On the taller slab left of the *Solens sønner* slab is this solitary route that mostly follows narrow cracks. There is some bolt protection where it is most needed. Start just to the left of the big cleft between the two slabs.
1) 5, 30m. Climb the black slab up to bushes. One bolt runner.
2) 7-, 55m. Make some hard moves up the small crack that splits the bulge then climb cracks up to a bolted stance.
3) 7, 30m. Climb the slab (bolt) up to crack, climb the crack and make delicate moves up a blank slab to a double-bolted stance.
4) 5-, 50m. Climb cracks to the right of the big offwith.
5) 5-, 30m. Continue up cracks up to the top of the slab.
FA. Thorbjørn Enevold, Arild Meyer 7.1998. "We are not really the Brothers of the Eagle. The name is strongly ironic. We just wanted it to match with rest of the names on the cliff."

❷ Solens sønner . 6

135m. *(Sons of the Sun)* A fine mixture of slab climbing and finger-cracks makes this a route not to miss - one of Lofoten's best climbs at the grade. It follows the thin vertical cracks up the left side of Sjøsvaet. Carry a modern rack, including small and medium sized cams. Double ropes are needed to protect the friction traverse on pitch 2, and for the descent. *Photo on page 125.*
1) 5+, 35m. This pitch is better than it looks. From the starting ledge, move left into the base of a grassy groove system. Climb straight up this to a flake on the right, chimney behind this block, then from its top, make a tricky stride across the gap. Climb up a short slab then traverse right to a good belay ledge in a corner.
2) 6, 50m. Climb up the short cracks above into an easier wide crack. From high wires (make them good ones) step back down 5m and make a precarious traverse left across the slab. Then step up into the prominent finger-crack which is very thin at the start and at the top. Climb the crack and step right to a fine stance with a double-bolt anchor.
3) 5, 30m. Climb the finger-crack up the left-hand side of the upper slab. When it ends, continue past a bolt to an excellent belay ledge on the left with a single bolt anchor - and a steady supply of fresh drinking water on the left.
4) 5, 20m. Move up the shoulder (bolt) then pad up the slab on the right past a second bolt before easier moves lead to the top and another nice belay ledge with another double-bolt belay.
FA. Ed Webster, Odd-Roar Wiik 16.8.1993. On their 3rd attempt.

❸ Månens døtre 6

140m. *(Daughters of the Moon)* This route has always played second fiddle to *Solens sønner* but after the typical Lofoten start, it develops into a great climb. It ascends the cliff's central crack system and the middle of the huge upper slab. Above the starting ledge is a right-facing flake with shrubbery - this is it.
1) 6- 24m. Climb up behind the flake, up a slab, through a bush, and then up a short, strenuous and muddy fist-crack to easier ground and a belay on flakes.
2) 5+, 30m. Continue up a grassy crack, then climb its bushy continuation crack which becomes a perfect clean finger-crack leading to a large belay ledge.
3) 5+ 30m. Climb up the slab above (just right of a bush) to a horizontal crack. Clip a high bolt, then step right and climb up a clean slab to a ramp protected by a second bolt. Now move up right to a tiny foothold belay stance (fixed nuts) at the base of the upper finger-crack.
4) 6- 55m. Climb the upper finger-crack until it ends, then move up and left then back right, past two spaced bolts, to a sloping ledge with a double-bolt belay.
FA. Ed Webster, Johan Sandberg 15.8.1993. On their 2nd attempt.

❹ Skåningen . . . . 5+

75m. *(A Man from Skåne - an area of southern Sweden)* A direct start to *Månens Døtre*. Doing the final pitch of *Månens Døtre* increases the quality and the difficulty. Begin at the base of the slab about 12m to the right of the flat ledge.
1) 5+, 20m. Climb up the slab (using cracks on the right for protection) for 15m. Make a hard move left around a bulge, then move slightly down to a grass belay ledge on the left.
2) 5+, 25m. Climb a V-groove above the belay, then head up a crack for another 10m until a thin traverse left leads into the base of the upper flake/dihedral system, and belay.
3) 5+, 30m. Climb flakes in the corner past some grass to the base of the upper finger-crack on *Månens Døtre*.
Abseil off here, or continue up *Månens Døtre* top pitch but be aware that this is harder than what you have just climbed.
FA. Johan Sandberg, Bo Andersson 7.1993

Superb autumn colours reflected in Djupfjord. Photo: Thorbjørn Enevold

The West · Henningsvær · Kalle · Kabelvåg · Svolvær · Trolltindan · Walking Peaks · Bouldering

The West

Henningsvær

Kalle

Kabelvåg

Svolvær

Trolltindan

Walking Peaks

Bouldering

Sjøsvaet

Sjøsvaet and Presten seen from below Pianokrakken on a glorious day.

Presten

Lille Presten

The West

Henningsvær

Kalle

Kabelvåg

Svolvær

Trolltindan

Walking Peaks

Bouldering

Presten

The West

Henningsvær

Kalle

Kabelvåg

Svolvær

Trolltindan

Walking Peaks

Bouldering

The West

Henningsvær

Kalle

Kabelvåg

Svolvær

Trolltindan

Walking Peaks

Bouldering

Colin Binks and Chris Craggs are just visible amongst the soaring rock architecture of Presten, tackling pitch 3 of *Vestpillaren* (6) - *page 148*. Photo: Sherri Davy

Linn Yttervik on *Vestpillaren* pitch 8
(6) - *page 148.* Photo: Nick Ashton

The unmistakable conical bulk of Presten *(The Priest)* dominates the coastal road running
out to Henningsvær. Lofoten's most famous cliff is known throughout Norway and its reputation has spread further afield. Its sheer nose of granite rises 400m above the sea in a single
majestic sweep.
There is a great collection of routes on the face and almost all are well worth doing.
Vestpillaren (The West Pillar), the original route on the face, ascends a system of cracks
and corners up the right-hand side of the nose. It is undoubtedly Lofoten's best known and
finest rock climb offering twelve pitches of varied and well-protected climbing, up a devious
but logical line, and on superb rock throughout. The two main features of the face are the
huge roof, which is tackled by *Reisen* and the *Codfather*, and the ledge running across the
face above the roof. This ledge is known as Storhylla and provides a useful connection point
between many of the routes.

Conditions
The barrel-shaped bulk of Presten faces all the way between southwest and north, catching
most of the weather, especially that which comes from the southwest and often brings
the rain. The rock is clean and quick drying, though some stubborn streaks do weep from
Storhylla after rain. As is to be expected on such a big cliff there are bits of loose rock so
some care is needed.

The West

Henningsvær

Kalle

Kabelvåg

Svolvær

Trolltindan

Walking Peaks

Bouldering

Colin Binks and Chris Craggs catching the morning sun on pitch 2 of *Vestpillaren* (6) - *page 148*. Photo: Tom Atle-Bordevik

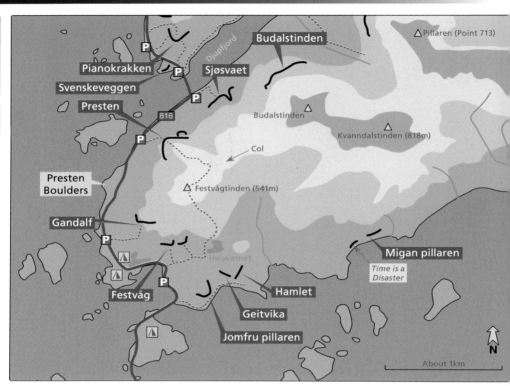

Approach

The routes can be approached directly from the road below. There is roadside parking for half-a-dozen cars in a lay-by directly below the big gully that delineates the right-hand side of the face. An intermittent narrow path leads from the left-hand end of this to the right-hand side of the face. See photo on page 82.

Descent or Retreat

Getting off one of the routes if the weather is threatening is relatively straightforward from the ledge of Storhylla and making a quick appraisal of your situation when you reach the ledge is a good idea. Once above Storhylla you are much more committed and any abseil descent is significantly more complicated and would almost certainly require leaving gear.

From the top of the mountain, descent is relatively straightforward but quite lengthy. Make sure you carry your approach shoes with you on the climb. From Presten's grassy summit, scramble southeast along the exposed ridge crest behind Presten (care needed in several places) to the col between Festvågtinden (541m) on the right, and Budalstinden (663m) on the left. From here the least complicated and safest descent (though it does involve some uphill work) is to follow the ridge rightwards to the summit of Festvågtinden and join the path that descends leading to Heiavatnet, the old Henningsvær reservoir and down to the road. Plan on 1 to 2 hours to get back to the road. The traditional descent has been to cross the ridge at the col and descend steep grass before heading right to access the ridge. It is easy to descend too far before striking out right towards the ridge though, in this event, it is possible to keep heading straight down the wide grassy gully until a traverse out right across the blocky hillside leads to the lake.

Lille Presten

Hanging on the lower left shoulder of Presten is a fine pillar of rock, 130m high and known as the Lille Presten *(The Small Priest)*. There are only two routes here and neither has proved to be popular.

Approach - Walk and scramble up the diagonal tree and bush covered ramp that runs up leftwards - connecting short gullies with more open slopes - 30 minutes minimum.

❶ **Muldvarpen**. . . . . 🔲 6- *A1*
100m. *(The Marmot)* The left-hand line starts up a groove with a prominent tree. Climb this and flakes to a stance, then spiral round to the right to gain the main central grooveline. Follow this to a fixed belay. Press on above to glory.
Descent - Abseil back down *Tarzan* (2 x 50m).
FA. Odd-Roar Wiik, Arild Meyer 1995

❷ **Tarzan**. . . . . 🔲 6-
100m. A two pitch route up the central groove that falls from the huge roof. Start up cracks and grooves to the left of the prominent water streak. Climb steeply to a stance in the base of the main groove, then continue up this to a fixed stance a short distance below the overhang.
FA. Odd-Roar Wiik, Johan Sandberg 1995

The West
Hennungsvær
Kalle
Kabelvåg
Svolvær
Trolltindan
Walking Peaks
Bouldering

A southwesterly and Presten wears a cloud cap - not a day to be up there.

Lille Presten

Help!
The Nord Norsk Klattreskole has long been the focus of Lofoten climbing, though sometimes it attracts the wrong kind of attention. The phone rings at odd times of day and night with questions such as, "How do I get down off The Goat?" or, "Should the path up Vågakallen be as steep as THIS?"

An abandoned car at the foot of Presten led to the police turning out, and they insisted that Thorbjørn met them on the road under the crag. When asked where the climbers might be he pointed up into the blackness, and after some discussion it was decided that everyone might as well go home to bed. The next morning the car had gone.

Rockclimbing

Kalle

Kabelvåg

Svolvær

Trolltindan

Walking Peaks

Bouldering

Descent - see page 136

Storhylla

A

A

Great Roof

A

Yppersepresten

A

Himmel og Helvete

1

Korstoget

3 4

Reisen

8

Vestpillaren

9

❶ Himmel og Helvete . 🏠 📷 🎿 ⬜ 7

560m. *(Heaven and Hell)* A climb of contrast; the first six pitches (Heaven) are great, up perfect cracks in white granite; the top half (Hell) follows a black basalt dike - unprotected and grassy. The route sees few repeats because of the upper half.

1) 6, 45m. Step right into the right-hand of a pair of grooves. Follow this to a thin crack and climb this to a belay ledge.

2) 4, 15m. Climb a short crack on the right to the top of a pedestal and good ledge.

3) 6+, 45m. Climb the superb Yosemite Dihedral to another good but small ledge.

4) 7, 35m. Continue straight up a difficult finger-crack. Where it ends in the middle of a blank wall, climb horizontally left with difficulty (and poor protection) on small edges into another thin, vertical crack on the left. Belay just above on a small stance. Sensational moves that you don't want to fall off!

5) 6, 30m. Jam the next finger-crack, then make unprotected moves up and left into yet another crack. Belay on a sloping ledge at the top of this.

6) 5+, 20m. Climb the next finger-crack to its top, then make a devious traverse left across the face to a belay ledge on the left side of the Potato Chip - a huge detached flake and wide crack, clearly visible from the road - the end of Heaven!

7) 5+, 50m. Traverse horizontally left (easy, spaced gear) until you can climb back right up a narrow grass ledge into the base of the upper corner - the start of Hell. Climb up angular black rock on good holds to a small grass ledge with tricky belays.

8) 5, 35m. Continue up the same line on good holds up black rock to a flake on the right. Belay higher on the left at a block. There is some grass and moss on this pitch.

9) 5, 35m. Climb a crack, traverse right across a thin flake, then move up and right to a stance at the base of the V-groove.

10) 6, 50m. Climb easily up the V-groove (capped by a triangular roof), then make unprotected moves left into the Green Caterpillar - a black basalt dike filled with a carpet of green moss. Unpleasant moves up this (5+ and usually wet) lead to a stance beside a large loose block.

11) 5+, 50m. Step right and climb a groove to a white block on the right, which is climbed to easier moves up flakes and cracks leading to a good belay ledge.

12) 5+, 35m. Head left onto the arete on clean rock, and finish up a crack to the top and redemption!

FA. Arild Meyer, Sjur Nesheim and Ulf Prytz made the first attempt on the general line in 7.1971. "... but luckily we got rained off before we got into trouble," said Arild. Niels Poulsen and Jørgen Sundby added the pitch 3 - Yosemite Dihedral - in 1989.
Ed Webster and Odd-Roar Wiik made the first complete ascent of the route on 12.7.1993 finishing at 1:30am the next morning.

Himmel og Helvete
The leftmost line on Presten; this one
follows a discontinuous crack system up
the far left-hand side of the face.
Approach - Scramble to the upper,
left-hand end of the grassy slope below
Presten - 20 minutes.
Descent - See page 136.

Potato
Chip

Storhylla

Yosemite
Dihedral

Descent - see
page 137

Storhylla

❷ **To krigere** . . . . 🔲 **7** *A3*
(*Two Warriors*) This difficult climb was the second full length route up Presten and was first done in the depths of winter! It starts
from the top of the steep grassy gully slightly to the left of centre. The climbing is characterised by strenuous mixed free and aid
climbing up to grade 6. The upper section of the route is in common with *Korstoget* which has pitches of 6+ and 7.
FA. Sjur Nesheim, Yngvar Julin from 25.11.1981 to 1.12.1981. They finished the route in a storm after having had a fire on their portaledge!

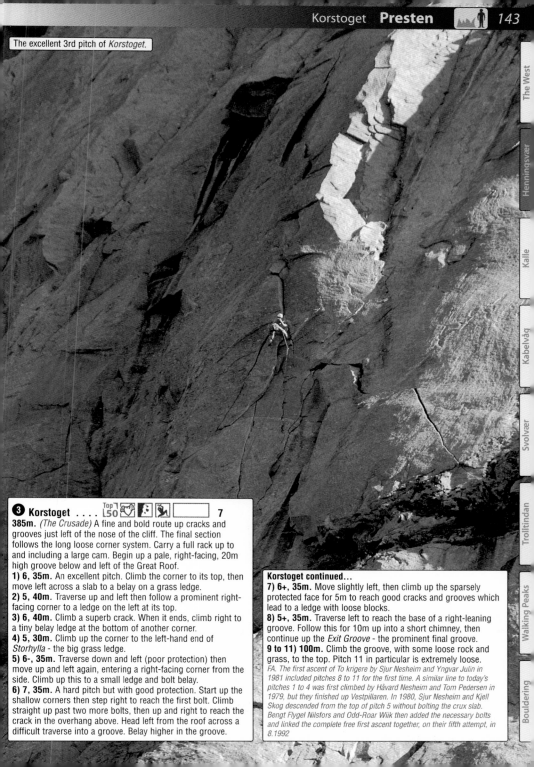

The excellent 3rd pitch of *Korstoget*.

The West
Henningsvær
Kalle
Kabelvåg
Svolvær
Trolltindan
Walking Peaks
Bouldering

3 Korstoget .... [Top 50] ☐☐☐☐ 7

385m. *(The Crusade)* A fine and bold route up cracks and grooves just left of the nose of the cliff. The final section follows the long loose corner system. Carry a full rack up to and including a large cam. Begin up a pale, right-facing, 20m high groove below and left of the Great Roof.

1) 6, 35m. An excellent pitch. Climb the corner to its top, then move left across a slab to a belay on a grass ledge.

2) 5, 40m. Traverse up and left then follow a prominent right-facing corner to a ledge on the left at its top.

3) 6, 40m. Climb a superb crack. When it ends, climb right to a tiny belay ledge at the bottom of another corner.

4) 5, 30m. Climb up the corner to the left-hand end of *Storhylla* - the big grass ledge.

5) 6-, 35m. Traverse down and left (poor protection) then move up and left again, entering a right-facing corner from the side. Climb up this to a small ledge and bolt belay.

6) 7, 35m. A hard pitch but with good protection. Start up the shallow corners then step right to reach the first bolt. Climb straight up past two more bolts, then up and right to reach the crack in the overhang above. Head left from the roof across a difficult traverse into a groove. Belay higher in the groove.

Korstoget continued...

7) 6+, 35m. Move slightly left, then climb up the sparsely protected face for 5m to reach good cracks and grooves which lead to a ledge with loose blocks.

8) 5+, 35m. Traverse left to reach the base of a right-leaning groove. Follow this for 10m up into a short chimney, then continue up the *Exit Groove* - the prominent final groove.

9 to 11) 100m. Climb the groove, with some loose rock and grass, to the top. Pitch 11 in particular is extremely loose.

FA. The first ascent of To krigere by Sjur Nesheim and Yngvar Julin in 1981 included pitches 8 to 11 for the first time. A similar line to today's pitches 1 to 4 was first climbed by Håvard Nesheim and Tom Pedersen in 1979, but they finished up Vestpillaren. In 1980, Sjur Nesheim and Kjell Skog descended from the top of pitch 5 without bolting the crux slab. Bengt Flygel Nilsfors and Odd-Roar Wiik then added the necessary bolts and linked the complete free first ascent together, on their fifth attempt, in 8.1992

❹ Ypperstepresten . . . . . . 🔲🔲🔲🔲 **6**

162m (+ 60m across Storhylla). *(The High Priest)* An indifferent start leads to superb climbing on the black dyke that splits the sheets of white granite below the Big Roof. Start below the left-hand end of the Big Roof at the base of a crack system that runs up the face. The start is up an open groove 20m right of the tall right-facing corner that is the start of *Korstorget*.

1) 6-, 45m. Bridge the groove (hard at the start) and continue for 20m, then traverse awkwardly right across a short face and follow more cracks up leftwards to a high belay ledge.

2) 5, 42m. Follow a left-facing chimney, or the more solid and easier cracks to the left, then continue up cracks up to a small stance (awkward belays) below the wide basalt overhang. It is worth considering belaying a little lower down (no real stance) and using the higher gear as runners to protect the next section.

3) 6, 30m. Either climb directly through the overhang (bold though good holds soon arrive), or traverse left to a grass ledge (same grade - different style), then move back right into the basalt dike. Continue up this by lovely climbing to a good ledge.

4) 5-, 45m. Continue up the basalt ladder which gives steady climbing, with spaced protection, in an amazing setting, to a stance just below the big grass ledge of Storhylla.

5) 3-, 60m. Traverse right along Storhylla, (don't forget the protection) around a rib, then across a slab before descending to the fixed anchor at the top of the *Vestpillaren Direct Start*. Four abseils lead back to the ground.

FA. Bengt Flygel Nilsfors, Aart Verhage 5.1992

Ypperstepresten

A pair of easier outings which follow lines up the lower face and pass the left-hand side of the Big Roof to reach the big grass ledge of Storhylla which cuts across the cliff at roughly half height.

Descent - Traverse right and climb down to the fixed belays at the top *West Pillar Direct Start* and make four abseils (one short and three long) back to the cliff base. Beware the crack below the lowest belay, it eats ropes!

❺ Biskopen . . . . 🔲🔲 **6-** *AO*

220m (+ 60m across Storhylla). *(The Bishop)* An intriguing line at an amenable grade with an exciting pendulum high on the cliff. Despite being the easiest way up the central section of the lower walls, it doesn't see much attention. Double ropes are a must.

1) 6-, 45m. As for *Ypperstepresten*.

2) 5+, 48m. Climb half of *Ypperstepresten's* second pitch, but climb straight up a slab via thin cracks. Pull through a small roof and climb up to a stance.

3) 5-, 35m. Continue up left-facing corners to a tiny stance.

4) 5 *AO*, **50m.** Traverse left, then continue straight up a line of flakes and holds to the left side of the Big Roof (this section is shared with *Reisen*). Now pendulum left to reach the upper, black basalt dike on *Ypperstepresten*.

5) and 6) 5-, 105m. As for *Ypperstepresten* pitches 4 and 5.

FA. Odd-Roar Wiik, Niels Poulsen 8.1992

The superb basalt ladder of the 4th pitch of *Ypperstepresten*.

Storhylla

5

7

3

4

6

8

9

The West

Henningsvær

Kalle

Kabelvåg

Svolvær

Trolltindan

Walking Peaks

Bouldering

The West

Henningsvær

Kalle

Kabelvåg

Svolvær

Trolltindan

Walking Peaks

Bouldering

Afternoon | 10 min | Bad weather

Reisen
The huge central roof of Presten is skirted by the two of the hardest routes on the face.
Descent - See page 136.

Close-up of upper section on page 151

Storhylla

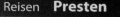
❻ The Codfather .... ⌈Top⌉ 🖼️ 🖊️ [ ] 7

465m. An excellent intricate route with some exciting moments. Carry a full rack including plenty of micro wires. Start at a vegetated bay between *Ypperstepresten* and *Reisen*.

1) 5, 45m. Climb easy slabs to the back of the bay then follow cracks leading towards the overlap to belay on a small ledge.

2) 6-, 25m. Climb to the overlap, pull through then move right and continue up cracks to a belay where they end.

3) 7, 30m. Climb to, and past, the left-hand side of the overlap and climb to a basalt dyke (shared with *Biskopen*). Move right for 5m to below the next crackline which is reached from the right by poorly-protected climbing. Belay 3m higher.

4) 7, 50m. Continue up the crack to its end, then make a difficult move right across the orange streak into the next crackline. Climb this up and right to the angle under the Big Roof.

5) 6+, 50m. Climb up then out right to a smooth groove. Head up and left, passing a large detached flake, then continue above this to a crackline leading rightwards across the slab to a stance on the left of the huge block on Storhylla.

6) 6, 55m. Climb the groove then move left and pull over the left edge of the overlap. Follow the crack to ledges below the prominent right-curving groove on the right side of the pillar.

7) 5-, 30m. Climb the groove to the point where it starts to lean to the right and becomes smooth - belay here.

8) 6, 35m. Continue up the groove until directly below a vegetated ledge, then cross the overhangs to reach the stance.

9) 6, 50m. Climb up and right to gain the grooves to the right of *Vestpillaren's* Slanting Corner and follow these (past a ledge leading across to *Vestpillaren*) continuing for another 10m until a move left reaches the stance at the end of *Vestpillaren* pitch 9.

10) 6, 55m. Follow *Vestpillaren* past the hollow flake, then continue rightwards up slabs and grooves to cross the top of the black dyke. Climb slabs and grooves until the peg on *Vestpillaren* pitch 11 can be reached. Climb to the *Vestpillaren* belay.

11) 3, 55m. Finish up the gully as for *Vestpillaren*.

FA. Mark Garthwaite, Mick Fowler 5.7.1999. A prolific 2 days for Mark and Mick who also completed the first ascent of Wee Beastie on Myggapillaren the previous day.

❼ Søndagskole turen . ☼ 🖼️ 🖿 [ ] 7

170m. *(Sunday School Outing)* A route to nowhere, though with some good and bold climbing.

1) 5, 45m. As for *The Cod Father*.

2) 6, 40m. Start as for *The Cod Father*, past the light grey spot, then move right into a weakness. Head up this, over small overlaps, by lovely run-out slab climbing and continue to a belay on a small ledge with space for "half an ass".

Søndagskole turen continued....

3) 7, 40m. Climb up the groove to a good runner then traverse left to good holds and runners up to the main groove. Continue diagonally to the left to reach the basalt dike on *Ypperstepresten*. Finish as for that route - **5-, 45m.**

FA. Robert Caspersen, Andy Cave 6.2006

❽ Reisen .... ☼ 🖊️ 🖼️ [ ] 7+

440m. *(The Journey)* A tremendous voyage of exploration up Presten's imposing central section. The route offers technical climbing on superb rock, but is poorly protected in several places. A double rack of cams (micro to large) is recommended, plus a double rack and full range of wires. Begin a few metres to the right of the open groove of *Ypperstepresten*.

1) 5, 20m. Climb up a corner, over a roof, and up to a belay.

2) 5+, 50m. Head up and right following a curving finger-crack (the higher of a pair of near-parallel cracks) to a belay below the tall corner.

3) 6+, 30m. Climb up the corner to an awkward layback/chimney slot and belay halfway up the slot.

4) 6+, 55m. Chimney the slot for 10m more, then make a serious traverse left for 20m before climbing up 20m to a belay just above the left end of the Big Roof.

5) 7+, 30m. Climb the groove until it is possible to traverse right 2m to some holds leading up to a block in the roof. Now traverse right, out along the block, on better holds (bold), then up to *Storhylla* - the big grassy ledge.

6) 6+, 40m. Head up and right on easy ground, then back left across a slab to a stance under a short, right-facing corner.

7) 6, 50m. Traverse left on big flakes to the left side of an arch (serious), then climb a crack to a stance below a finger-crack.

8) 6+, 55m. Jam up the finger-crack to reach a long groove which gives great climbing to a belay.

9) 5+, 40m. Continue up the groove for 15m until it ends, then climb cracks to a stance below a right-facing corner - the *Direkte-Utsteget* of *Vestpillaren*.

10) 7, 40m. Climb the sustained groove - a great pitch.

11) 6+, 30m. Continue up the corner past a hard bulge then head up easier ground to the top.

FA. Tom Cosgriff, Sjur Nesheim 9.7.1993. The first ascent took 11 hours and was done with all nut protection.

The West

Henningsvær

Kalle

Kabelvåg

Svolvær

Trolltindan

Walking Peaks

Bouldering

The West

Henningsvær

Kalle

Kabelvåg

Svolvær

Trolltindan

Walking Peaks

Vestpillaren

Regarded as Lofoten's finest route, it announced a new level of difficulty and commitment when first climbed by Arild Meyer and Brynjar Tollefsen in 1978. Every climber who is up to it should do this route once in their lifetime, offering as it does a superb experience - long, interesting and well protected but never too difficult. It has been done in just under an hour! There are two starts to the route, the direct and *Original starten* up the huge gully on the right, there are also a variety of finishes. The combination described below is far and away the most popular way of doing the climb - other variations are described opposite and on page 150.
Descent - See page 136.

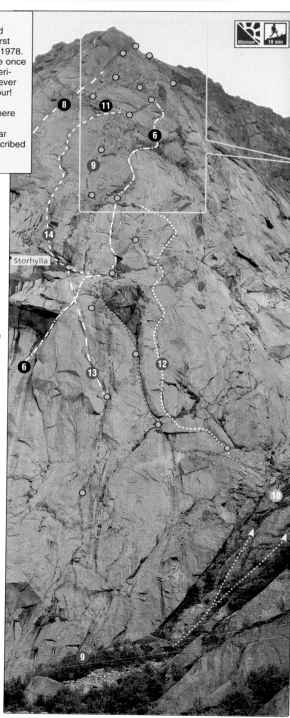

9 Vestpillaren . . . . . [Top 50] 6

467m. *(The West Pillar)* The normal ascent time is 6 to 8 hours although an efficient team should manage it in less. From the parking area on Route 816, follow a small path up grassy slopes and scree for 10 minutes towards the right-hand base of Presten, and the start of a steep water-washed gully filled with grass and some loose blocks. Begin approximately 20m to the left of this, up the central one of three shallow corners.
Photos - cover, pages 5, 10, 66, 132, 134 and 135.
1) 5+, 45m. Climb up a right-slanting groove for 15m, then traverse left 10m across an easy ledge to a nice crack which leads to a small ledge with fixed belay.
2) 6-, 40m. Start up a small groove, followed by more broken ground leading to a flake/block on the left. Climb this, then make a hard move up into a thin finger-crack which leads to easier climbing up a crack to a fixed belay.
3) 6, 50m. Climb straight up the narrow groove (hard but safe) by thin finger jamming and laybacking. At its top, head left up a diagonal ramp which leads to a fixed belay and small stance.
4) 5-, 20m. Continue up a short wall and groove then easy slabs to a fixed belay on the right edge of Storhylla.
5) 4, 30m. Move right across the ledge, climb cracks up the right side of the huge block to a belay on its top.
6) 6-, 45m. Climb straight up thin cracks and neat grooves to another good ledge, then traverse 20m left across the ledge (some rope drag and loose rock) to a belay on a higher ledge to the left below a superb looking groove.
7) 6, 45m. Difficult moves lead up the shallow groove. Follow the flake above until it becomes a thin crack, then step left into a parallel crack system. Climb straight up the fine sustained crack into the big left-facing groove and take a semi-hanging belay above a bulge in the corner.
8) 5+, 40m. Continue laybacking up the groove then head right up an easier slabby groove and belay on either of two ledges at the base of the Slanting Corner.
9) 6, 40m. *The Slanting Corner.* Layback and jam the right-leaning groove - sustained and awkward, especially with a sack on - to a tiny ledge. After a rest, continue up left then back right (or up the thin vertical crack on the right - harder) and belay up to the right at a block.
10) 4+, 30m. Climb up and left across ledges to a large loose flake jammed in a groove. Climb carefully up and right past the flake, then continue left up a chimney groove to reach a small belay ledge with several blocks.

Vestpillaren continued...
11) 5, 35m. Follow the open groove up and right to its top, then move down and right for several metres, before traversing horizontally right past a fixed peg and make delicate moves around right into the grassy exit gully.
12) 3, 55m. Scramble up the grassy gully to the top.
FA. Arild Meyer and Brynjar Tollefsen made the first ascent on their first try on 18.6.1978 (14 hours). The team carried their courage in their rucksac - pitons of all sizes, bongs and skyhooks. Meyer and Tollefsen swung leads, but high on the face, "we became very wet and cold." The upper section was climbed during a heavy rainstorm. "Shall we go down now?" asked Brynjar when the rain began. "Absolutely not!" replied Arild, typically determined to push on no matter what, and the pair succeeded. Twelve days later Arild returned with Finn Tore Bjornstad and made the first ascent of the Normal avslutning (Normal Finish) on 30.6.1978.
The first free ascent was done by Hans Christian Doseth and Håvard Nesheim using the Original avslutning in 6.1979.
The popular Slanting Corner pitch of the Normalavslutning was first climbed by Helge Stokstad and Harald Henden in 1982.

⑩ Vestpillaren original starten 🔾 [   ] **5+**
A good set of pitches which can be combined with *Klokkeren* (page 150) to offer a different way up the face. Start up and right from the normal start at the steep gully filled with grass and loose blocks. Climb this for 55m (either the grassy buttress or water-washed groove on the right - a rope is advisable). Belay where the angle eases.
1) 4, 40m. Climb a short wall (loose) then traverse left for 20m across ledges and climb up towards the start of the huge left-facing groove. Belay on a ledge by some big flakes.
2) 5, 40m. Follow the steep corner with a crack and several good rests to a belay on a small grass ledge.
3) 5+ 35m. Continue up the groove to the roof and make a tricky traverse left for 10m then climb straight up cracks to Storhylla and a fixed belay. Choose a way on, or abseil off.
FA. Arild Meyer, Brynjar Tollefsen 18.6.1978. As part of Vestpillaren.

⑪ Original avslutning . . . . 🔾 🖊 [   ] **7**
(Original Finish) On the first ascent of *Vestpillaren* the team were attracted to the fine leaning grooves in the crest of the pillar.
9) 6-, 40m. Traverse left across a face for 5m, then move down and left under an overhang. Climb through this and follow cracks and flakes for 25m to a belay ledge.
10) 4+, 45m. From the right end of the ledge, follow the grooves and cracks rightwards up broken terrain to a ledge.
11) 7, 35m. Traverse left to gain the large right-slanting groove. Climb the strenuous corner to a sloping stance.
12) 7-, 35m. Continue to, and past, a bulge in the upper part of the groove then climb thin cracks until it is possible to move left to the finish. Belay on a good ledge, then scramble up to the top.
FA. Arild Meyer, Brynjar Tollefsen 18.6.1978

The West
Henningsvær
Kalle
Kabelvåg
Svolvær
Trolltindan
Walking Peaks
Bouldering

⑫ Himmelen kan vente . . . [Top L50] 🖊 ☐ **6+**

310m. *(Heaven Can Wait)* This hybrid route has some great climbing and a sensational finish high on the buttress. A large cam or two will come in useful.

1) 4+, 25m. As for pitch 1 of *Original starten* (page 149) but move up to a stance at the foot of a left-trending groove.

2) 6+ (or *A0***), 50m.** Traverse left to reach the long crack and climb this - sustained - until it curves over and forms a flake. Either free climb the arete on the left, or the thin crack up and right with a quick pull on a nut. Belay on the ledges just above.

3) 3+, 30m. Up easy ground to a belay at the foot of a groove.

4) 6-, 40m. Climb the right-leaning corner and the continuation crack to reach a small stance on the left.

5) 5-, 40m. Climb the big leaning corner on *The Codfather* almost to its end, then head out left to a belay.

6) 6+, 35m. Continue up the corner to the stance below the Slanting Corner on *Vestpillaren*.

7) 6+, 30m. Head out left onto the face and climb this diagonally leftwards (not obvious and poorly protected) to a small stance.

8) 6+, 35m. Climb up and left into a long crack and follow this to a wild stance under the roof that caps the wall.

9) 6+, 25m. Traverse left under overhang, climb the corner, and then move out right under the overhang to a sudden ending.

FA. (Pitches 2 and 3) Helge Stokstad and Harald Henden climbed the initial crack system (plus the Slanting Groove pitch of the Vestpillaren) in 1982. The whole route as described, with the exciting finish - Patrik Fransson, Thorbjørn Enevold 15.6.1997

⑬ Variasjon til en variasjon 〰 🏃 ☐ **6+**

150m. *(Variation on a Variation)* Tackles the left-slanting crack system just to the left *Vestpillaren* pitch 3.

1 and 2) 6-, 85m. As for *Vestpillaren Direct*.

3) 6+, 45m. Step left and climb the clean, left-slanting crack/corner up to a small ledge and belay.

4) 4, 20m. Continue up easy cracks to Storhylla.

FA. Odd-Roar Wiik, Niels Poulsen 9.1992

⑭ Klokkeren . . . . 〰 ☐ **7-**

450m. *(The Bell Ringer)* A popular set of pitches on the upper central portion of Presten, up a parallel crack/groove system just to the left of *Vestpillaren's* upper section, rejoining it below the Slanting Corner.

1 - 4) 5+/6, 145m. Climb the start of *Vestpillaren* or use *Original starten* for a bit of variety.

5) 5-, 50m. Storhylla is split towards its right side by a slab. Climb up to the right side of the slab (passing left of an abseil anchor), then traverse left across the slab for 10m until you can climb up through blocks and grass to the base of a black section of rock slightly on the left. Face climb up this and belay at the foot of a right-facing groove at the right margin of the large, smooth face.

6) 6-, 35m. Excellent climbing up the groove above the belay for 10m, then face climb up and right into another prominent, left-facing corner system. Belay on a small ledge on the right at a flake.

7) 6-, 40m. Step back left into the corner, climb past some loose rock, then head over a bulge to enter the next groove (also left-facing). Climb this to two large stacked flakes and pass these carefully to a tiny ledge down on the left with a fixed belay.

8) 7-, 24m. Follow a shallow corner up and right to a fingertip crack with thin moves and excellent climbing up to a short crack on the right (fixed piton) continue to the roof then move right to the stance on *Vestpillaren*.

9 to 12) 6, 160m. Finish up *Vestpillaren*.

FA. Tommy Nilsson and partner made the first ascent of the route, using some aid on pitch 7, in 1984 or 1985.
FFA. Tim Hansen, Ingun Raastad Summer 1986

Vestpillaren Variations

There are a number of variations on *Vestpillaren*, which make suitable objectives once you have done the classic route.

Descent - See page 136.

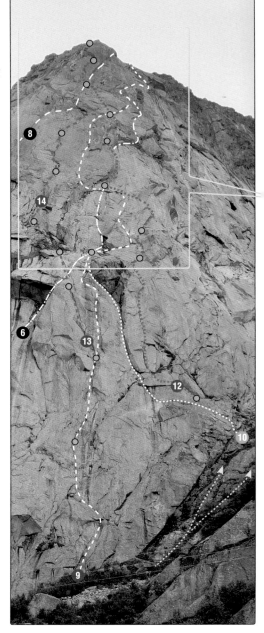

The West
Henningsvær
Kalle
Kabelvåg
Svolvær
Trolltindan
Walking Peaks
Bouldering

Descent - see
page 136

The West

Henningsvær

Kalle

Kabelvåg

Svolvær

Trolltindan

Walking Peaks

Bouldering

orhylla

The Harley Davidson Wall

A fine wall, north facing and hidden in a steep gully between Gandalf and Presten. The best bit of rock is a fine grey wall seamed by three drainage streaks/cracks, which are the first three climbs.

Approach - Make a steep 20 minute scramble up the gully below the cliff from a couple of parking spaces right under it. Avoid the blocky scree in the centre of the gully for the easiest (and safest) line. From the gully, exit right and scramble up to ledges below the wall.

① Massor av kubik . . . . 🎴 ⬜ 6

50m. *(Plenty of Cubic Capacity)* The left-hand crack leads to a ledge system and possible belay. Move right and continue up the corner to where it ends. Move out left onto the cracked face and climb this to the top of the wall.
Descent - Abseil off or walk down to the right.
FA. Patric Fransson, Anders Lundkvist 1990s

② Spinning Wheel . . . . 🎴 ⬜ 7

30m. The central crack system gives hard climbing as far as the overlap. Pass this and continue up easier ground to the ledges. Finish up the previous route or move right and abseil off.
FA. Anders Lundkvist, Krister Jonsson 1990s

③ Easy Rider and the Fat Boy . 🎴 ⬜ 6

30m. Climb the right-hand of the trio of cracks through a bulge early on then continue to the overlap which is passed on the right. Finish up the easy groove above to ledges. Abseil descent.
FA. Patric Fransson, Krister Jonsson 1990s

④ Full fart . . . . 🎴 ⬜ 7

25m. *(Full Speed)* The groove in the right-hand side of the face leads leftwards, then bypass the bulges and step right to get through the overhang. A thin crack leads to an easy groove and the ledges.
FA. Krister Jonsson, Anders Lundkvist 1990s

⑤ Sportster . . . . 🎴 🎴 ⬜ 7

20m. A fine thin crack up just right of a big corner leads to a break. Traverse left along ledges to the abseil descent.
FA. Krister Jonsson, Erik Berglund 1990s

> These routes have not been checked, the grades and lines are those given by the first ascensionists and the pitch lengths and quality ratings are estimates - care required.

LO Profile - Johan Sandberg

Johan has been a wannabe climber for almost 20 years and has spent most of his adult time managing software projects all over the world. In the last 5 years, the focus changed dramatically towards his new family members, Mia and Leo.

Lofoten: My first encounter with Lofoten was with the climbing school back in summer 1990, when it was located in Kalle. I was fortunate enough to have Thorbjørn (now a lifelong friend) as an instructor, who took my friend Patrik and myself up great routes like *Gandalf*, the *Spurven* and *Bare blåbær* in splendid weather - one of my best weeks ever. Then Lutta and Thorbjørn bought and created the legendary climbing cafe where I worked during the first couple of summers. What a place, what a bar, what a fantastic atmosphere (indescribable, must be experienced). Here, I have downed the best tasting pints in the midnight sun after 'mini epics' on the crags. Nothing can beat that. That said, I will do my best to return every summer to Lofoten as long as I can crawl (out of the cafe?).

Favorite Route(s): I always start at the Gandalf wall which is an excellent introduction, with *Gandalf*, *Guns 'n' Roses* and *Gollum*. If too crowded, I head for *Applecake Arete* or *Lys og skygge* on the Pianokrakken. When warmed up, I head for other classics like *Spurven/ Colibrien* link-up with its spectacular friction and the *Ørneryggen* with its fantastic airy grand finale. The *Vestpillaren* is always my ultimate goal, but before that I have to climb *Lundeklubben* to measure my capabilities. Finally, the best part is to break new ground and complete new routes - infinite potential all over Lofoten!

The Story: During the first 7 months of 2007, I got paternity leave for Leo. I started practicing the old art of climbing again in the Stockholm area and booked all of July for Lofoten. Unfortunately, my wife Catrine could only join us for the last two weeks, hence I arranged for an *au pair* for the entire month. The *au pair* in combination with amazing weather for the entire month led to large amount of climbing time! As usual Thorbjørn had a few projects to work on and we decided for a 100+ metre line that looked very promising. After several tries over two weeks we made it to the top including ground up cleaning of mud and huge rocks. What a climb! What a come-back! *Venus Passagen* at Rørvika is a future classic in the range of Gandalf, if you ask a biased first asensionist.

The West

Henningsvær

Kalle

Kabelvåg

Svolvær

Trolltindan

Walking Peaks

Bouldering

Gandalf

The West

Henningsvær

Kalle

Kabelvåg

Svolvær

Trolltindan

Walking Peaks

Bouldering

The West

Henningsvær

Kalle

Kabelvåg

Svolvær

Trolltindan

Walking Peaks

Bouldering

The second pitch of *Gandalf* (5) - *page 163* - the classic of the cliff.

This near-roadside cliff is a great destination for Lofoten climbers, offering several classic routes at amenable grades. The routes are quite long - up to four pitches - the approach only takes a few minutes and there is an easy walk-off. Generally the rock is good, though the occasional loose block or flake needs care. The accessibility and the grade spread, plus the sunny aspect, mean that the cliff is popular and queues are not unheard of - though at least you can check your route before leaving the road!

For something a little more taxing, the nearby Silmarillion Wall should be checked out, with its hard aid routes and steep free climbs.

Approach   See map on page 184

There are several parking spots opposite the cliff around the free camping area. Follow a path up over a rocky bluff, past the Henningsvær water pipe and towards the cliff, which is only five minutes from the car.

Conditions

The crag faces south and gets the sun for much of the day. It is also slightly sheltered from southwest winds and large sections are surprisingly quick to dry so it is possible to grab a route at any time of the day (or night!) if the weather suddenly improves.

Gandalf and Silmarillion cliffs.

157

The West

Henningsvær

Kalle

Kabelvåg

Svolvær

Trolltindan

Walking Peaks

Bouldering

Colin Binks and Chris Craggs on the great classic of *Gandalf* (5) - *page 163* - Gandalf.
The leader is in the same place as in the double page spread on the previous page. Photo: Sherri Davy

The West

Henningsvær

Kalle

Kabelvåg

Svolvær

Trolltindan

Walking Peaks

Bouldering

Walk off descent

The Ear

Live Aid

On the left-hand side of the face the crag disappears into a gloomy gully that only gets the sun early in the day. This used to be home to a solitary aid route *Live Aid*, though nowadays there is a selection of hard free climbs here, and a newer aid route.

Descent - Either by abseil, or walk down the ridge.

Opposite the Live Aid wall is a short face of good rock split by a finger-crack that doesn't reach the ground, and a curving 'bow' feature to the right. Two tiny routes have been claimed here - Super Guide, 6, the thin crack (Arild Meyer 1980s solo, in his Alpine boots) and the flake and blank wall to the right - Bowmore, 6, (Nick Ashton 1990s).

➊ Fremmed på veien 7

60m. *(Stranger on the Road)* A very steep route which takes a direct line up the left-hand side of the wall. It has a couple of bolt runners at the start of the second pitch.
1) 6-, 30m. Climb flakes and pockets up to a ledge with a bolt belay. The gear is a bit lacking at the start of this pitch.
2) 7, 30m. Climb the strenuous groove past bolts, then follow cracks and flakes up into the base of the steep layback groove. Climb this to a bolted belay.
Descent - Abseil from the bolts or walk off leftwards.
FA. Thorbjørn Enevold, Trond Solberg (point of aid in the groove) 1992
FFA. Erik Grunnesjö, Arild Meyer 8.2006
The bolts were placed before the decision to ban the use of bolts on established crags. They have been hiding in the shade all these years.

➋ Kaptein Sabeltann . . . . A2+

60m. *(Captain Sabretooth)* An aid route taking a steep line up the rock to the right of *Fremmed på veien*. The first pitch leads to a stance on *For Cod's Sake*. Continue up this (free or on clean aid) then a bit of *Hot Fisk...* to eventually bale out at a high pendulum point which enables an escape left.
FA. Odd-Roar Wiik, Trond Helge Hansen 1995

➌ Live Aid A3

85m. A tough aid route, the first on this part of the wall. Despite some claims, it hasn't really been free climbed!
1) A3, 15m. Start up an expanding flake, continue up the rurp/bird-beak crack, splitting the black rock, to a bolt belay by The Ear.
2) A2+, 25m. Start up loose flakes then follow the crack above to a bolt belay on a small ledge.
3) A2+, 45m. Aid climb the broken rock above, using skyhooks and bashies, to reach the final crack. Up this to a bolt belay.
FA. Odd-Roar Wiik, Neils Poulsen 1.1994. Ascent made by headtorch.

➍ For Cod's Sake . 7

75m. A line which uses the start of *Live Aid* before heading away left to find a devious but logical way up the cliff.
1) 7, 15m. Start up *Live Aid* but keep right where it heads left up the rurp crack, to reach the old two bolt belay on *Live Aid*.
2) 7-, 25m. Layback around the Ear, then do an airy leftwards traverse and climb up to the next bolt belay.
3) 6, 35m. Layback the flake, then traverse left to the steep layback groove on *Fremmed på veien* (possible stance if the rope-drag is bad). Climb this strenuously to bolt belays.
Descent - Abseil from the bolts or walk-off leftwards.
FFA. Dave Musgrove, Nick Ashton 10.8.1998

➎ Hot Fisk, Jumping Weasel 8-

85m. A tough outing that was touted as a free ascent of *Live Aid*. It is likely that the first ascensionists were confused by the geography of the wall.
1) 8-, 40m. Start right of *For Cod's Sake* and climb the flakeline to reach the base of a steep groove. Climb this then move left to the stance on *Live Aid*.
2) 8-, 45m. Traverse leftwards on slightly alarming flakes to a corner. After a few moves up the corner make an exposed move right and up to gain rightward slanting cracks. Follow cracks to easier ground.
FFA. Dave Barnes, Robin Thomas 24.7.2004. Really the name should have been Hot Fisk, Jumping Røyskatt!

The West
Henningsvær
Kalle
Kabelvåg
Svolvær
Trolltindan
Walking Peaks
Bouldering

Gandalf and Festvåg cliffs from Henningsvær with Festvågtinden above.

Tynne ting

The slabby central section of the cliff only has a small set of routes. They are all poorly protected and, unsurprisingly, they see little attention.
Descent - Abseil off - 35m to the ground.

5 Edderkoppen 7-
40m. *(The Spider)* Start below the left-hand end of the big slanting overhang in the middle of the wall.
1) 6-, 25m. Trend right, passing underneath a black water streak, to reach a flake. Pull through the roof and belay on a small stance just above the lip. A bold **Direct Start** is possible to the right.
2) 7-, 25m. Traverse left using the crack, then move up and follow the continuation back rightwards to the bolts on the abseil line and an easy descent. A more direct version of this pitch is technically easier but much less well protected, better to go the long way round!
FA. Odd-Roar Wiik, Patrik Fransson 1994

6 Tynne ting 6
35m. *(Thin Things)* Another bold pitch up the slabby rock below and right of the lower abseil point. The name is pointer to the lack of protection. Start just left of a block at the base of the slab. Climb leftwards up the unprotected slab to ledges, then straight up past a thin hollow flake to a (rather old) bolt. Step right (tricky) into the upper flake system and climb easier cracks and corners straight up, then left, to the abseil bolts.
FA. Odd-Roar Wiik, Niels Poulsen 9.1991

7 Nøttolfs fristelse . . . 7-
45m. *(Nøttolf's Temptation)* A line based on the black water streak just to the left of the diagonal overlaps.
1) 6+, 25m. Climb the poorly-protected wall, trending rightwards up flakes, then pull through the bulges to a stance on the left.
2) 6, 20m. Traverse left along the flake into *Tynne ting* then climb straight up to the abseil bolts.
FA. Odd-Roar Wiik, Patrik Fransson (one point of aid) 7.1995
FFA. Patrik Fransson and Anders Lundquist shortly after.

The West

Henningsvær

Kalle

Kabelvåg

Svolvær

Trolltindan

Walking Peaks

Bouldering

Ali Kennedy making the steep moves into the groove of *Gamle rev* (6) - *page 163*. Photo: Tim Wilkinson

Walk off descent

A

Lots of sun | 5 min | Sheltered

13

8

9

10

11

12 14

See next page for an
alternative viewing
angle of these routes

The West

Henningsvær

Kalle

Kabelvåg

Svolvær

Trolltindan

Walking Peaks

Bouldering

❽ Førstereisgutten 7

95m. *(The Boy's First Journey At Sea)* The thin crack and right-hand edge of the diagonal overhangs. The hard climbing is above the main groove and protection is good.

1) 7, 40m. Climb broken ground to a crack leading to the groove. Climb it then traverse up and left to a rest at the overhang. Continue up the crack above to a good stance.

2) 6-, 45m. Climb a good crack, move across some ledges, then go up the large left-facing groove to a stance on a small ledge above the top of the steep section.

3) 3, 10m. Scramble up easy ground to reach the top set of *Gandalf's* abseil anchors.

FA. Odd-Roar Wiik, Thor Solberg Kvande 3.8.1993

❾ Gamle rev 6

95m. *(Old Fox)* The attractive twinned groove system in the centre of the face gives sustained and well-protected jamming. Popular and worthwhile. Start below a black slab (sometimes wet) below the main corner. *Photo on pages 12 and 161.*

1) 6, 45m. Climb easily to the base of the groove, then layback and jam up the corner until a harder move leads leftwards at the top into easier cracks and a corner. Belay on a ledge on the left.

2) 6-, 50m. Continue up a groove with a hand-crack to a grassy ramp, then climb a short awkward finger-crack on the right to another ledge. Finish up an unlikely looking thin finger-crack up the steep wall above to jugs and an easy finish.

2a) 7, 20m. Revungen *(Fox Club)* Step right from the stance and climb the thin cracks right of the arete - tiny wires protect the run-out up the slab above - scary! Take a belay then add another pitch to the rest of *Gamle Rev.*

FA. Ed Webster, Thorbjørn Enevold 25.7.1993
FA. (Revungen) Asgeir Larsen, Jonatan Rask 6.2007

❿ Tromsø ekspressen . 6

95m. *(The Tromsø Express)* A fine route up the most prominent of the parallel grooves in the centre of the cliff. Three well-protected crack pitches make for a great route.

1) 6, 40m. Climb the black slab, step right and make a quick pull into the base of the groove. Follow it by laybacking and jamming to its top. Step right and climb up into a thin left-facing groove which leads to an excellent belay ledge on the left.

2) 6, 30m. From the right end of the ledge, climb a thin vertical crack just to the left of a grassy groove. Continue up cracks and flakes then move right onto a sloping belay ledge.

3) 5, 25m. Step right, climb the left side of the flake, then finger jam up an arching thin crack on the left.

FA. Håvard, Sjur Nesheim 1979 or 1980. They may have used a different finish to the one described.
FA. (Pitch 2) Ed Webster, Thorbjørn Enevold 1993

⓫ Lost Gandalf 5-

This variation start to one of the adjacent routes is rather grassy though it does see quite a few ascents and queues are rare.

1) 5-, 40m. Head up the grassy crack system to better climbing, good jamming leads to the black ledge at the top of the crack. Move right and belay on *Gollum.*

2 and 3) Finish up *Gollum*, or move left to gain the first belay of *Tromsø ekspressen* if you are up to it.

Gandalf

The fine broad buttress that makes up the main bulk of the cliff is home to many of its best routes. On the left are a compelling set of groovelines and to the right some striking cracklines - almost all of these give classic climbs.

Descent - Either head left (west) around the cliff top and then down a short ridge to the lower left end of the cliff (see photo on page 156). Alternatively, abseil from the bolt anchors at the top of *Førstereisgutten*, make two abseils (42m and 34m). - see previous page for line.

⓬ Gollum 5

100m. An excellent and well-protected crack climb up the parallel crack system a few metres to the left of *Gandalf*. Almost as good as its classy neighbour.

1) 5, 40m. From the tip of a block, jam up the fine crack, stepping left once, and continuing to a sloping stance.

2) 5-, 35m. Continue up the same crack, past a ledge, to a short slab. Climb the slab, then move up thin cracks in the steeper wall above, on good holds, to a good sloping stance.

3) 5-, 25m. Step right, then climb the right side of a prominent flake (shared with *Tromsø ekspressen*) but move right to easier cracks and the top.

FA. Arild Meyer, Sjur Nesheim 1985

⓭ Gandalf's kamin .... 5+

100m. *(Gandalf's Chimney)* A more strenuous and awkward finish to *Gandalf* and easily combined with *Lost Gandalf*.

1) 5, 40m. As for *Gandalf* or *Gollum* (or use *Lost Gandalf* and traverse right if the other lines are busy).

2) 4, 20m. Climb up and left up a knobby slab about 5m left of the *Gandalf's* overhang. From a ledge, climb a corner on the left, then climb up to a grass ledge below an orange chimney.

3) 5-, 50m. Squeeze up through the chimney to an exit on large holds, then follow the awkward crack above to a sloping ledge on the right. Move up left and finish up *Gollum*.

FA. Odd-Roar Wiik, Kjell-Arne Andreassen 5.1989

⓮ Gandalf 5

100m. A Lofoten classic up the highest part of the cliff by a fine series of pitches, each interesting, varied and well protected. Start up the left-facing groove behind a tree and a large boulder at the right side of the face. *Photos on page 154, 157.*

1) 5, 40m. Climb the narrow groove, passing a small overhang, then continue up a short slab to stance by a good crack. Avoid belaying on the loose blocks over to the right.

2) 5-, 35m. Traverse 5m to the right, climb the juggy overhang and awkward groove just to the right. Continue past a possible stance below the steep headwall split by a vertical crack. Cross the tricky slab leftwards and pass the arete, then climb up good finger-cracks to a belay in the prominent yellow niche of the Eagle's Nest. Care needed with rope drag on this pitch.

4) 5-, 25m. From the Eagle's Nest, step right around a small corner - exposed and delicate for a few moves - then follow an easier crack straight to the top.

4a) 6+ 25m. The original (and much harder) finish goes straight through the lip of the Eagle's Nest via a strenuous jamming crack.

FA. Arild Meyer, Kjell Ove Storvik, Brynjar Tollefsen 5.1978. Not by today's standard route. They climbed left around the pitch 2 overhang, then aid climbed straight through the crack above the Eagle's Nest ledge. Later parties added the now traditional second and third pitches and free climbed the Eagle's Nest Direct Finish.

The West · Henningsvær · Kalle · Kabelvåg · Svolvær · Trolltindan · Walking Peaks · Bouldering

Lots of sun | 5 min | Sheltered

The West
Henningsvær
Kalle
Kabelvåg
Svolvær
Trolltindan
Walking Peaks
Bouldering

Walk off descent

A

13
16
17
18
19
20
21
22
23
19
9 10 11 12 14 15

⑮ Guns 'n' Roses . . . . . . ⌐50⌐ ⌐ 6-
100m. A nice varied route - steep, satisfying, well protected and on excellent rock. The route sees plenty of action. There has been plenty of discussion about the star rating of this climb, you will just have to do it so you can join in!
1) 5, 40m. Start up a crack with a tree in it and climb straight up over a small overhang, then up the arete on the right using a finger-crack. Belay on a ledge just below the *Gandalf* overhang. Many teams struggle up the grassy groove round to the right - this IS NOT the route, so get back on the proper line now!
2) 6-, 25m. Climb the right-hand crack directly through the *Gandalf* overhang, then continue up the vertical jamming crack in the steep headwall above to a tiny stance.
3) 6-, 35m. Continue directly up a series of vertical finger-cracks in orange rock keeping just to the right of the Eagle's Nest belay on *Gandalf*. Finish up a groove and hand-crack just to the right of *Gandalf's* final section.
FA. Sjur and Håvard Nesheim climbed the vertical hand-crack on pitch 2 in 1979, calling it Kvite spøkesla (White Ghosts) because it was the first time they had ever used chalk. Odd-Roar Wiik and Gunnar Austrheim climbed all of pitches 2 and 3 in 1990, using a start up the crack system round to the right of pitch 1. The route as described was first climbed by Thorbjørn Enevold and Truls Seines in 6.1993.

⑯ Krympefesten . . . . ⌐ ⌐ 6+
100m. *(The Shrinking Party or 'Wetting the Baby's Head')*
This combination of pitches has several hard sections of climbing. Rather lacking in line though with interesting moves. Start as for *Guns 'n' Roses* under the crack with a prominent tree. Carry a full range of cams.
1) 6, 40m. Climb up the first 5m of *Guns 'n' Roses*, step left, then climb a thin finger-crack following it through two overhangs to a belay on a ledge below the *Gandalf* overhang.
2) 6+, 25m. Traverse right under a white, A-shaped overhang, - hard to protect - then swing out right, climb up a crack, and traverse left to a position below the prominent vertical crack of *Guns n' Roses*. Hand traverse strenuously right along a horizontal crack then follow cracks to a ledge and belay.
3) 6-, 35m. Climb a short groove to join *Guns 'n' Roses*.
FA. Ed Webster, Johan Sandberg 5.7.1993. The hand-traverse pitch had been climbed before.

The grassy groove and the cracks to its right have been claimed many times over the years (1500 according to some sources). Although the climbing is okay, if a little vegetated, the lines run out of anywhere to go after the first pitch. Really, the routes to the left are a better use of your time.

⑰ Vår pump . . . . ⌐ ⌐ 7-
85m. *(Spring Pump)* The cracks and ramps in the steep rock round to the right of the arete of *Guns 'n' Roses* to a finish up the prominent beckoning hanging crack far above. Take a couple of big cams.
1) 6+, 45m. Climb a crack then, at its top, trend right up the rampline that leads to a second crack. Climb this to a belay over to the right of a large perched block.
2) 7-, 40m. Climb the cracks, then move out right to below the hanging bottom-shaped crack. Struggle up into this (hard to climb and harder to grade) to reach easier ground. Trend left to finish.
FA. Odd-Roar Wiik, Patrik Fransson (with some aid) 30.4.1995
FFA. Patrik Fransson, Thorbjørn Enevold 5.1995

Guns 'n' Roses
The right-hand side of the face swings round to form a steep wall. The classic of *Guns 'n' Roses* is far and away the most popular climb here, sadly the routes further right are a bit hard to have mass appeal.
Descent - Walk off leftwards or locate the central abseils above *Førstereisgutten*.

⑱ Three Lions on the Shirt . . . ⌐ ⌐ 7-
85m. A steep direct start to *Vår pump* combined with an easier, though still worthwhile, finish.
1) 7-, 40m. Climb to, and up, a steep flake then continue past a bush before trending left to reach the top of the ramp on *Vår Pump*. Continue up this to the belay.
2) 5, 45m. Trend left up a series of cracks and grooves, all the way to the cliff top ledges.
FA. Nick Ashton, Vidar Kolstad 1.7.1998

⑲ The Caveman . . . . . ⌐ ⌐ ⌐ 8-
85m. A direct and arduous outing with some great and steep climbing after the worrying start.
1) 7, 35m. Start in the back of the dark recess and climb loose overhanging rock (difficult to protect) to a flake and runners. Continue up and right to join *Rasmus expressen* and follow this to its stance.
2) 8-, 50m. Head out right, then follow the overlap back left to join *Rasmus expressen* at the top of the right-leaning corner. Above this, step back right and continue direct via some superb climbing. This long pitch can be split with a belay.
FA. Robert Caspersen, Andy Cave 6.2006. Onsight and without falls.

⑳ Rasmus ekspressen ⌐ ⌐ ⌐ 8-
80m. *(The Rasmus Express)* In its day Lofoten's hardest free climb offering high quality technical climbing. Begin on the far right-hand side of the cliff in a gully below the overhanging wall. Belay in a corner next to a large flake.
1) 6+, 35m. Step up on the flake, bridge a couple of moves then pull left onto the wall. Traverse left for 6m, then head up an overhanging bulge on good holds to a crack which leads to a semi-hanging belay in an uncomfortable niche.
2) 8-, 45m. Climb up the groove and undercut rightwards then move up a right-leaning corner. Step up and left to reach a vertical crack. Climb past a stubborn bush, then up easier cracks and grooves to the top (shared with *Vår pump*).
FA. Tom Cosgriff, Sjur Nesheim (with one fall) 5.7.1993. The day Rasmus Enevold was born.

㉑ Souhaila Andrawes . . . . ⌐ ⌐ A3
80m. A mixed route that tackles the imposing leaning wall above the start of *Rasmus ekspressen*. A full aid rack is required including hooks, birdbeaks and copperheads.
1) *A2+, 20m, 2) A3, 15m, 3) A2+, 20m, 4) 6, 25m.* The line and stances marked on the topo are slightly speculative although it is thought that it shares its upper pitch with *The Caveman*.
FA. Jonas Tetlie, Knut Fausa Storvik 1/2.8.1999

The final two short climbs are on the upper walls.

㉒ Blondie . . . . ⌐ ⌐ 6-
15m. A short clean slab on the upper wall is split by a thin crack.
FA. Kirster Johnson and NNKS students 1996

㉓ Grus i øgat . . . . ⌐ ⌐ 6
15m. *(Dirt in Your Eye)* The short strugglesome crack passing the left-hand side of the huge jammed block.
FA. Peter Restorp, Erik Westling 2001

The West
Henningsvær
Kalle
Kabelvåg
Svolvær
Trolltindan
Walking Peaks
Bouldering

The West

Henningsvær

Kalle

Kabelvag

Svolvær

Trolltindan

Walking Peaks

Bouldering

Silmarillion Wall

The rightward extension of the Gandalf wall forms a fine tall buttress of excellent orange granite. Although clearly seen from the road, and relatively easy to get to, the first route on the wall wasn't added until 1999. Now it is home to a small selection of hard climbs which you won't have to queue for.

Approach - From the parking, walk past Gandalf and scramble up the boulders to the base of the face in about 10 minutes.

Descent - Make 4 abseils down the line of *Simarillion*, or walk off leftwards - 20 minutes back to the road.

❶ Silmarillion 7

165m. The original route of the face. A fine and long expedition forcing its way up the left-hand side of the face. Start at a prominent pillar that leads towards a chimney formed by a large flake and a groove to its right.

1) 6, 50m. Climb the pillar and then the chimney above before moving right and climbing the crack to a stance. Belay (large cam) below the continuation crack.

2) 5, 10m. Climb the crack then move left to a tree belay on the big ledge system. Move the belay rightwards to another tree.

3) 7-, 25m. Follow the groove left then straight up (3 pegs) to a small ledge. Undercut belay and belay on cams above a flake.

4) 6+, 45m. Head up the curving orange groove then continue direct (passing to the left of an abseil station) up the groove to a stance by the great roof.

5) 7, 20m. Traverse right then make hard moves up the overhanging crack (big cams) before continuing more easily to a small stance. A spectacular and exposed pitch.

6) 3, 15m. Straightforward slab climbing leads to a tree at the top of the crag.

Descent - Abseil back down the line (15m, 45m, 40m, 50m) or walk off left - 20 mins.

FA. T.Sieger, F.Moell 4.7.1999. The ascent took 7 hours.

❷ Set Trippin' A3

115m. A rather arduous approach leads to fine and hard aid climbing on the central wall. It looks likely that the lower pitches could be free climbed but subsequent ascents have avoided these by heading up the gully on the right as for *Daei!* The route could really do with being pushed on upwards to tackle the upper overhangs. Start in the centre of the face, directly below the great block jutting out of the upper roofs and just right of a tree-filled groove.

1) 5 *A2***, 40m.** Follow cracks and overlaps right then back left to reach the upper part of the tree-filled groove (plenty of grass). Now climb rightwards round the overhangs to a ledge and belay.

2) *A1***, 35m.** Step left and climb the curving groove then trend right and climb cracks past the left-hand edge of the conspicuous wide roof. Continue up the easy grassy groove to a stance on the left-hand end of the huge ledge system.

3) *A3***, 40m.** Step left past loose blocks and climb a thin crack to a short bolt ladder and on into the 'copper-head groove'. Above this, continue to a grassy niche then step left and climb cracks and a right-trending ramp (huge loose stuff to the left) to a double-bolt belay below the frowning overhangs. Abseil descent.

FA. F.Rapp (roped solo) 10.1999

The final two routes are located on the upper right-hand side of the wall above the big grassy ledge system. They are both reached by the black-streaked gully that bounds the right-hand side of the face.

❸ Daei! 8- *A2*

165m. A spectacular and hard outing that breaches the roofs on the upper right-hand side of the cliff by some wild climbing. Start at the base of the gully that defines the right-hand side of the cliff.

1) 4+, 45m. Climb the clean white slabs left of the streaks into a corner and continue to a niche with a high peg belay.

2) 3, 40m. Continue up the gully for 10m until a grassy ramp runs out to the left onto the crest of the buttress. Follow this up and down to a belay on spikes.

3) 6-, 30m. Climb a series of flakes and cracks, with harder moves where it steepens, to reach a small stance and nut belays.

4) 8-, 30m. Now the fun begins! Climb up to the roof and bridge past its narrowest point. Follow an undercut flake out left, passing a couple of grooves, to a point below the crack that splits the roof. Difficult moves up to the roof lead to a good hold out left then hard pulls on thin flakes are needed to gain a belay in a crack above the overhang.

5) 7- *A2***, 20m.** Start free as far as a small sidepull. Then, when the crack becomes too thin, aid up it to a groove and climb this to reach bolt belays in the roof above the ledge. Walk off left.

FA. Robin Thomas, Andrew Norton 18.7.2004

❹ The Pels of the Fisk 8

140m. Another route in the hard and wild mould, with some desperate jamming in an out-there situation. The name means *The Scales of the Fish* - in Norwenglish!
Start as for the previous climb.

1) 4+, 45m. As for *Daei!*

2) 3, 25m. As for the second pitch of *Daei!* but scramble to the highest point of the ledge and a tree belay.

3) 6, 30m. Climb cracks left of the arete, heading for the big roofs, until it is possible to move right past a big loose block and climb out to a small stance on the edge of the void.

4) 8, 25m. Make an alarming leftwards traverse above the roof to reach a sharp-edged flake, from where a long and blind reach gains the bottom of the jamming crack. Thug up this (desperate) until things begin to ease (after about 8m) at which point easier climbing leads up the groove to a grassy exit onto a ledge.

5) 5+, 25m. Move left along the ledge and climb the short corner to the top.

FA. Robin Thomas, Simon Devidiers 23/24.7.2004

Walk off descent

The West

Henningsvær

Kalle

Kabelvåg

Svolvær

Trolltindan

Walking Peaks

Bouldering

Festvåg

The West

Henningsvær

Kalle

Kabelvåg

Svolvær

Trolltindan

Walking Peaks

Bouldering

Tim Wilkinson on the superbly positioned *Skiløperen* (6-) - *page 178* - on the upper
walls of Store Festvåg with Henningsvær in the background. Photo: Ali Kennedy

The West

Henningsvær

Kalle

Kabelvåg

Svolvær

Trolltindan

Walking Peaks

Bouldering

Lille and Store (Little and Big) Festvåg are two of the closest cliffs to Henningsvær. They are a pair of excellent crags with a number of interesting and varied routes, which mostly tackle grooves and cracks. From a distance the cliffs look a little loose, but in fact the rock is extremely solid and well-featured offering excellent climbing on clean rough granite.

Approach   See map on page 184

Park at a lay-by (room for half-a-dozen cars) on the outside of the bend a couple of hundred metres west of the outer bridge (Engøysundet bru) on Route 816. The two cliffs stand next to each other and are visible above the road. Walk along the road (away from Henningsvær) to the next bend, then turn right into the shrubbery at the old granite foundations of what was a holding tank for the Henningsvær water supply. Follow stone steps up the foundation's right-hand side. This is the start of the Festvågtinden path - the path that leads up the back of the valley to the Heiavatnet reservoir hidden on the shoulder high above and on to Festvågtinden. To reach Lille Festvåg, scramble left around several large boulders, then head straight up the hillside to the cliff base. For Store Festvåg continue up the Festvågtinden path until level with the base of the cliff then cross the scree (many loose blocks - care required though there are vestiges of a path) to reach the foot of the wall.

Conditions

The crag faces pretty much south and gets the sun for much of the day. Parts of the cliff are slightly sheltered from southwest winds and, despite being part of a huge hillside, the cliff is quite quick to dry. The rock is generally clean and lichen free.

The Gandalf and Festvåg cliffs seen from Engøya, the island between the two Henningsvær bridges.

Festvågtinden (541m)

Jammen, Jammen

Spring Wall

Store Festvåg

Lille Festvåg

Silmarillion

Gandalf

P

The West

Henningsvær

Kalle

Kabelvåg

Svolvær

Trolltindan

Walking Peaks

Bouldering

P

Store Festvåg path

Lille Festvåg path

Dramatic positions on the last pitch of
Lundeklubben (6) - *page 177* - Store Festvåg.

The Spring Wall

A grey slab located up and left of Lille Festvåg. Two crack systems running up the slab can be seen from the road - both give single pitch routes on good rock. From the base of Lille Festvåg, traverse left across the slope to ledges below a broken buttress under the slab. Head left and carefully solo up ledges and grass for 45m to reach the start of the routes. The names refer to two unusual north Norway delicacies.

① Mackøl og måsegg . . . . ⟨2⟩ 🪨 [____] **5+**
45m. *(Mack Beer and Gull's Eggs)* Well-protected finger-jamming up the lovely left-hand crack, past one short steep section in the middle, to a stance on the right. Abseil from a fixed nut anchor. Mack Beer is a popular product of the world's most northerly brewery.
FA. Ed Webster, Odd-Roar Wiik 6.5.1994

② Gammelosten . . . . ⟨1⟩ 🪨 [____] **5+**
45m. *(The Old Cheese -* smelly but tasty!) Climb straight up the right-hand of the two cracks - there are some tricky moves near the top up a shallow groove. Abseil off from the fixed nut anchor.
FA. Odd-Roar Wiik, Ed Webster 6.5.1994

Månedans

③ Månedans . . . . Top 50 🪨 [____] **6+**
95m. *(Moon Dance)* Two less interesting pitches lead to a fine finish up the overhanging groove and exposed top slab. The route is generally well protected.
1) 6-, 30m. At the left-hand end of the lower cliff band, jam up a short steep crack to slab and then a grassy ledge. Continue up a V-groove to a small stance.
2) 5, 35m. Step left and climb a left-facing corner (some loose blocks) to reach easier climbing up columns to another small stance below the last pitch - a spectacular leaning groove.
3) 6+, 30m. Jam and bridge up the sensational, overhanging, groove corner (sustained) until it ends, then follow finger-cracks first to the left, then back right up the exposed slab and an easier finish on the right.
FA. Ed Webster, Odd-Roar Wiik 10.7.1993

④ Singer . . . . ⟨1⟩ 🪨 🧗 [____] **7**
95m. ... as in 'sewing-machine-leg!' A varied outing up the bold rib split by a finger-crack right of *Månedans* and the wide fissure above. Bring a good selection of small wires and a few big cams.
1) 5+, 20m. From just left of a low cave, climb cracks up to a big grassy ledge and a belay.
2) 6+, 45m. Climb a groove then follow thin cracks up a steep slabby wall, with some bold climbing linking the crack systems. Continue for a short distance to belay on a tiny ledge.
3) 7, 30m. Move right to below a leaning groove that splits the overhangs. Jam the initial crack strenuously to eventually reach easier climbing up the top corner.
FA. Odd-Roar Wiik, Niels Poulsen (3 points of aid on the last pitch) 6.1992.
After climbing two other pitches at the start, Arild Meyer free climbed the top overhang with Ottar Skog in October 1993.

⑤ Shine a Light . . ⟨1⟩ 🪨 🧗 🪨 [____] **6+**
95m. Plugs a gap with some good climbing, though only the third pitch is new. Start 3m right of the lowest point of the cliff.
1) 5, 20m. Climb past the left-hand end of the low overlap and up left-slanting twin cracks in a groove to the big grassy ledge.
2) 6+, 25m. Climb the thin finger-crack with difficulty until easier climbing leads to another grassy ledge. Move left to belay at the foot of a long groove.
3) 6-, 20m. Climb the groove and cracks above it to a good stance out on the right.
4) 6, 30m. Step back left into the continuation groove and climb left then right to gain the crack splitting the roof with difficulty. Jam up this to enter the hanging groove where things ease.
FA. Andrew Norton, Klaus von Aynaten 21.7.2004

⑥ Lille vikke vire . . . . ⟨1⟩ [____] **7-**
95m. *(Incy Wincy Spider)* A nice direct line up the centre of the face with a couple of good pitches. Start as for the last climb.
1) 5, 20m. As for *Shine a Light.*
2) 6+, 45m. As for *Shine a Light* climb the thin finger-crack with difficulty until easier climbing leads to a grassy ledge. Continue past a higher grass ledge (possible stance) and up a rib (some loose rock) to a stance on the left below the yellow overhangs.
3) 7-, 30m. Climb the groove, then head to and through the overhangs to access the narrow hanging groove above. Climb this (hard) and finish up the continuation crack.
FA. Kirster Jonsson, Johan Reuterholdy 7.1996

⑦ Blod eller gull . . . . ⟨2⟩ 🧗 🪨 [____] **6**
95m. *(Blood or Gold)* A strong line up the right-hand side of the buttress in two big pitches, though other stances are available along the way if needed. Slightly spoilt by the scruffy middle section, but well worth doing anyway.
1) 6-, 55m. Start up the curving groove in the right-hand side of the lower face, then climb an off-width crack behind a flake then easier cracks and grooves to a stance on top of a small pedestal.
2) 6, 40m. Nice moves lead up the steep pocketed face and through a roof to gain the upper groove. Finish up this or, better, out on the exposed arete to the left.
FA. Thorbjørn Enevold, Johan Sandberg 6.1992

⑧ Blod eller gull Right-hand Finish
. . . . ⟨1⟩ 🪨 [____] **7+**
95m. Originally done as finish to *Lille vikke vire.*
1) 6-, 55m. As for *Blod eller gull.*
2) 7+, 40m. From the stance, trend right and climb the prominent crack splitting the roof then trend right up the buttress above.
FA. Odd-Roar Wiik, Trond Helge Hansen 1997

Månedans

Lille Festvåg is the left-hand of this fine pair of cliffs, tall and barrel shaped and seamed with many cracks and grooves.
Approach - From the start of the Festvåvtinden path, scramble left around several large boulders, then head straight up the hillside to the cliff base.
Descent - Abseil from a tree into the gully between Lille and Store Festvåg, then make a second abseil from a fixed nut back to the cliff base.

Abseil into gully

A

The Spring Wall just to the left

8

6

Approach to the Spring Wall

3

4

5

7

Store Festvåg

Gaukerisset
The right-hand side of Lille Festvåg consists of a tall buttress that swings round to form a steep sidewall. There is a small set of climbs here with *Gaukerisset* being the popular one.
Descent - Make two abseils into and down the gully.

Abseil into gully

---

9 Studenten . . . . 🔲 🗲 🏃 [   ] 7
75m. *(The Student)* An unbalanced route with one hard move.
1) 5, 45m. Meander up the cliff's right-hand arete to a good ledge below a left-leaning groove.
2) 7, 30m. Climb up the severely overhanging groove, and its easier continuation, to the top.
FA. (Pitch 1) Thorbjørn Enevold, Johan Sandberg 7.1992. Odd-Roar Wiik and Thorbjørn Enevold completed the route in 6.1993 - breaking a key foothold on the crux in the process.

10 Måken Sven . . . . 🔲 🗲 [   ] 6+
70m. *(Sven the Seagull)* A similar but harder line to *Gaukerisset* up the rock to the left of its crack, giving fine sustained jamming.
1) 3+, 30m. A straightforward pitch up the gully, or the rock to its right, to a belay underneath the crack.
2) 6+, 40m. Start up *Gaukerisset* crack, but where this starts to trend right by a small bush, climb up and left into the steep groove which gives fine sustained jamming until past a small roof, at which point things begin to ease.
FA. Aina Konradsen, Stein Stenkjær 3.7.1999

11 Gaukerisset . . . . ⎡Top⎤⎣50⎦ 🗲 [   ] 6
75m. *(Cuckoo Crack)* A fine crack high on the sidewall. An easy approach pitch gets you into the gully and up to its base.
1) 3+, 30m. As for *Måken Sven.* A straightforward pitch up the gully, or the rock to its right, to a belay underneath the crack.
2) 6-, 45m. The easy initial crack leads to tricky moves right and up to gain the main crackline. Climb this by fine sustained moves as it slices up the steep smooth wall. Excellent climbing.
FA. Odd-Road Wiik, Thorbjørn Enevold 6.1993. On the first ascent, Odd-Roar promised to belay part-way up the crack, but it was so good that he led it all, with a cuckoo singing in the background.

Store Festvåg

The bigger of the two Festvåg cliffs has a high concentration of good routes with easy access and is quick drying with a sunny aspect.

Approach - As for Lille Festvåg, but just uphill from the old granite block foundation, head to the right through several large boulders, then follow the Festvågtinden track up the back of the valley until you can traverse horizontally left across a very loose scree slope to the cliff base - take care!

Descent - Walk down around the cliff's right-hand side, back past the base of *Skiløperen*.

⑫ **Skomaker Grus** . . . . ☝1 [____] 6+

(Grus the Cobbler) A five pitch route that makes the most of the rock at the left-hand side of the cliff and has two alternative starts. If you are happy to accept a little bushwhacking between the pitches, you will be rewarded by a pleasant and long route. The individual pitch grades and lengths were not recorded by the first ascensionist, though the pitches are separated by good stances. A sense of adventure is required.

FA. Thorbjørn Enevold (Skomaker) with a party, and Odd-Roar Wiik with another party (Grus) more or less on the same date in 1990. Nobody could remember who went first, so they added the two names together to share the fame and glory. Odd-Roar Wiik and team did the left-hand start.

⑬ **Johan Boyer** . . . . ☝1 [____] 5+ AO

75m. Named after a well-known Norwegian 19th century writer. A short route that runs up to the grassy terrace up and left of the Island. Start just to the left of a shallow groove.

1) 5+, 40m. Climb up the centre of a steep cracked slab to a small overlap split by a thin, vertical finger-crack. Jam up this - steep to start - to a big ledge with a large rock sitting on it.

2) 5 AO, 35m. Climb up the crack directly behind the boulder (one point of aid to start) and continue up the cracks above to a possible stance. A short pitch up a slab split by a crack leads to the ledge. Scramble off right, or continue up *Den Siste Viking*.

FA. Thorbjørn Enevold, Morten Solberg, Trond Solberg 5.1992

⑭ **Vikingjenta** . . . . ☝1 🪢 [____] 6+

75m. *(The Viking Girl)* A free variation to Johan Boyer's second pitch climbing the next crack system to the left.

1) 5+, 40m. As for *Johan Boyer* to the ledge with its boulder.

2) 6+, 35m. Climb up a strenuous slightly overhanging parallel-sided crack to a flake, then climb up a shallow groove, step left then back right and follow a thin crack up to the terrace.

FA. Ed Webster, Maria Hannus 16.7.1993

The wall below the terrace has a series of cracks which have been climbed for many years but recently folks have started claiming them so we have decided to list them. They all belay at a big ledge with trees and a huge horizontal block. Abseil descent, or walk off rightwards along the terrace. They are named after characters in a famous Norwegian book about Lofoten fishing - Den Siste Viking.

⑮ **Kristaver** . . . . 🪢 [____] 6-

25m. The left-hand crack system, starting through the black overhang. Quite sustained.

⑯ **Marja Myran** . . . . [____] 6-

25m. Climb through the centre of the overhang to enter the easier upper cracks.

⑰ **Elezeus Hylla** . . . . [____] 5+

25m. Climb the right-hand crack through the black bulges then follow the flakes above. A bit grassy but nice enough.

⑱ **Kanales Gomon** . . . . [____] 5+

25m. Start on the right and follow parallel cracks, trending slightly left, until it is possible to sidestep the bulges to reach the belay.

Lundeklubben

The right-hand side of Store Festvåg has some superb long routes including the classic *Lundeklubben*.

Approach - All climbs on this side start behind a rocky outcrop known as The Island. Scramble around to the right-hand side of this, then up and left up to a small, grassy terrace where you can leave your sack.

Descent - Walk down around the cliff's right-hand side past the base of *Skiløperen* to The Island.

Lots of sun | 20 min

Descent

The Stone
Sausage

20

21 22   23

19   The Island   24

The Terrace

25   26

Approach

⑲ Den Siste Viking . . . . . . 🔲🖳 ⬜ 6
90m. *(The Last Viking)* The first route done on the cliff tackles the steepest central portion. The route can be extended by starting up *Johan Boyer* though the normal start is reached by walking to the left end of the Terrace from The Island.
1) 5, 20m. Head up to a belay at the base of the fairly prominent left-facing corner just to the left of the Stone Sausage, the reddish bulging pillar near the cliff's centre.
2) 6, 45m. Climb up the corner system in a long pitch, moving left around a roof at the top via a few thin moves. Continue and belay at the top of a short crack.
3) 5, 25m. Follow another crack, cross a slab rightwards and finish up the big right-trending groove.
FA. Thorbjørn Enevold, Lutta Fagerli 5.1992

⑳ Running for Rasmus 🔲🖳🔲 ⬜ 7-
90m. An interesting combination of pitches featuring some difficult jamming. Just left of *Lundeklubben* and *Luksusdyret*, at a short overhanging finger-crack. Pitch two - a narrow right-facing corner with a finger-crack in the back, is visible just to the left of *Lundeklubben* groove.
1) 7-, 20m. Climb the strenuous overhanging finger-crack to better holds and, a little higher, a small stance.
2) 6+, 35m. Continue up the crack directly above (as for *Luksusdyret*), then undercling right into the slim groove in the arete. Finger jam and layback up this and belay on a good ledge on the left.
3) 6+, 35m. Head up the crack above (possible belay on *Lundeklubben*) then continue direct up the cracks splitting *Lundeklubben's* final spectacular slab, with one very thin move at the start.
FA. Ed Webster, Thorbjørn Enevold, Truls Seines 4.7.1993

The next two climbs start at the high point of the grassy col behind the rocky tower of the Island.

㉑ Luksusdyret . . . . 🔲🖳 ⬜ 6
90m. *(The Luxury Animal)* A line up cracks up the face just right of the groove that bounds the Stone Sausage.
1) 5, 25m. Climb up and left onto the white prow of rock (just to the left of *Lundeklubben*) then climb a good jamming crack to a stance at its top.
2) 6, 40m. Follow the same crack system straight up, taking the crack through the notch in the roof above. Continue up the crack, around the left side of a small roof and belay on a ledge.
3) 5, 25m. Step right, then climb a steep crack, making a hard move over a bulge, then follow the groove to the top.
FA. Bengt Flygel Nilsfors, Aart Verhage 5.1992

Running for Rasmus
Finishing the new route later to become *Running for Rasmus*, Thorbjørn saw his car driving past down on the road. Believing that the mother-to-be was heading to the hospital he started running. Approaching the car he realised that Ed Webster was not far behind. Ed with his amputated toes from Everest and with the nickname 'the turtle' really went for it down that slope. Every night at the pub, the next week, you could hear in an American dialect, "I didn't run very fast, and I didn't run very far, but I did run!"
For the record, it was a false alarm. Rasmus was not born until a few hours later, with his father present. He did arrive quickly though, and thus provided the name for the first grade 8 route in Lofoten - *Rasmus ekspressen* done by Thomas Coscriff.

㉒ Lundeklubben . . . . [Top 50]🖳 ⬜ 6
90m. *(The Puffin Club)* A great classic, very popular with varied and sustained climbing up the striking right-facing corner and cracks above The Island. *Photos on pages 42, 171, 179 and 180.*
1) 6-, 35m. Climb up an easy groove then step right onto a blunt arete. Move right again into a big right-facing corner which is climbed to a good ledge.
2) 6, 35m. Follow the steep corner above, passing the bulge, and continue up a crack until it fades. Move right into another crack which leads to a ledge. Hand traverse 3m left and climb an easier crack to a large sloping ledge. The crack contains hidden delights.
3) 5+, 20m. Move up and left to another ledge then finish up the zig-zag cracks in the steep slab. Time for the photo!
FA. Arild Meyer (The Old Puffin), Thorbjørn Enevold (The Young Puffin) 5.1992

㉓ Straight Albatross . . . . 🔲 ⬜ 6
90m. A good direct line leading to an unusual finish.
1) 5+, 20m. Climb cracks to a belay below a black-streaked slab.
2) 6, 45m. Climb up cracks in the slab to gain the cracked groove immediately right of pitch 2 of *Lundeklubben*. At the top of the groove, step left and climb a difficult bulge at a thin vertical crack and flake. Belay at the horizontal break above.
3) 6-, 25m. Climb up, then undercut a crack to the right into a flaring chimney with a hidden cave.
FA. Starting up Lundeklubben, Thorbjørn Enevold and Lutta Fagerli climbed part of pitch 2 (not the crux) plus all of pitch 3 in 5.1992
FA. (as described) Thorbjørn Enevold 1990s

㉔ Wandering Albatross . . . . . . 🔲 ⬜ 6
95m. A meandering variation to the previous route.
1) 6-, 35m. Climb a prominent 5m tall corner, stepping back right onto a grass ledge. Continue up cracks in a V-groove to a sloping belay ledge on the left.
2) 6, 35m and 3) 6-, 25m. Traverse directly left to join and finish up *Straight Albatross*.
FA. Ed Webster and Tormod Klepper 1.7.1993

㉕ Fire forsøk . . . . . . 🔲🖳🔲 ⬜ 7-
80m. *(Four Tries)* A sustained crack climb, the crux of which might require a bit of staying power.
1) 6-, 35m. Climb up the wide crack in an orange corner on the right side of the wall to a small ledge. Belay here, or continue up the wider cracks leading up leftwards to a stance.
2) 5+, 25m. Up finger-cracks to easier climbing which leads to a large sloping ledge. The final steep wall is split by a single beautiful, and yet quite intimidating, crack.
3) 7-, 20m. The very strenuous widening crack in the centre of the steep wall gives a tussle - big cams help.
FA. Thorbjørn Enevold, Aart Verhage, Bengt Flygel Nilsfors 5.1992

㉖ Four Pitch Route . . . . 🔲 ⬜ 6-
80m. A four pitch easier alternative to *Fire forsøk*.
1) 5, 15m. Climb the flake and wall to a small stance.
2) 6-, 20m. Continue up the wall and pass the overhang with difficulty to reach a small stance in the base of a groove.
3) 5, 25m. Climb the groove then gain the crack on the right and climb this then the bulge on the left to a good stance.
4) 5+, 20m. Start up the off-width crack then bridge out to the rock spike on the left and climb on top of it. Clip the bolt and do delicate moves up the slab to finish.
4a) 6+, 20m. Finishing straight up the crack is **Trollmannens uløselige mysterium** *(The Wizard's Unsolvable Mystery)* and needs a couple of very big cams.
FA. Thorbjørn Enevold, Trond Solberg 6.1994
FA. (Trollmannens...) Odd-Roar Wiik, Trond Helge Hansen 1996

Skiløperen

The short steep face that overlooks the gully is home to a trio of climbs. On the left is the tough *Riz Raz* and in the centre is the ever-popular crack *Skiløperen*. As the wall is passed on the decent route it is well worth stopping off to tick this particular classic.

27 Riz Raz . . . .   **7+**
30m. The steep wall to the left of *Skiløperen* was originally a hard aid route *Alpinisten*. Now it gives an even harder free climb although on a slightly different line. Start 10m left of *Skiløperen*. Follow the cracks rightwards by sustained climbing to the eventual sanctuary of a narrow ledge. Trend back left above the overlap to reach the base of a wider crack and finish up this. **Alpinisten** goes direct from the narrow ledge by tricky aid climbing. The lower section can be done on nuts at *A1+*, the upper wall remains much harder *A3*.
FA. Øyvind Utby, Andreas Capjon 24.7.2004
FA. (Alpinisten) Anders Bergwall, Odd-Roar Wiik 1.1993

28 Skiløperen . . . . Top L50   **6-**
30m. *(The Skier)* The striking crackline in the sidewall is very photogenic. It is easily ticked when descending from having done one of the longer routes on the front of the cliff. Some jamming is required low down, followed by hauling on jugs as the route gets steeper, leading to a tricky section passing the roof.
Photo on page 168.
FA. Arild Meyer, Thorbjørn Enevold 5.1992

29 The Joker **6-**
35m. The right-trending crack leads to a ledge and possible stance. Step right again and commit to the hollow-sounding flake. Climb up this to better holds, then step right and finish up the rather scruffy slab.
FA. Nick Bassnett, Roger Brown (alts) 11.8.2005

High up in the valley, right of Store Festvåg is a beautiful steep sheet of rock with a fine route. See photo on page 170 for the rough location of this route.

30 Jammen, Jammen . . . . **6+**
Start over some blocks to reach a right-facing groove. Climb up this to a roof then follow an overhanging jamming crack leftwards to a belay on good ledge. Finish up a chimney. It is a little mossy but very nice if you like jamming.
FA. Øvind Utby, Andreas Capjon 23.7.2004

The West

Henningsvær

Kalle

Kabelvåg

Svolvær

Trolltindan

Walking Peaks

Bouldering

A climber approaching the base of the main groove of
Lundeklubben (6) - *page 177* - on Store Festvåg.

The West

Henningsvær

Kalle

Kabelvåg

Svolvær

Trolltindan

Walking Peaks

Bouldering

The West

Henningsvær

Kalle

Kabelvåg

Svolvær

Trolltindan

Walking Peaks

Bouldering

Climbing Efficiently

It goes without saying that on a long route you'll need to take everything you need with you. Depending on the length of the route this could mean a guidebook and a few snack bars; a water bottle, waterproofs, a head-torch and trainers for the descent; or even a porta-ledge, stove, dehydrated meals, sleeping bags and spare hardware.

Each route will be different, and before starting you'll have to balance the extra hassle of carrying things against the extra usefulness of having them with you. Only with experience will you know what is best, and even the most experienced big wall climbers sometimes get it wrong.

If you are the kind of climber who clips many things to your harness 'just in case' you find a use for them, you may want to reconsider your strategy. With descent shoes, waterproofs and water to carry as well as your rack it is easy to encumber yourself enough to seriously affect your ability to climb, not to mention spoiling much of the enjoyment you are hoping to have. So trim your rack carefully. Do you need a full set of cams, or will a select few suffice? Is there any point in taking both a belay device and a figure-of-eight descender? Do you need a full-weight locking krab on every sling?

The big problem with taking too much gear is the extra time it takes to carry it. One virtual certainty is that if you take overnight gear you will end up using it, as carrying it will slow you down so much you'll be left with little choice.

While staying safe is obviously high on the list of priorities, achieving this can be as much about moving quickly and efficiently as it is about belay systems and ropework. In Lofoten daylight is not usually a problem, especially in June, but your body will still get just as tired so careful planning is still needed to avoid having to climb or descend when exhausted which almost inevitably leads to serious mistakes.

A common error made by climbers more used to single-pitch routes is that they don't climb fast enough. On single-pitch routes of 15 to 20m or less, you may well need to place gear every couple of metres or so since there could be a very real chance of a ground fall. Doing this on a pitch of 50m or more will take a very long time, as will sorting that amount of gear again on each stance. Like it or not, if you're going to move efficiently on a big route you'll have to resist the temptation to put lots of gear in when it isn't very hard!

Further time can be saved by missing belays (stances) - long double ropes will make this much more possible.

Based on text from the **Multi-pitch** chapter of **Trad Climbing+** by Adrian Berry and John Arran, published by Rockfax 2007 - see cover flap

Climbers enjoying the ever-popular Lundeklubben (6) - page 177 - Store Festvåg, as the mist swirls around the high peaks.

Kvanndalstinden (818m)

Geitvika

HENNINGSVÆR
BRYGGEHOTEL

The West

Henningsvær

Kalle

Kabelvåg

Svolvær

Trolltindan

Walking Peaks

Bouldering

Henningsvær to Kalle

Vågakallen (943m)

Migand pillaren

The West

Henningsvær

Kalle

Kabelvåg

Svolvær

Trolltindan

Walking Peaks

Bouldering

The view along the coast looking northeast from Henningsvær.

The spectacular section of coast between Henningsvær and Kalle is one with a huge amount of potential - the small set of routes described here is just a taster. The approach to the more remote cliffs is a little laborious though - a friendly fisherman might be a useful.

Around the first major headland are the hidden bays of Geitvika and of Gullvika. The latter is superbly situated and well hidden at the base of the long gully that falls from the col between Festvågtinden and Budalstinden. Around Geitvika are three areas that have seen a little development, and beyond them the rock goes on and on.

Ed Webster's 1994 Lofoten guide referred to the first developed bit of rock, with the route *Pan*, as Gullvika svaet (Golden Bay Slab) though the slab actually overlooks the smaller Geitvika (Goat Bay) just to the west. We have decided that probably the least confusing option is to rename the cliff now rather than let the error roll on down the years.

It is said that the traverse of the coast between Henningsvær and Kalle is a great outing that only takes a couple of hours. It may be worth investigating on a rest day - expect to spot loads of new routes.

Approach
There is parking by the landward side of the outer bridge by Henningsvær. Vague paths and scrambling lead eastwards along the coast. The rough path is sometimes close to the sea, and occasionally higher to avoid the occasional cliff that drops straight into the water at high tide.

Conditions
The whole area faces southeast towards the distant mainland and catches the morning sun. Much of the rock sticks well out of the hillside and should dry relatively rapidly and it is also sheltered from southwesterlies.

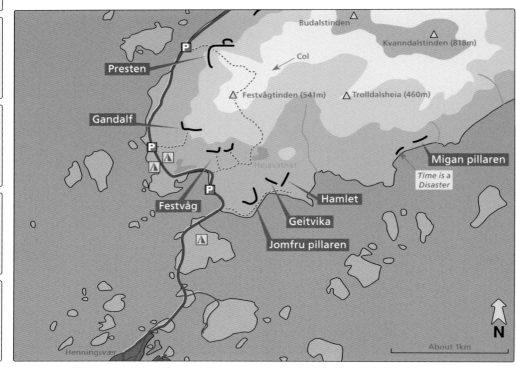

The West
Henningsvær
Kalle
Kabelvåg
Svolvær
Trolltindan
Walking Peaks
Bouldering

The West

Henningsvær

Kalle

Kabelvåg

Svolvær

Trolltindan

Walking Peaks

Bouldering

Arild Meyer looking pretty in purple on the first ascent of the remote *Migan pillaren* (6+ *A0*) - *page 190*. Photos: Odd-Roar Wiik

The West
Henningsvær
Kalle
Kabelvåg
Svolvær
Trolltindan
Walking Peaks
Bouldering

Descent

Jomfru pillaren

On rounding the first headland an impressive barrel-shaped buttress appears high up on the left. Jomfru pillaren *(Virgin Pillar)* only has one route at present, though there is scope for others, the most obvious one being the long corner system round to the right. The base of the face is reached by a short steep scramble.

Approach (see map on page 184) - Park in the lay-by on the landward side of the outer bridge on Route 816. Scramble east around the headland. A more direct approach across the spur might be possible too.

❶ Vårkåt . . . . . [Top 50] [ ] ████ **7**

(Spring lust) A steep and powerful route tackling the superb crack system splitting the big rounded pillar overlooking Geitvika. The line is unmistakable, tackling the prominent line of cracks and grooves. The whole line has been thoroughly cleaned so there is little chance of getting lost. Bring PLENTY of cams!
1) 7-, 35m. Climb the crack to an overhang then the continuation to its end. Traverse left to another crack leading to a ledge.
2) 6+, 35m. The crack leads past a blank section, and a niche, to a torrid off-width below a small stance.
3) 7, 35m. Follow the crack, then make a thin traverse right into another steeper crack and storm up this to a stance.
4) 5-, 30m. Climb discontinuous cracks then move out right past a loose flake to the arete. Climb past a tree to the top.
Descent - From the top of the cliff, take the path leftwards then down from Heiavatnet lake.
FA. Odd-Roar Wiik, Nils Paulsen, Truls Seines (some aid) 1994
FFA. Odd-Roar Wiik, Patrik Fransson 1995

Geitvika

Set above the right-hand side of the small valley, and almost opposite Jomfru pillaren, is a prominent golden coloured slab that is clearly visible from Henningsvær. The original route here was climbed back in 1992, and three more climbs have been added since.
Approach - Park in the lay-by on the landward side of the outer bridge on Route 816. Scramble east around the headland until below a loose gully which leads up to the grassy ledges at the cliff base. See photo on page 11 for approximate location.

❷ Aprilsnarr . . . . . [1] ████ **6-**
110m. *(April Fool)* A route that makes the most of the left-hand side of the face by an interesting zig-zagging line. Start at a ledge below and right of the big loose gully that bounds the face
1) 5+, 35m. Climb the thin crack in the face then, at its top, trend right up the ramp to a belay in the big alcove.
2) 6-, 45m. Step round the exposed arete and follow the ramp to its end. Traverse back left then follow the diagonal crack to a good ledge on the left.
3) 4+, 30m. Step left and climb easy ground to the top.
FA. Ragnar Ekker, Knut Fausa Storvik 1.4.2002

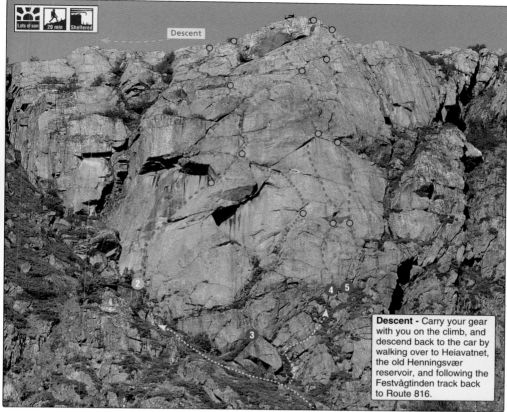

Descent

Descent - Carry your gear with you on the climb, and descend back to the car by walking over to Heiavatnet, the old Henningsvær reservoir, and following the Festvågtinden track back to Route 816.

❸ Landstrykere .... 6+
135m. *(The Tramps)* A line up the central section of the face. Start under the grassy rampline that runs up towards the prominent niche in the centre of the cliff.
1) 5+, 45m. Start up the short wall then follow the bushy ramp until the crack that runs rightwards up the face leads to a stance on the nose.
2) 6, 30m. Climb along the overlap then head up the thin crack in the face, trending slightly left, then follow deeper cracks leftwards to a small stance where *Aprilsnarr* arrives from the left.
3) 6+, 30m. Continue direct up the black streaked wall until *Aprilsnarr* arrives from the left again, then step left to a stance.
4) 4+, 30m. Head straight up the face taking the easiest line.
FA. Mie Kastet, Odd-Roar Wiik 7.2007

❹ Pan 7-
125m. A fine climb up the thin crack system in the steep clean slab on the cliff's right-hand side. A very full rack is required for the sustained second pitch. Scramble up a right-trending bushy ramp to a good ledge below the initial crack.
1) 5, 30m. Climb up a short wall, then step left into the thin crack which is followed to a good belay ledge.
2) 7-, 35m. Jam up a crack on the right and step left to the base of a classic finger-crack in a steep slab. Climb this straight up (very sustained) to a right-trending crack and a troublesome overlap. A difficult final move over this bulge gains a small belay stance.

Pan continued...
3) 6+, 30m. Climb straight up another steep vertical crack to easier climbing.
4) 5-, 30m. Follow a finger-crack on the left, then go diagonally right up easy slabs. Finish up a short corner on the right.
FA. In 7.1992, Odd-Roar Wiik and partner made the general first ascent of the route, including pitch 2, where they used 1 point of aid on the crux overlap. Ed Webster and Thorbjørn Enevold made the first free ascent of the route described here on 12.7.1993

❺ Mordar Anders .... 6+
130m. *(Anders the Murderer)* A good four pitch route up the right-hand side of the face, though there is some doubt about the precise line and pitch grades. Start from the highest grass ledge as for *Pan*.
1) 30m. Traverse out right to gain the base of a crack, then climb this and its thinner continuation to a stance in the niche.
2) 35m. Climb out of the apex of the niche and follow the thin cracks to its end. Move right then continue up to reach a good ledge with a belay at its left-hand end below a groove.
3) 35m. Climb the groove to its end then continue up the thin crack above to eventually arrive at a good ledge.
4) 30m. Easier climbing leads rightwards to the top.
FA, Krister Jonsson, Anders Lundkvist 1997

The West
Henningsvær
Kalle
Kabelvåg
Svolvær
Trolltindan
Walking Peaks
Bouldering

Hamlet Wall

Beyond Geitvika is a rocky ridge that runs down the hillside towards the sea and tucked in beyond it are a set of short sheltered walls that were developed in 2007 with a small collection of climbs. Interestingly this was first discovered and climbed on by Anders Lundquist and Johan Sandberg in the 1990s. They called the cliff the Hamlet Wall but, when questioned, that was about all they could remember - the routes they did must have made quite an impression!
Approach (See map on page 184) - The wall is a little further along the coastline from Geitvika.

⑥ Frozen in Time . . . . ☐ **5**

1) 5, 25m. Climb the right-trending and streaked slab (the grassy crack to the left is tricky to avoid) to gain the wide crack left of the overhangs. Step right and climb the right-trending groove, past the 'frozen in time' block, to a small recessed ledge.
2) 5, 20m. Squeeze up the awkward constricted slot to gain the slab above and follow the crack to grassy ledges.
Descent - Move left across grassy ledges carefully to reach a fixed nut belay. A 45m abseil reaches the ground.
FA. Nigel Redshaw, Lex Pearce 12.6.2007

⑦ Shark Ride . . . . ☐ **5+**

Start at a block at the lowest point of the buttress.
1) 5+, 25m. Climb the crack 1m right of the block until tricky moves left and right reach its continuation. At the end of the crack, mantel up and left to a thinner crack and continue to a good ledge.
2) 5+, 20m. Climb steeply then step right onto the arete at a flake runner. Ride the arete to a good ledge and block belay.
Descent - Abseil from the block - 45m.
FA. Nigel Redshaw, Lex Pearce 13.6.2007

Up and to the right is the other developed piece of rock - Cask Strength Buttress - split by a series of attractive cracks. The route names are all Scottish whiskeys.

⑧ Tamnavulin . . . . ☐ **5**

35m. The left-hand crack leads past a niche to a broken wall on the left. Climb this and the finger-crack above to the ledge.
FA. Lex Pearce, Nigel Redshaw 10.6.2007

⑨ Uigeadail . . . . ☐ **5+**

35m. Layback up the right-facing ramp and climb past an undercut flake to a small ledge. Bridge the twin crack above to access the corner on the left then climb this and the crack above.
FA. Lex Pearce 3.6.2007

⑩ Milburn 25 . . . . ☐ **5+**

35m. Climb the right-hand of the three cracks (loose block at 5m). Continue up the right-hand side of a large flake then jam the bulge to reach a good belay ledge.
FA. Lex Pearce, Nigel Redshaw 3.6.2007

Geitvika

Hamlet Wall

Shark Ride

Cask Strength

The West

Henningsvær

Kalle

Kabelvåg

Svolvær

Trolltindan

Walking Peaks

Bouldering

Looking down the upper arete, and into the approach gully, on the first ascent of *Shark Ride* (5+). Photo: Nigel Redshaw

The West

Henningsvær

Kalle

Kabelvåg

Svolvær

Trolltindan

Walking Peaks

Bouldering

Descent

11 Time is a Disaster . . . . 〔1〕 [   ] **5-**
90m. This remote route is reached by boulder hopping and scrambling eastwards for about 30 minutes (easier at low tide) from the Henningsvær bridge, passing first Geitvika and then the Hamlet Wall.
1) 4+, 40m. Climb the rib forming the right-hand side of the slab to a belay in the bottom of a wide groove 2m right of a roof/overlap.
2) 5-, 40m. Traverse left under the roof/overlap and pull onto the slab above. Climb this, trending right to reach a groove and jamming crack, and climb this to a juniper bush. Step right on the undercut arete and climb this in a fine position to a thread belay at a large flake.
3) 4+, 10m. Continue up the arete to the top.
Descent - Make two abseils down the grassy groove 5m to the left of the top of the route - one of 50m and one of 40m, old slings are in place.
FA. Nigel Redshaw, Alex Pearce 20.7.2005

Migan pillaren
An extensive and impressive section of rock which is the seaward slope of Kvandalstinden. Only two routes have been recorded here so far though the scope is massive.

12 Migan pillaren . . . . 〔2〕 [   ] **6+** *A0*
A seven pitch route up the tall, triangular and attractive white cliff. It is reached by boulder hopping from the Henningsvær side. The first ascent team described it as one of their most memorable routes, so maybe it is worth three stars, you will just have to go and see. If it doesn't look an adequate challenge, keep heading east for bigger and better things. *Photo page 185.*
Descent - Walk down to the left.
FA. Arild Meyer, Odd-Roar Wiik 1995

Kvanndalstinden (818m)

Vågakallen (943m)

12

The West

Henningsvær

Kalle

Kabelvåg

Svolvær

Trolltindan

Walking Peaks

Bouldering

One of the better-looking unclimbed buttresses along this coast Photo: Thorbjørn Enevold

The West

Henningsvær

Kalle

Kabelvåg

Svolvær

Trolltindan

Walking Peaks

Bouldering

Henningsvær

Kvandalstinden

Vågakallen

Storpillaren

Glåmtind

Trollfestningen

Paradiset

Honnikornsvaet

Løva

Kongstinden

Urdstabben

Finnvika

Tjeldbergvika hornet

Tjeldbergvika Left

Svolvær

Sandvika

Kabelvåg

Urdstabben

The West

Henningsvær

Kalle

Kabelvåg

Svolvær

Trolltindan

Walking Peaks

Bouldering

Fløya

Svolværgeita

Skråpillaren

Kalle

The West

Henningsvær

Kalle

Kabelvåg

Svolvær

Trolltindan

Walking Peaks

Bouldering

Colin Binks and Sherri Davy on *Stiv kuling* (5+) - *page 203* - one of the many fine short climbs on the left-hand side of Paradiset Main Cliff.

The West

Henningsvær

Kalle

Kabelvåg

Svolvær

Trolltindan

Walking Peaks

Bouldering

The West

Henningsvær

Kalle

Kabelvåg

Svolvær

Trolltindan

Walking Peaks

Bouldering

The Kalle area offers some of the most contrasting climbing you will find on Lofoten. Dominating everything is the immense northeast face Vågakallen with its two striking pillars - Myggapillaren, and the mighty Storpillaren. The routes on Storpillaren are long undertakings including a few internationally acclaimed lines like the original *Storpillaren* (7), *Freya* (8) and *Storm Pillar* (7+). An ascent of one of these is not to be underestimated but even the lesser undertakings on Storpillaren and Myggapillaren are big climbs which require experience and pre-planning.

In complete contrast to this is Paradiset - a set of small crags dotted across a complex area of walls, gullies and boulders. This is a great spot for getting a feel for rock climbing, with the pleasant easy routes on the Main Cliff always popular, and is the main reason that the NNKS was originally set up here back in the 1970s. The solid rock and sublime setting by the glittering sea help turn the place into a magical spot. Most of the routes in this area have been climbed for years but never properly documented. This book covers them in greater detail for the first time but there are certainly more quality lines in the area waiting to be discovered.

The other crags in this section are mostly on the flanks of the ridge which swings round from Vågakallen towards Kalle, forming the open valley of Øvredalen. The cliffs of Alcoholveggen and Trollfestningen offer more multi-pitch climbs in a friendlier environment than Vågakallen. There are also a few other smaller crags plus the outlying peak of Glåmtinden.

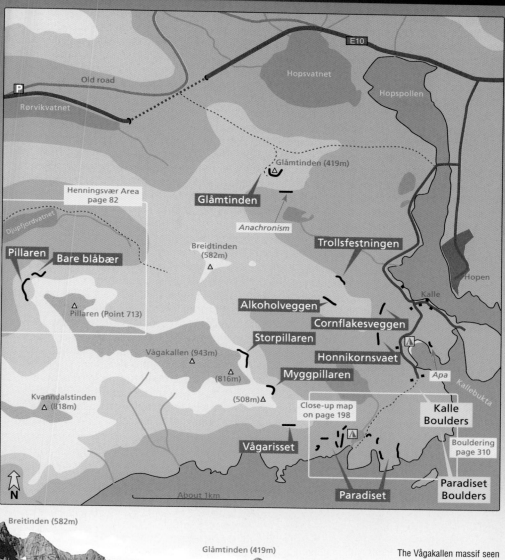

The West

Henningsvær

Kalle

Kabelvåg

Svolvær

Trolltindan

Walking Peaks

Bouldering

P

Old road

Rørvikvatnet

Hopsvatnet

E10

Hopspollen

Glåmtinden (419m)

Glåmtinden

Henningsvær Area
page 82

Djupfjordvatnet

Anachronism

Pillaren

Bare blåbær

Breidtinden
(582m)

Trollsfestningen

Hopen

Kalle

Pillaren (Point 713)

Alkoholveggen

Cornflakesveggen

Vågakallen (943m)

Storpillaren

Honnikornsvaet

Apa

Kallebukta

Kvanndalstinden
(818m)

(816m)

Myggpillaren

(508m)

Kalle
Boulders

Close-up map
on page 198

Bouldering
page 310

Vågarisset

N

About 1km

Paradiset

Paradiset
Boulders

Breitinden (582m)

Glåmtinden (419m)

The Vågakallen massif seen
from Sandvika Camping

Paradiset is located just to the southwest of the tiny fishing village of Kalle, 5km along the coast as the gull flies from Henningsvær. It is a superb area of granite cliffs and boulders set beside the sparkling sea, with distant views of the mysterious mountains of the mainland. Paradise is one of Lofoten's most popular climbing destinations for a variety of reasons; the high-friction quick-drying rock, a great collection of easier climbs, the seascape, the impressive views of Vågakallen soaring high above, the beautiful jamming cracks and the wild camping close to the cliffs.

Traditionally many of Paradiset's climbs have not been named or documented, though this policy has been slightly inconsistent over the years. This lack of information, combined with the complex nature of the various gullies, walls and boulders, has meant that climbers have tended to focus on the obvious cliffs, missing out on some great routes elsewhere. This time we have described most of the major routes although there are certainly more that have been done over the years. In some cases we have made up names for these routes to give them a bit of character and uniqueness. If the documenting of these routes with their new names offends, please feel free to ignore them and go exploring, getting lost among the rocks, sun, rain and surf of Paradiset; just as it ever was.

Approach   Also see main map on page 197

From the E10 to the east of Kabelvåg, turn south on Våganveien (also called Hopsveien) at signs for Hopen and Kalle Rorbu. Drive south then in a dip at 0.8 km, turn right onto a dirt road that leads over a stone causeway across the estuary. Drive 2.7 km to the fishing village of Kalle, then turn right, still on a dirt road, up a short, steep, bumpy hill. Just over the brow is a public beach and grassy camping area by the beach at Kallebukta. There is also free camping, drinking water and a smelly and much overused toilet here. At 3.3 km on this same dirt road, turn right along a small dirt track and park in a small, grassy parking area (at 3.4 km). Walk east to Paradiset across a field, following a well-worn track (keep left in the low-lying areas to avoid the swamps) to reach a small wild campground beside a fresh water stream and delightful lake. The main section of cliffs lie directly ahead, and several other outcrops are located to either side of the path. A small trail branches left towards a fairly prominent armadillo-shaped boulder on the left - the Butter Arms Boulder.

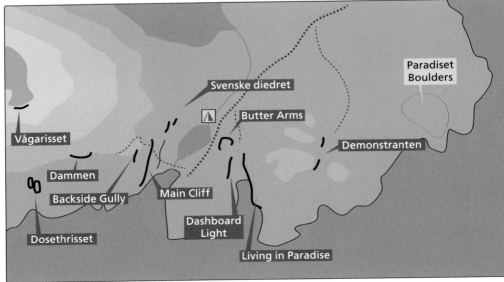

Paradiset

Vågakallen (916m)

199

The West
Henningsvær
Kalle
Kabelvåg
Svolvær
Trolltindan
Walking Peaks
Bouldering

Vågarisset

Storpillaren

Butter Arms

By the Dashboard Light

Approach
to Living in
Paradise

Vågakallen and its mighty Storpillaren tower high
above the popular climber's playground of Paradise.

Dosethrisset

These large boulders must have fallen from the flanks of Vågakallen aeons ago. They are home to a few routes and are set in a pleasant location are a short distance above the high-tide mark.

Approach (see map on page 198) - Take the ramp, as for the Main Cliff, to the flat area but continue up and right to higher ledges (see photo on page 204) then head around to the right of the deep gully that cuts rightwards from the Main Cliff. Follow vague tracks and rocky steps then drop into the next gully (Backside Gully) at a big jammed boulder before heading towards the sea. Climb down a short steep corner then head out onto the golden granite slabs.

The West

Henningsvær

Kalle

Kabelvåg

Svolvær

Trolltindan

Walking Peaks

Bouldering

The first climb is to the left and behind the Dosethrisset face.

① Jesus 6-
14m. Gain the groove and crack from the right and follow it to a leftward exit.
FA. Bent Svinnung, Bjørn Braathen 1982

② Grandiosa 6
14m. *(A popular pizza)* Bold climbing up the blunt rib and ramps to the left of the fierce thin crack.
FA. Oskar Alexandersson

③ Dosethrisset . . . . . . [Top 50] 7
14m. *(Doseth's Crack)* This notoriously strenuous finger-crack found on the biggest boulder in the area, facing the sea. Climb straight up the crack to hard moves to gain the slanting ramp. The tempting flakes on the right are supposed to be avoided for the grade 7 although the amount of chalk on them suggests they usually aren't. Finish up the ramp with difficulty. Escape from the top of the block is a little problematical. *Photo on page 49.*
FA. Hans Christian Doseth, summer 1979. It had previously been an aid route.

④ Smutthullet . . . . 7+
14m. *(Loophole)* The left-slanting crack is hard work.
FA. Daniel Bidner early 1990s. It had previously been aided.

⑤ Gelbe kante 6-
15m. *(Yellow Edge)* A bold (though it is often top-roped) route up the striking jutting arete to the right of *Dosethrisset*. Undercut through the bulges at the start round to the right then climb flakes, trending left to finish up the arete. Protection is poor.
FA. Toby Foord-Kelsey, Toby Archer 7.2002. Initially top-roped by Arild Meyer and Magnar Osnes in 1984

mid afternoon | 20 min | Sheltered

The West

Henningsvær

Kalle

Kabelvåg

Svolvær

Trolltindan

Walking Peaks

Bouldering

Migan pillaren

Dammen

The Boulders

Approach

To mid afternoon | 20 min | Sheltered

Dammen

(The Lake) A short slabby wall with three excellent jamming cracks plus some harder stuff. Sadly the Lake is only shallow so there is no deep water soloing here.

6 No Place to Flounder. . . 7-
14m. A hard start gains flakes and small cam runners. Finish boldly to the left up the rounded arete.
FA. Max Durson, Will Wykes 12.6.2004

7 Venstre risset. . . . . 4+
14m. The left-hand crack to a finish on the right.

8 Venstre risset direkte 6
14m. A desperate move gains the base of the jamming crack

9 Tynn 6-
14m. A tricky start reaches the rattly flakes then step left and climb the fine sustained thin crack.

10 Sentrums risset . . . . . . 4+
14m. The central crack and shallow groove give an excellent pitch with some rattly flakes.

11 Krabbe 5
16m. Follow the ramp leftwards, cross *Sentrums risset* and finish up the right-hand crack in the slab.

12 Høyre risset . . . . 5+
14m. Climb the crack past a spike, gain the right-hand continuation, then exit to the right.

13 Diederet . . . . 3+
14m. Trend left up the leaning groove - good holds and runners.

Backside Gully

The gully crossed between the Main Cliff and Dosethrisset contains a couple of steep cracks that give worthwhile jamming. They are in the shade in the morning and are a little slow to dry.

1 Biff Tartar . . . . ⟨2⟩ 🗲 ☐ 6-
20m. *(Raw Beef)* Jam and bridge the deep groove to a steep exit. Make sure you carry some large cams.
FA. Arild Meyer and partner, mid 1980s

2 Feber . . . . ⟨1⟩ 🗲 ☐ 7-
14m. *(Fever)* Climb a short leaning wall to reach a crack in a slanting groove. Finish over a small roof at the top.
FA. Arild Meyer (top-rope) 1985

Main Cliff

A fine wall tapering down towards the sea, which offers some excellent short routes on great rock. They are mostly named after different weather conditions.
Approach (see map on page 198) - Scramble up the grassy left-trending ramp to the left of *Svenska diedret* to a flat area then follow a ledge to the right of a gully (a little exposed, but with large holds) to reach the open slabs below the cliff.

3 Stormvarsel . . . . ⟨1⟩ 🗲 ☐ 5
20m. *(Storm Warning)* A pleasant route traversing above the waves. Start at the lowest point of the ramp and climb cracks to reach a horizontal break which leads left. Hand traverse along this then climb straight up slabby rock to the top.
FA. Ed Webster, Odd-Roar Wiik 26.7.1991

4 Lett bris. . . . . ⟨1⟩ ☐ 4
16m. *(Light breeze)* The long bubbly crack above the base of the ramp gives a good lower grade pitch.

5 Liten storm . . . . . . ⟨1⟩ 🧗 🧗 ☐ 5+
16m. *(Storm)* Either of two cracks leads to a junction. Continue with difficulty up the yellow streak to reach easier ground.

6 Full storm . . . . ⟨1⟩ 🧗 ☐ 5+
16m. Climb the crack system in the steepest part of the face to hard moves up to, and past, the highest break.

7 Malabarsk . . . . ⟨1⟩ 🧗 🧗 ☐ 6
16m. *(The perfect storm* - named after the Malabar Coast). The central line on the wall has a testing finale up a thin flake. Bolder than the other routes hereabouts.

Backside Gully

8 Sterk storm 6
16m. *(Major storm)* The right-hand crack system.

9 Orkan 5
14m. *(Hurricane)* The wide crack/narrow chimney is steep.

10 Sterk kuling . . . . 5+
14m. *(Howling gale)* Twin cracks with a steep and awkward exit.

11 Laber bris 4
16m. *(Gentle breeze)* The juggy groove on massive holds to an exit on the right.

12 Stiv kuling . . . . 5+
14m. *(Strong gale)* Trend right to gain the flakes and climb these to a finish up the scoop above. *Photo on page 194.*

13 Liten kuling . . . . 5+
18m. *(Gale)* The left-hand crack is a good pitch. Climb it to the ramp then balance right until an upward exit is possible.

14 Frisk bris . . . . 5+
14m. *(Fresh breeze)* Steep climbing on amazing holds, first right then left to the ramp. Finish above and right.

15 Heavy Weather 5
14m. Juggy climbing leading to an exit through the bulges.

16 Værvarsel 5
14m. *(Weather forecast)* The right-hand crack leads to a fork, finish to the right or left (a little harder).

Beginners' Wall

The right-hand side of the Main Wall at Paradiset is a great place to learn the basics - perfect rock, short pitches, excellent runner placements, good stances and an easy walk-off. Describing the myriad routes here would tax the most dedicated guidebook writer and in truth all the cracks can (and have been) climbed for many years.

We have left the page blank so that you can record the climbs you did on your visit, when and who with, give them a name and a grade - in fact a way to try your hand at guidebook writing.

This area is much used by instructional groups, please give them some space as they practice the skills that will take them on to greater things.

17

18

19

20

21

Descent

Approach to left-hand side

A Climbing Introduction

Start up one of the lower cracks, placing protection on the way. Belay on the mid-height ledge then bring up your partner. Finish up one of the cracks in the top wall. Once your partner has arrived, shake hands then descend and do another one. Repeat until pooped.

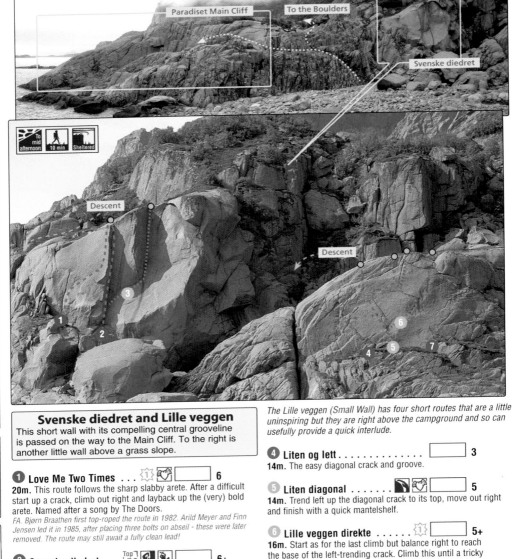

Svenske diedret and Lille veggen

This short wall with its compelling central grooveline is passed on the way to the Main Cliff. To the right is another little wall above a grass slope.

❶ Love Me Two Times ... 6

20m. This route follows the sharp slabby arete. After a difficult start up a crack, climb out right and layback up the (very) bold arete. Named after a song by The Doors.
FA. Bjørn Braathen first top-roped the route in 1982. Arild Meyer and Finn Jensen led it in 1985, after placing three bolts on abseil - these were later removed. The route may still await a fully clean lead!

❷ Svenske diedret ... 6+

22m. *(The Swedish Corner)* The left-hand of two deep grooves is a popular testpiece. An awkward start leads to easier bridging then a hard move to gain the upper corner and a sprint for the top.
FA. Originally and aid route, two Swedish climbers made the first free ascent in the early 1980s.

❸ Kakadu 6-

24m. Start up *The Swedish Corner* then pad right across the slab to gain the right-hand groove. This is easier but lacks much in the way of runners (RPs and not much else) until just short of the top. Double ropes are a good idea.
FA. Krister Johnsson 5.1996. Originally done on aid.

The Lille veggen (Small Wall) has four short routes that are a little uninspiring but they are right above the campground and so can usefully provide a quick interlude.

❹ Liten og lett 3

14m. The easy diagonal crack and groove.

❺ Liten diagonal 5

14m. Trend left up the diagonal crack to its top, move out right and finish with a quick mantelshelf.

❻ Lille veggen direkte ...... 5+

16m. Start as for the last climb but balance right to reach the base of the left-trending crack. Climb this until a tricky mantelshelf reaches the final short crack.

❼ Lille høyre .... 4+

14m. Trend right to flakes and a grassy ledge. Hand traverse out left and pull up for the top.

The West

Henningsvær

Kalle

Kabelvåg

Svolvær

Trolltindan

Walking Peaks

Bouldering

Colin Binks working out the best way to tackle the precarious and strenuous moves to gain the final groove on *Svenske diedret* (6+).

Dashboard Light

Butter Arms

This pseudo-boulder is actually the end of a rocky bluff overlooking the lake and wild camping spot. It is the first buttress encountered on the approach and is worth a quick visit. The views from the top are great.

❶ Butter Arms `Top 50` 🪨🪨🪨🪨🪨 **8+**
16m. The leaning groove and desperate thin crack will leave you with arms like butter and fingers like claws! Climb the groove to its top (7- to here) then, after a blow, go for glory up the slanting crack. Well-protected by small cams, but very hard work.
FA. Ed Webster, Odd-Roar Wiik 5.8.1991. They aid climbed the top crack on nuts. FFA. Håkon Hansen 2.8.1998. He gave it 9- initially.

❷ No Butts . . . . 🪨 **?**
16m. The open project up the steeply leaning rib will be mighty tough if anyone ever completes it. It was originally bolted by 'Crazy Martin', an Austrian - a victory of aspiration over ability!

Dashboard Light

Opposite Living in Paradise and behind and left of the Butter Arms boulder, is a fine slab - 40m high facing the morning sunshine.
Approach (see map on page 198) - Walk past the left edge of the Butter Arms boulder, over a small col, then scramble down the slab into the bay.

❻ Back to Paradise . . . . 🪨 **3+**
35m. The cracks in the left-hand side of the hanging shield have an awkward start, then lead left before finishing straight up the slab.

❼ Too Wide for Paradise . . . . . 🪨 **3+**
35m. Climb the big flake followed by the off-width to the left, or the undercut flake to the right. Finish up more wide cracks.

❽ By the Dashboard Light . . . . `Top 50` **4**
40m. The thin crack up the centre of the slab (not much gear) leads to a finish up the corner above. Excellent.

❾ Heart of Paradise . . 🪨🪨🪨 **6+**
40m. The bold right-hand side of the slab leads to taxing moves into the hanging groove above.
FA. Colin Binks, Chris Craggs 28.7.2007. This may have been soloed by Arild Meyer in the 1980s, in his rubber boots, whilst setting up a top-rope for his students, or maybe it was the one to the left!

❸ Butter Fingers Direct . . . 🪨🪨 **5**
24m. Variations on the original. A short struggle gains the hanging groove, then follow the cracks of the regular route before making a bold finish up the front of the final block.

❹ Butter Fingers . . . . 🪨🪨 **5**
22m. Worthwhile. Scramble up the groove on the right then climb the left-trending flakes to a break. Shuffle left and finish up the awkward widening crack to the summit.

❺ Butter Balls . . . . 🪨 **3+**
20m. Start as for *Butter Fingers* but follow pleasant cracks right of the arete throughout. A safe lead.

Descent

Approach

Colin Binks on *By the Dashboard Light* (4).

'X' Marks the Spot

This wide wall has a small selection of climbs in a sunny setting. The X-shaped cracks identify the wall.
Approach - From the Butter Arms boulder, head down the left-hand side of the wide gully to the wall, which is opposite *Dashboard Light*.

10 X-citing . . . . 5+
26m. Start 2m left of the block at the edge of the wall. Climb to the bulges then move left and pull through on X-citing rock to a ledge. Finish up flakes and a slab above.

11 Generation X 7-
22m. A fine climb. From the left-hand boulder climb the wall to the basalt blobby bits, move right (thread) and climb the blank section to a break. Move left to more blobs then follow the crack rightwards to the X-tension of *Ayers Rock*.
FA. Jason Porter, Mike Ayres 29.7.1996

12 Ayers Rock. . . . . 6+
22m. From the right-hand boulder, pull into a scoop and climb steep ground on good but X-traordinary holds to reach the base of the crack. Climb this as it widens from fingers to hands.
FA. Matt Heason, 'Max' 20 August 1996

13 A Cry in the Dark . . 6+
22m. Use the same start as *Ayers Rock* but trend right up the steep wall to the base of the right-hand crack. Layback and jam this until it eases. The harder of the pair and it is X-cellent!
FA. Jørgen Sundby, Niels Paulsen 1990s

14 X-crement . . . . 5+
22m. Climb the steep wall to the base of the chimney (sometimes damp) and gain it with difficulty from the left. The upper chimney is easy and loose - the right arete is better. The name says it all!

'X' Marks the Spot

Descent

Approach - not high tide

Living in Paradise

A set of sea cliff climbs which are worth seeking out for some fine climbing in a secluded setting. The right-hand routes start right at the waves at the left edge (looking out) of the inlet. A traverse right on narrow ledges above the sea (not high tide) leads to a stance round the arete at the base of an easy groove that leads to a steep narrow chimney above.

❶ Paradise Regained . . . . 🔄 🧗‍♀️ ☐ 6

30m. Climb the fingery wall (bold) then move left to a flake. Up this to a ledge at the base of a leaning groove. Gain this awkwardly, then more of the same up the next groove to an easier finish up the crack on the right.

❷ Traverse of the Cods . . . . . 🔄 ☐ 5+

55m. Start up *Seaside Special* but traverse left all the way to a steep corner-crack and a stance. Finish up this.

❸ Seaside Special . . . . . 🔄 🏄 ☐ 5+

30m. An interesting outing. From the stance move left onto the arete and climb it trending left up slabby rock. A crack leads to a short steep wall which is passed using a good spike. Continue leftwards up a tricky slab to finish.

❹ Living in Paradise . . . . . 🔄 Top 50 🏄 ☐ 5

20m. From the stance move up and right to reach the crack. Climb it by sustained well-protected fun.

FA. Ed Webster, Odd-Roar Wiik 5.8.1991. Probably done before.

❺ Lost in Paradise . . . . 🔄 ☐ 5

20m. The right-hand crack is followed to its end then finish up the fine slab. A right-hand start is about the same grade though with less gear. *Photo on page 7.*

Chris Craggs and Colin Binks enjoying *Living in Paradise* (5) a hidden gem that has always been a little tricky to locate. The fact that the action shot in the old guide was reversed didn't help. Photo: Sherri Davy

Demonstranten

This small collection of climbs is situated to the south of the approach path to Butter Arms and the camping area. The 'Demonstranten' (demonstration) routes are many folks' first contact with rock climbing since they have always been popular with the local climbing schools.

Approach (see map on page 198) - Branch left from the main path shortly after the marshy area. Head across undulating ground until the twin cracks of *Demonstranten* appear down on the right in a steep gully. *Kveldskosen* is further down the same gully. The exact whereabouts of *Rått kjøtt* remains a bit of a mystery though!

① Kylling vingen . . . . . . 🎒 💪 [   ] 5+
15m. *(Chicken Wing)* The most prominent of the steep wide cracks on the wall on the seaward end of the gully. Old school climbing, old school grade, and the name gives a clue about the best approach.
FA. Arild Meyer and friends 1980s

② Kveldskosen . . . . 🎒 ⬅️ [   ] 7
8m. *(A Cozy Thing to Do in the Evening)* The impressive roof crack - 'the *Separate Reality* of Lofoten' - is actually best done in the morning when it catches the sun. Jam the crack that splits the underside of the huge boulder jammed in the gully.
FA. Arne Nybråten (top-rope) 7.1981

③ Demonstranten . . . . 🎒 [   ] 4
17m. The left-hand of the two attractive slanting cracks gives a pleasant pitch. It is commonly spilt into two pitches by those who are 'learning the ropes'.

④ Demonstranten direkte . . . . 🎒 [   ] 5
17m. The right-hand crack is a touch steeper and more sustained.

⑤ Master Class . . . . 🎒 ✏️ [   ] 6-
16m. The steep crack on the right is accessed from a convenient boulder and gives a short pumpy tussle.

A shot from the first day of a climbing course in the 70s. Tom Pedersen and Finn Tore Bjørnstad showing how it is done on *Demonstranten*.
Photo: Kjell Ove Storvik

The only other named route in the area is the elusive Rått kjøtt. The route is thought to be in an inlet between Living in Paradise and Demonstranten - if you locate it please let us know. The vague original description is preserved below for posterity.

⑥ Rått kjøtt . . . . 🎒 💪 [   ] 6+
10m. *(Raw Meat)* "Located closer to the sea, inside a sort of cleft, near Butter Arms. Climb a hard-to-protect steep wall to gain a shallow, flaring, left-slanting fist crack."
FA. Arild Meyer, Sjur Nesheim, Håvard Nesheim mid-1980s

The West

Henningsvær

Kalle

Kabelvåg

Svolvær

Trolltindan

Walking Peaks

Bouldering

'Fontainbleau' Folly

In the 1980s a pair of German climbers spent some time exploring the headland beyond *Demonstranten* and created a bouldering circuit with a good number of problems that ran out towards the sea. When locals came to check it out they were shocked to find the start of the circuit marked with a yin-yang symbol, and the problems were marked on the rock with paint 'a la Fontainbleau' with a series of arrows and names. They were not very pleased about the complete disregard of the local ethic of leaving places exactly as you find them.

Nearly 30 years on, most of the paint marks have faded away though the yin-yang symbol remains as a landmark to this short-sighted folly. There is still some great bouldering out there though, and in a magic setting, just tread lightly.

Mathias Strømquist pondering the
problems of the *Vågarisset* (6+).
Photo: Erik Grunnesjö

Zig Zag . . . . 6+
195m. This seldom climbed route has three good crack pitches
plus some typical Lofoten terrain. Start about 40m to the left of,
and slightly higher than, the base of *Vågarisset*.
1) 5+, 45m. Climb a thin finger-crack through a bulge to reach a
slab split by another vertical crack. Belay above on a ledge below
some big overhangs.
2) 30m. Traverse left below this overhanging section to reach
some grassy ledges.
3) 6-, 45m. An awkward and strenuous crack leads into a steep,
grass-filled chimney. Climb the chimney to a big moss-covered
ledge, and move out right to a belay.
4) 10m. Continue along the ledge around a block, and belay on
top of a block, just below the start of the next crack system.
5) 6, 45m. Climb straight up a steep, beautiful finger-crack
(**5+** *A0* with 2 points of aid) which soon eases back and widens
before narrowing again just below a big belay ledge.
6) 5+, 20m. Walk right for about 5m, then climb a crack straight
up to an overhang where the crack widens. Finish up the right-
facing corner above.
FA. Arild Meyer, Bjørn Braathen, summer 1982

Vågarisset
The impressive buttress above Paradise is home to a
pair of infrequently climbed routes. There is little doubt
that if this buttress was anywhere else in the world it
would be covered in quality climbs since the rock is of
great quality. The descriptions here are from the 1994
guide.
Approach (see map on page 198) - Scramble up
grassy ledges and small outcrops from the area above
Paradiset Main Cliff from where the crack of *Vågarisset*
can be easily seen.
Descent - As for *Myggpillaren* - see page 215 - down
ledges and gullies to the west..

Vågarisset . . . . 6+
About 170m. *(The "Daring Crack" of Vågakallen)* This is the
striking, vertical crack splitting the cliff. It is a sustained, fist-sized
crack. Carry plenty of large cams.
1) 6, 30m. Climb steep cracks in red rock through a roof and up
to a belay stance below the main soaring crackline.
2) 6+, 40m. Fist jam and layback up the strenuous, parallel-sided
and never-ending crack. It is usual to abseil from here.
3 - 5) Several more pitches were climbed on the first ascent, but
the exact line of the route, and grade of the pitches, is not known.
FA. Hans Christian Doseth, Finn Jensen 1979

Vågakallen

Vågakallen (916m)

Approach to
Storpillaren

Storpillaren

Myggpillaren

Approach along the
edge of Kallevatnet

The West

Henningsvær

Kalle

Kabelvåg

Svolvær

Trolltindan

Walking Peaks

Bouldering

Magnificent Vågakallen with the soaring
Storpillaren rising above the remains of the
winter snows. Photo: Thorbjørn Enevold

Erik Grunnesjö climbing the free variation to pitch 4 of *Storpillaren* (7) - *page 221*. To the left is the groove climbed by the original route and above it soars the groove of *Genus Locy*. The trail-rope is clipped to aid the second as he jumars. Photo: Jonas Dahlstrup

With its huge rock precipices on almost every side, Austvågøy's dominant and most beautiful mountain presents an impressive and daunting challenge. Any ascent to its remote summit is an experience not soon forgotten, especially if the climb is made in clear and sunny weather, as it should be for safety. The summit panorama of sea, sky and neighbouring peaks, with the islands of Vestvågøya, Flakstadøya and Moskenesøya to the southwest, and the Norwegian mainland to the south, is truly unforgettable. Attempting the peak in poor weather is a bad idea; route finding (ascending or descending) on the upper sections of the mountain is difficult enough even on clear days.

The peak offers a variety of technical routes as well, ranging from the standard classic scramble of *Sydveggen* (see page 301) which is also the normal descent. To the Yosemite-like (always excluding the weather of course) *Storpillaren*, up the North Face. This latter route set the standard for many years but this has now been eclipsed by the huge lines of *Storm Pillar* and *Freya* over to the left.

Approach   See map on page 234
From the parking at Kalle, head towards Paradiset for about five minutes then cross the stream and follow vague paths round the southwest shore of Kallevatnet and on up into Øvredalen until under the face. Thirty minutes to the foot of the face, and an hour to the base of Storpillaren.

Conditions
The pillar faces east and southeast, gets sunshine until around midday. Although reasonably rapid drying, the altitude and aspect make it a settled weather venue only. Also snow at the base and on the face, make the entire cliff out of season until mid-July in normal conditions.

The West

Henningsvær

Kalle

Kabelvåg

Svolvær

Trolltindan

Walking Peaks

Bouldering

Traditional descent down south side

Ear

1

2

(icons: Morning, 15 min, Bad weather)

Myggapillaren

Myggapillaren is the left-hand and more elegant of the two clean pillars on the face of Vågakallen rising above the shores of Kallevatnet.
Approach (See map on page 234) - Starting from the path between Kalle and Paradiset, walk along a good path around the west side of Kallevatnet to the base of Myggapillaren. Scramble up the base of the pillar.

❶ Wee Beastie 6
160m. A line near the left-hand edge in four pitches. Start 50m up the slope to the left of the groove of *Mygga*.
1) 4, 50m. Pad up the slabs until they steepen to eventually reach a belay on the left at a small tree.
2) 6-, 55m. Climb up the buttress then go around the right-hand side of the ear-shaped feature that dominates the left-hand side of the buttress. Belay on small ledges above the ear.
3) 6, 25m. The thin crack above gives excellent climbing.
4) 4+, 30m. Move up and leftwards to a well-positioned jamming crack in the arete overlooking the gully.
FA. Mark Garthwaite, Mick Fowler 4.7.1999

❷ Mygga . . . . 5+
240m. *(The Mosquito)* Not a real Lofoten classic but this route has a lot of good climbing and is quite popular. Grass and bushes detract a bit from the overall quality.
1) 4+, 45m. Start up a V-groove in the left toe of the pillar. Step left at its top and climb a bit higher to a belay above an overlap on a small ledge with a block.
2) 5-, 40m. Traverse right across the blank slab to a ledge with a fixed nut. Continue up and right across the slab and into a shallow groove with a small stance.
3) 5, 35m. Climb the easy V-groove to another fixed nut, then step left across a short slab into a crack which leads into a groove with small trees and a belay on the right.
4) 4+, 20m. Step right to a layback flake that leads into the V-groove - the route's major feature - which is capped by a huge bulging chockstone. Continue up the groove, past bushes, to a small belay ledge (peg belay).
5) 5+, 25m. Climb the groove above to the bulge (peg) which requires some tricky bridging. Continue with difficulty up the strenuous corner-crack and belay on a ledge on the left.
6) 5-, 20m. Walk up the grass above, then climb out right around a small roof. Layback up the steep corner forming the right-hand side of the huge jammed chockstone at the top of the main V-groove, to a good stance.
7) 5-, 20m. Follow easier cracks up to another long narrow and comfortable belay ledge. Peg on the right.
8) 5+, 35m. From the left-hand end of the ledge, hand traverse left along a horizontal crack (peg - very exposed) into another crack and climb up to a ledge. Continue up and left, following a higher crack to another good ledge.
9) 2, 30m. Finish left easily into the shrubbery above.
FA. Bo Nyborg Andersen, Sverre Søgaard 6.1974. They managed to drop a bag containing most of their pitons from high on the route. The name Mygga was given by a later team of climbers.

Descent - The original descent route involves scrambling to the top of the ridge then descending down the steep, bushy slopes on the opposite (south) side of the buttress summit (see photo on page 221). More recent parties have abseiled back down *Mygga* instead (6 x 50m) - you may want to leave some equipment behind to reinforce the anchors.

The West | Henningsvær | Kalle | Kabelvåg | Svolvær | Trolltindan | Walking Peaks | Bouldering

Close-up of this section on page 222

â = bivi spot

Storm Pillar and Freya

Once known for obvious reasons as 'The Bonatti Pillar of Lofoten', this massive arrow-head of sheer granite dominates Vågakallen's intimidating North Face. Currently two routes tackle the impressive left-hand side of the pillar - on the left *Storm Pillar*, put up by Mike and Louise Turner in 2003 and, on the right, *Freya*, put up by Robert and Daniela Jasper in 1998. Both routes feature hard free and aid climbing, with little in the way of fixed gear, and should be considered as very major undertakings for teams experienced in long multi-day ascents.

Approach - From the edge of Kallevatnet, scramble up scree and rough ground to the face, heading to the right of the huge curving roof.

Descent - Both routes eventually join *Storpillaren* on its pitch 9, one more pitch leads to the pillar crest. Either follow this, and the rest of the climb, to gain the South Face and an easy descent (see page 221) or alternatively, abseil back down the route.

❶ Storm Pillar ... 7+ A3

865m. An almost free ascent of the left-hand side of the face on superb rock. Pitch 11 may eventually go free at around 7c+ with pre-placed gear. Gear needed is a set and a half of cams (to 4), a full set of nuts and micro wires, lost arrow and knife-blade plus hooks. The first ascent team thought it would make an awesome candidate for a one day ascent, though the second ascensionists were less sure - portaledges will probably be needed by most teams. Start to the right of the fall-line from the pillar where a white left-trending and left-facing groove offers a way to outflank the huge black overhangs directly under the pillar.

See photo and stories on page 218.

1) 6-, 50m. Climb leftwards up the groove to belay.
2) 7-, 40m. Continue left with hard moves through the roofs.
3) 7, 25m. Head left (bolt) past the base of the long flake/groove system of *Freya* to a stance beyond it.
4) 6-, 30m. Move left and climb a groove to ledges.
5) 6+, 40m. Trend left across the slabs to a stance under the big diagonal overhang - serious.
6) ?, 30m. Trend up and right to a stance. No grade given.
7) 6+, 60m. Break through the overhangs and continue to a stance in the grass fields above.
8) 6-, 45m. Continue up the rocky buttress above to reach ledges at the First Bivi-site.
9) 7, 55m. Cross the gully then climb the steep groove to the base of the soaring corner above.
10) 7+, 55m. The fantastic overhanging corner gives a magnificent pitch.
11) 7, 50m. Continue up the black corner to the Second Bivi-site on a stance at the base of a steep crack.
12) A3, 55m. Aid climb the steep crack in the smooth steep wall, with some hard free moves in the middle of the pitch.
13) 6+ A1, 35m. Climb over a roof and on to a stance below the 'Fab Flake'.
14) 6+, 50m. The Fab Flake is followed out right then back left to a stance in the base of a long groove.
15) 6+, 45m. The groove leads to the base of a huge square block perched on the wall.
16) 6+, 30m. The 'Tunnel Pitch' heads behind the huge block. The top of this was the Third Bivi-site.
17) 6- A2+, 55m. Aid up the crack then free climb to a stance by a big block.
18) 6, 60m. Climb right then left, past a roof, then move back right and climb to the point where *Storpillaren* comes in from the right.
Descent - Follow *Storpillaren* to the summit, or descend by abseil.
FA. Mike 'Twid' Turner, Louise Thomas 9.2003

❷ Freya ...... 8 A3+

800m. A major undertaking up the central groove system on the pillar. The first ascent - which was filmed - took five days. The climbing is mainly free with bold climbing on the lower walls and some super-sustained cracks in the big groove. There are also three pitches of aid which requite a lot of small gear. Portaledges may be needed, the only decent bivi-ledges are above pitches 7 and 21. Apart from the belay bolts (which provide a viable escape route) the climb has minimal fixed gear - a peg on pitch two and a bolt on pitch three.

1) 6-, 50m. Climb leftwards to a belay.
2) 7-, 40m. Continue left with hard moves over an overhang.
3) 7, 45m. Head left (bolt) to the base of the long flake/groove system and belay a short way up it.
4) 7-, 45m. Climb the groove past some loose blocks.
5) 7-, 35m. Continue up the groove.
6) 6+, 40m. More groove and flake climbing with an excursion out left at about one third height. Bolt belays.
7) 4, 40m. Easier ground leads to a block belay and the site of the First Bivi.
8) 2, 60m. Head left to gain the big grassy ramp then climb this to a belay.
9) 4+, 65m. Continue to bolt belays at the top of the ramp.
10) 6-, 30m. Climb past the right-hand side of a roof and up a crack to a good stance. Bolt belays.
11) 6-, 30m. Slabby rock leads to a stance at the base of the Y fork in the road.
12) 6+, 25m. Follow crack and slabs leftwards to a stance at the base of the huge groove system - bolt belays.
13) 7-, 30m. Climb the left wall of the groove, past loose blocks, until it is possible to get back right into the groove. The right-hand side of a small overhang leads to a good small stance - the Second Bivi-site and base-camp for the battle to come.
14) 8, 25m. Desperate climbing up the groove.
15) 8-, 20m. More of the same.
16) 8, 30m. ... and yet more, following the undercut flake system up and right to a bolted stance just left of the arete.
17) A3+, 35m. Move round the arete and climb the thin crack that splits the 'mirror' slab, to a hanging stance.
18) A3, 20m. More aid climbing on up the thin crack to a ledge.
19) ?, 30m. Cracks lead to a bolted belay - no grade given.
20) 7-, 25m. Climb past the side of the huge roof, and the right-hand side of the next one with difficulty, then follow an easier crack to a double-bolt belay on a huge ledge system.
21) -, 20m. Traverse left along the ledge to a great stance in an overhung niche - the perfect bivi-spot.
22) 6 A2+, 25m. Climb the back of the niche then exit left and climb the crack before pegging the left-curving crack to a double-bolt stance back on the ledge.
23) 6-, 60m. Climb leftwards over loose rock then climb a huge groove, exit left to its top. Continue to a stance on the shoulder.
24) 6, 60m. This is pitch 18 of *Storm Pillar*. Climb right then left, past a roof, then move back right and climb to the point where pitch 9 of *Storpillaren* comes in from the right.
From here either follow *Storpillaren* to the Summit, or descend by abseil.
FA. Robert Jasper, Daniela Jasper 7.1998

The West / Henningsvær / Kalle / Kabelvåg / Svolvær / Trolltindan / Walking Peaks / Bouldering

The West

Henningsvær

Kalle

Kabelvåg

Svolvær

Trolltindan

Walking Peaks

Bouldering

Storm Pillar (7+ A3)

Louise Turner following the long groove on pitch 16 (6+). Photo: Twid Turner

First Ascent

After climbing around Henningsvær for a pleasant few days, Louise Thomas and I were both taken by the stunning 700m Storpillaren - the 'Bonatti Pillar of Lofoten' - on the north face of Vagakallen. Were this superb granite pillar in Yosemite, it would have a dozen or more routes on it but, in 2003, it only had four. The first route - *Storpillaren* (7- *A2*, E3, 5.10c/d, 600m) - was established in 1980 by Bjornstad, Meyer and Skog. The most recent climb - *Freya* (8 *A3+*, E5/6, 5.12+, 800m) - by Daniela and Robert Jasper, was put up in 1998 and includes thirty pitches of climbing, most of which go free at 7 to 8 (5.11+ to 5.12-). We were amazed that nothing had gone up the left-hand side of the face through a big shield of overhanging rock.

With a view toward creating a big-wall free route, we started to climb. The first two days we fixed 200m of rope and hauled five days' worth of food and water up to our high point. A further three full days of climbing brought us to the summit. The climbing was on fantastic rock, and all but one pitch and a couple of short sections went free. Most pitches were 6+/7- (E3/4, 5.10/11) with occasional 7/7+ (E5, 5.12-). The overhanging aid pitch went at A3 with lots of pegs.

The weather was perfect until we reached the summit. At our top bivvy we spent more than two days in a massive storm - rain and sleet poured over our ledge fly like a waterfall. It was quite exciting. After a couple of days the rain subsided and we abseiled to the ground in ten hours. We called our route *Stormpillar* (7+ *A3*, E5, 5.12, 750m). I reckon the one aid pitch would go free at sport 7c+ or 8a.

Mike 'Twid' Turner, GB

Twid Turner involved with the 'fantastic overhanging corner' of pitch 10 (7+.) Photo: Louise Turner

The West

Henningsvær

Kalle

Kabelvåg

Svolvær

Trolltindan

Walking Peaks

Bouldering

Second Ascent

From June 16 to 18, Vasek Satava and I made the second ascent of *Storm Pillar* on the Storpillaren of Vågakallen. The route was first climbed in September 2003 by Louise Thomas and Mike Turner and they gave it the grade of British E5 6a and A3.

We had a small amount of information from Twid and felt it might be possible for us to make a free ascent. We got a detailed topo from the climbing cafe in Henningsvær. On the first day we onsighted the lower slabby part of the wall and slept at a grassy spot above the big terrace (top of pitch eight). Next day we continued, planning to make a free ascent of pitch 12 - the first aid pitch. However, we met three 'ugly' pitches, including the very steep 'water-fall' - pitch 11 - which had been given the grade E4 5c. We managed to onsight this hard pitch - the grade was a joke. Above, we discovered that we would be unable to bivouac, as we were not carrying a portaledge.

It took us over three hours, using all the gear we had, to overcome the A3 pitch. Without resting for part of the day, we couldn't even attempt to free this pitch. We also felt that we would probably need to replace much of the gear or drill a few bolts. Although there was gear every half-metre in the crack, it was generally poor.

We continued up, looking for a place to rest, but there wasn't a ledge big enough even to sit on, so we continued through the night, which was still quite light at this time of year.

At the top of pitch 16, which we reached at 9am, we found a big square block that we could sit on and sleep for three hours in the morning sun. After this rest we climbed the A2+ pitch, which again might be possible to free except for problems with the old gear. Above, easier pitches led to the top of the pillar. After taking photos we abseiled the route. Due to overhangs and poor belays, abseiling was almost as adventurous as the climb, but we made it down in a few hours.

During my visit to Wales in 2004 I tried to understand the British grading system. Here in Norway I stopped worrying about it, accepting that just about anything could fit any grade.

Pavel Jonak, Czech Republic

The West

Henningsvær

Kalle

Kabelvåg

Svolvær

Trolltindan

Walking Peaks

Bouldering

Belay at the
top of pitch 12

Storpillaren

The classic route of *Storpillaren* is identified by a series of steep, left-facing grooves on the right-hand side of the main pillar. The first ascent of this serious route was originally done in 20 pitches in 1980 and the climb was not repeated for 13 years. The route is best done when completely dry, as the normal top section involves an unprotected slab which would be near impossible when wet, though this can be avoided by some grunge climbing - see description. Carry 2 sets of cams and a full set of wires including micro wires.

Approach - Walk past Kallevatnet and continue past the huge gully that defines the right-hand side of the pillar until exposed ledges lead back left across the face, across the gully (loose) and up to the foot of the pillar.

5

4

4

3

Close-up of this
section on page 222

2   1

Lower pitches
hidden

❸ **Storpillaren** . . . . . . [Top][50] 🖊️📷[ ] 7
500m. *(The Great Pillar)* A Lofoten classic - long remote and
serious, though less so on all counts, than the routes to the left.
The route received its long overdue first free ascent in 2001,
though it is still normally done with some aid (**6**- *A1*) where
needed. Start on the grassy shoulder under the right-hand side of
the pillar at a conspicuous groove. *Photo pages 10, 17 and 214.*
1) 5, 45m. Climb up the corner/groove, then up a slab to a belay
on the right side of a huge block.
2) 6-, 30m. Move left and down, traversing back up until you
reach a stance at the right-hand edge of a ledge at the base of a
left-facing groove.
3) 7-, 40m. Move left into the base of the groove (old stance in
the base of the chimney on the left). The groove is hard to start
then good climbing leads to the top of the corner. Climb the
left-hand of two cracks up to a narrow ledge (possible stance).
Continue up a short hard groove and the continuation crack
system (some loose rock) to the ledge of Storhylla.
4) 7, 40m. Climb the tough diagonal jamming crack into the
big groove and continue up a chimney to a tiny ledge. The main
corner - the original line - can be climbed at **6**- *A1*.
5) 6, 20m. Start up a wide crack to a ledge, then climb the
prominent left-facing corner to a sloping ledge.
6) 7-, 35m. Climb the big chimney, then move up a narrow
right-trending ramp to a good belay ledge.
7) 6+, 20m. The sustained left-facing corner leads out under a
roof, then up to a stance in a niche.
8) 6-, 40m. Continue up the steep face left of the stance - tricky
to protect and to find the easiest line.
9) 5, 55m. Head straight up the face, following the easiest line,
then follow an easier groove back to the right to a stance.
10) 5, 50m. Move right into a crack which is just to the left of
a large groove. Continue up broken ground (poor protection) then
traverse right for 30m to a stance.
11) 4, 45m. Climb up and right to the groove/gully. At its top,
move left around an arete onto the left side of the ridge and climb
the face up and to the right to a huge flat ledge.

Storpillaren continued...
12) 4, 50m. An easy pitch (BIG loose blocks) up the right side of
the ridge leads to a ledge 15m below the top of the ridge. Climb
up and left to gain the ridge crest.
13) 3, 40m. Follow the ridge up then down, to a fixed belay.
14) 30m. Abseil then down climb another 20m to reach a gap and
bolt belays.
15) 6-, 35m. Climb cracks to a tiny ledge (old peg) then move
left onto a blank slab (poor nuts). Now move right and layback an
arete (bold) to a ledge with many loose blocks.
16) 5, 45m. Climb around the left side of a pinnacle onto steep
grass with loose blocks - from here up is the only way out. Make
a hard move at the end onto the flat ridge above, and relief!
15 and 16 alternative) 5. The final two pitches can be avoided by
abseiling 20m down to the right and doing two pitches of 'mungy'
grade 5 to reach the crest. This is less good than the normal
route, but at least it is a fair bit easier.
*FA. Arild Meyer, Kjell Skog, Finn Tore Bjørnstad 7.1980. They took 26 hours.
On a prior attempt by Meyer and Skog in 1979, they reached the top of pitch
7 but stopped since it was the middle of the night and they had no water. On
the last pitch attempted, Arild ran out of karabiners so started tying slings
round the rope. After he fell they decided it was time to call a halt! The route
was not repeated until 1993 when Odd-Roar Wiik and Niels Poulsen climbed
it in 13 hours.*
*FFA. Odd-Roar Wiik, Robert Caspersen, Arild Meyer 2001. The young
hotshots brought the grand master along because they needed someone to
lead them up the last grotty pitches.*
*In 2006 Jonas Dahlstrup and Erik Grunnesjö did the route car-to-car in 12
hours - and that is moving!*

> **Descent -** There are two options, both long and tiring.
> **1)** Head left across ledge systems onto the South
> Face then climb to the summit of Vågakallen before
> descending the South Face route until it is possible to
> cross the col and descend to Djupfjord.
> **2)** Instead of heading to the col leading to Djupfjord,
> descend Myggandalen and hike back along the
> coastline to Kalle. This looks short and takes you to
> your starting point, but there is much rough going and
> boulder hopping.

The West

Henningsvær

Kalle

Kabelvåg

Svolvær

Trolltindan

Walking Peaks

Bouldering

Genus Locy

These two variations make the most of the rock on either side of the main section of *Storpillaren*. *Genus Locy* is a little devious in the lower part, but there is a lot of good climbing on the route and some long pitches. Bring plenty of gear, from micro wires up to big cams.

Approach (and Descent) - As for *Storpillaren* - see page 221.

Storhylla

Genus Locy .... ☒▨ ▢ **6+** *A2+*

...0m. If you get stuck in a queue on *Storpillaren*, or have already ...ne it half-a-dozen times and fancy a change, here is one idea.

5, 45m. As for pitch 1 of *Storpillaren* - climb up the right-...cing corner, then a slab to a belay on the right of a huge block.

6+ *A0*, **50m.** From the block, traverse left until it is possible ...move down and round into the long crack system that falls ...om the chimney left of *Storpillaren's* third pitch. Climb the crack ...nin) with a little aid, to a stance with fixed gear at the base of ...e chimney.

-, 45m. Abseil down the ramp to a stance at its foot.

6+ *A0*, **58m.** A rope-stretching pitch up the crack and into the ...ge groove. This requires some big cams and little aid around ...ree-quarters height. Belay in the chimney above. Plenty of size 1 ...d 2 cams were used.

3, 15m. Easy climbing up the chimney to Storhylla.

A2+, **55m.** Climb the main corner (*Storpillaren's* original line) ...t transfer into the long groove on the left. Climb this - thin at ...id height where a good number of micro wires will be needed ...then proceed on easier aid to a poor stance.

A2+, **50m.** Continue up the groove (nowhere else to go!) past ...hollow block, to reach a stance between the roofs - a heap of ...res required, all sizes up to 8. *Freya* comes up from the left to ...ach this same stance.

6-, 55m. Move right and climb the groove to the break, then ...ove right again and join *Storpillaren* on pitch 8. Continue up this ...bold and not obvious. The pitch can be split in the niche on the ...ght if required.

- 16) 6, 350m. Finish up *Storpillaren*.

...l. Martin Jakobsson, Fredrik Rapp 2.7.2003. Pitches 3,4 and 5 were done ...v Arild Meyer and Nils Paulsen "a long time ago" in a free attempt on ...torpillaren.

⑤ Søring variant .... ☒▨ ▢ **6+** *A1*

95m. *(Southern's Variation)* Another variation about which little is known. From the stance below *Storpillaren* pitch 3, climb the groove left of the huge chimney to a stance then traverse right to gain the grooveline in the crest of the pillar. This gives three more pitches, before joining *Storpillaren* on the sloping ledge above pitch 5. Although this route has a hardest pitch of 6+, the next pitch of *Storpillaren* is **7**.

FA. Anne Grete Nebell, Bjarte Bø 1997

Lo-Profile - Erik Grunnesjö

I was born in 1984 in Sweden and I came to Lofoten for the first time in 2004 and have been working as an instructor at the climbing school since then.

My Lofoten: It's hard to choose a favourite climb. Nothing beats the *Vestpillaren* in the midnight sun of course, but there are many more great climbs on Presten. If you climb the four first pitches of *Korstoget*, then the four next on the *Klokkeren* and finish with the last four on the *Reisen*, then you are up to something good. And then there is *Storpillaren* of course...

My story: It was a very wet day, guiding on *Bare blåbær*. I was with Matthias Stromqvist and leading the first group of clients. It was raining a lot and the last pitch was very slippery. I came to the belay with a struggle, and it was Matthias's turn. Then the rain stopped, and typically Lofoten, the sun came out and dried the rock in a minute. Matthias had his big smile on, "You should have waited five minutes", he shouted. I tried to get revenge, by emptying my water bottle on the crux. Unfortunately he did it anyway, and I got my just deserts.

Eric Grunnesjø atop *Storpillaren*, just as the weather starts to change - time to get a move on! Photo: Jonas Dahlstrup

Tactical Leading

The traditional approach, and in many cases the most efficient, is to 'swing leads' so that each climber of a pair leads alternate pitches. There are several advantages. Firstly, the belayer stays in place so there is no need to spend time changing positions. Secondly, if you paid the ropes out carefully onto the ledge as your partner seconded the previous pitch, they should now be pulling from the top of the pile as your now-leading partner climbs on ahead. The third advantage is that the second may already have most of the gear needed to lead with, having taken it out of the previous pitch.

If you decide not to lead through and need to switch belayers on a stance, then you will find it much quicker and easier if you've used slings rather than the climbing rope to equalise the belay. Many people carry a cordelette (a long loop of rope or tape) specially for this purpose, as it may easily be knotted to exactly the lengths required. The changeover is then simply a matter of clipping into, and un-clipping from, a single equalised attachment point. If you have belayed using the ropes to equalise the belay then the changeover process can get messy and often the easiest way to sort the problem out is for leader and seconder to untie and swap their rope ends. Of course before untying you need to make absolutely sure you'll still be attached securely while you do so, which isn't always as easy as it sounds.

When climbing in a group of three there are extra considerations. To move faster it is a good idea for two climbers to second the pitch on a separate single rope simultaneously. A competent leader should be able to belay the ropes independently but it is worth trying this on easy ground first to get used to how the system works. Changeovers at stances can be very complicated due to the number of belay points and the fact that ropes always need to be untied and tied each time. In this case it is even more sensible for each member of the party to have their own belay sling which is independent of the ropes. This frees the ropes up to enable the leader to always access the top ropes on the coil pile.

A final tip for moving fast when on easy ground is by climbing together. This is where the leader sets off with all the gear, placing it sparingly but in good solid placements. When the full rope is run out the second starts to climb removing the gear as normal. Both climbers keep climbing but modify their climbing pace to take up the slack in the rope. The leader stops and takes a belay when they have run out of gear, reached a hard section, or are tired. Obviously this technique is for experienced teams only but it is a very fast way of climbing on long routes.

Based on text from the **Multi-pitching** chapter of **Trad Climbing+**
by Adrian Berry and John Arran, published by Rockfax 2007 - see back cover flap

Congestion on *Bare blåbær* (5-)
- *page 116* - in Djupfjord.

The West

Henningsvær

Kalle

Kabelvåg

Svolvær

Trolltindan

Walking Peaks

Bouldering

Lo-Profile - Hanna Mellin

I was born in 1979 and I am now almost grown up! I work for 80% of my time in a climbing shop in Göteborg, Sweden

Lofoten is one of the most magic places on Earth with the midnight sun in the summer, and the mountains rising from the blue sea. It has so much potential to do what ever you want - climbing, skiing, alpine, hiking and kayaking.

My Lofoten: I been trying to visit Lofoten every year since I went to an Outdoor Pursuits Centre in Kabelvåg, it is my way of charging my batteries for the up-coming year. Lofoten is the place that taught me the most about myself and my climbing ability and in Lofoten everything is possible. The first time I came to Lofoten there was so many routes I wanted to climb, it was like giving a bag of sweets to a child. In a week we had climbed many of the classic routes and spent so long approaching them that my legs were so sore, I couldn't walk upstairs or sit down comfortably by the end of the week.

Favourite routes: *Vestpillaren* on the Presten, *Bare blåbær*, *Pan* and *Storpillaren*.

My stories: Vågakallen in the winter is a magic climb that I was pretty eager to do and after turning back near the top, we were back for a second go. After digging out a snowbound bivi and seen the sun disappear we knew we were in for a long night in our sleeping bags. Somehow one of the guys had brought a bottle of wine up in his pack and warmed it under his down jacket and with a big smile brought it out for us, and at just the right temperature. We had a wonderful evening and summited the next day.

Storpillaren is something that we had been looking at a couple of years before we had amassed enough courage to attempt it. We were walking in under the baking sun and were getting spanked by the low birches so we were very happy to start climbing. After a long day and a long night (we climbed through the night in the midnight sun) our blood sugar was getting low after too little to eat. On the descent, when we had been going for around 20 hours, a friend Kristin came and met us with chocolate, cordial and sandwiches that were the best I had ever tasted. A short time after that it started to rain, so soaked to the skin we got a ride to the Klatrecafe to get a shower and sauna and then it was straight to bed.

Clearing cloud on Breidtinden

The West

Henningsvær

Kalle

Kabelvåg

Svolvær

Trolltindan

Walking Peaks

Bouldering

The West

Henningsvær

Kalle

Kabelvåg

Svolvær

Trolltindan

Walking Peaks

Bouldering

Nordryggen

Lofoten's best low-grade 'Alpine' rock climb. An excellent tour of Vågakallen can be had by ascending the north ridge and descending the south face route - *Sydveggen* (page 301). Twelve pitches, plenty of scrambling, plus a sizeable approach and descent make for a long day out.

1 Nordryggen . . . . Top 50 **4+**

505m. Start on the right of the col, at the base of a small groove.

1) 4, 20m. Climb the groove up to a belay.

2-3) 80m. Grade 2 to 3 scrambling leads around the corner to the left, then up the ridge for 2 rope lengths.

4) 3, 45m. Move around a loose corner on the left and climb mossy blocks to the Lunch Ledge below a prominent vertical chimney.

5) 4+, 25m. Climb the chimney past several chockstones. Go through a tunnel on the right, then back left to a belay. Wet near the top.

6) 3+, 20m. Head up a short wall then move right around a corner to a belay near the bottom of a gully.

7) 3, 20m. Climb straight up the ridge, staying to the left of the gully, to blocks and a belay.

8) 4-, 30m. Follow the ridge and climb up a shallow corner.

9) 2, 30m. Easy scrambling leads up to the base of a slab split by a jamming crack.

10) 4+, 25m. Climb the crack up the slab by jamming and laybacking, to a good ledge under a large bulge in the ridge.

11) 4+, 35m. Traverse right across a big flake (and move slightly downwards) then leave the flake. Traverse right across a short wall into a chimney. Climb straight up the chimney to regain the ridge crest.

12) 2, 175m. Follow the slabby ridge (tricky at the start), then scramble up the ridge to a gap which requires a jump to cross. Continue more easily to the summit.

Descent - Use the standard south face route *Sydveggen* (page 301) back over the Vågakallen/Kvanndalstinden col, then down to the Djupfjorden parking spot at the fjord entrance where your chariot awaits.

FA. Arne Randers Heen, Lars Nordby 6.1939

The Chimney

Lunch Ledge

The Start 1

Vågakallen (943m)

Sun and shade | 90 min | Bad weather

The West

Round arete

Henningsvær

The Gap

Kalle

The Jamming Crack

Old approach - From Glåmtinden, follow a horizontal trail on the right to the saddle, then follow the ridge southwest until you can traverse west to the saddle between Breidtinden (582m) and Point 398m. Contouring back south, sheep trails lead into the upper Djupfjorden valley followed by a scramble up scree and a left-trending ramp to a notch below the steep, upper portion of Vågakallen's north ridge.

New approach - Nowadays it is more common to park at Djupfjorden's entrance, hike all the way along the Djupfjorden path to the upper end of the lake then follow tracks up the steep valley to the base of the ridge (see page 112 for photo of the first part of this approach). Either approach takes one and a half to two hours.

Kabelvåg

Svolvær

Nordryggen

Trolltindan

Old approach from Glåmtinden

Walking Peaks

New approach from Djupfjord

Bouldering

Djupfjordvatnet

The slabby and sunny side of the attractive valley, opposite the soaring Storpillaren on Vågakallen. It is home to the fine slab of Alkoholveggen, which has the popular route *Rom and Cola*, plus a couple of other isolated routes including the long ridge scramble of *Småkallanryggen*. The valley isn't particularly popular but the setting is magnificent.

Ed Webster belayed at the bottom of a shaft of sunlight, on a new route on Alkoholveggen . Photo: Odd-Roar Wiik

Approach   See map on page 234

To approach from the parking at Kalle, head towards Paradiset then cross the stream. Follow a good path around the left (west) side of Kallevatnet, past Myggapillaren, and along the sandy beach at the end of the lake. Cross the stream that runs into the lake, then head north up the right-hand side of Øvredalen, avoiding wet areas by keeping as much as possible on the clean slabs on the right. For *Flua på veggen* and *Småkallanryggen*, bear right when heading up from the lake.

Conditions

The cliffs face south and so get plenty of sun, though they do take quite a lot of drainage and take a few days to dry out after rain. Fortunately their condition can be checked from the start of the approach.

Vågakallen (943m)

Storpillaren

Myggapillaren

Breidtinden (583m)

Lille Vågakallen (498m)

Alkoholveggen

Flua på veggen

Øvredalen

Kallevatnet

P

The West

Henningsvær

Kalle

Kabelvåg

Svolvær

Trolltindan

Walking Peaks

Bouldering

Alkoholveggen and Småkallanryggen seen from the start of the approach walk.

The West

Henningsvær

Kalle

Kabelvåg

Svolvær

Trolltindan

Walking Peaks

Bouldering

Øvredalen

Alkoholveggen

A fine crag with a selection of big routes and a substantial approach. The cliff is easily identified by its maze of right-trending overlaps, black water streaks, plus several prominent vertical grooves to the left of centre. Apart from *Rom and Cola*, the routes see little (if any) attention.

❶ A Wee Nip . . . . 🗒️ [ ] 7-
65m. A short route that nips up the smaller buttress on the left-hand side of the main section of the cliff. Start under corners that lead towards the prominent crack of the second pitch, which is up the left wall of a deep corner complete with a conspicuous black streak.

1) 7, 25m. Scramble up the right-hand side of the slabby toe of the buttress until a flake (gear) to the left can be reached. Make very thin moves left to a good hold then follow easier cracks to a stance in the base of the groove.

2) 6+, 15m. The strenuous jamming crack in the left wall of the groove gives good climbing.

3) 5+, 25m. Climb towards the overhang then move out right onto the well-positioned arete. Finish up the cracks.

Descent - Abseil from the tree to the ground (2 x 60m ropes).
FA. Jonathan Bertalot, Jim Church 10.7.2002

❷ Återstilleren . . . . 🗒️ [ ] 6
270m. *(Hair of the Dog)* A long line that links a series of cracks and grooves up the left-hand edge of the tallest part of the cliff. It has some long pitches and sustained climbing.

1) 6, 40m. Trend left into the base of the groove and climb it (peg) to a small stance.

2) 6, 40m. Continue up the groove (peg) then move left to a bolt then back right to a long crack. Climb this to a belay.

3) 5, 50m. A continuation crack leads to easier ground where cracks and grooves lead to the large grassy ledge (on Descent 2).

4) 6, 50m. Climb cracks past the right side of an overlap then trend right and climb the long crack to its end. Move left and back right to a ledge with blocks at the base of a groove.

5) 6, 50m. Climb the groove, and its continuation, until an exit to the right is possible. Move right (grassy) then climb right again to the base of a good crack. This is most easily reached from the right and leads to a belay at a horizontal break.

6) 5, 40m. A short crack leads to easy ground then the ridge.
FA. Martin Jakobsson, Krister Johnson 19.6.1999

❸ Famous Grouse . . . . . . 🗒️ 🖉 [ ] 7-
240m. An intricate route up the long groove system that is the main feature of the centre of the cliff. Start under the groove, about 100m left of the start of *Rom and Cola*. The pitch lengths are estimates.

1) 6, 45m. Climb grooves and slabs to a small stance.

2) 6+, 45m. Traverse right under the series of overhangs then continue up the awkward groove to a big ledge.

3) 7-, 20m. Trend left to the large groove and climb this with difficulty to a belay on top of the hanging flake.

4) 5-, 40m. Traverse out right then follow the cracks running diagonally up to a ledge with big block.

5) 5+, 20m. Traverse left - poorly protected - then continue across to a stance a short way up the soaring groove.

6) 5+, 30m. Climb the groove - a great pitch.

7) 6+, 40m. Start with a tough overhanging groove then follow hard cracks up the rib (a little aid was used on the first ascent due to wet conditions) to a good ledge.

8) 2, 20m. As for pitch 7 of *Rom and Cola*.
FA. Andreas Christiansen, Ragnar Ekker, Lars Ekker, Knut Storvik 1998

❹ Rom and Cola . . . . . . 🗒️Top 50 🔲 [ ] 5+
265m. Satisfying and popular with a variety of fine slab and groove climbing. Interestingly, the line in the old guide was slightly in the wrong place though folks seemed to manage anyway. Protection is sometimes sparse and route finding is not always easy until all of the initial overlaps have been bypassed on the left. Fine situations with sustained and enjoyable climbing and almost no loose rock or grass! The route stays wet early in the season. Start under a pair of converging flake/grooves.

1) 5, 50m. There are two narrow grooves at the start. From a block, traverse right then climb the right-hand groove to a small ledge and possible stance. Continue to the top of the same groove and belay on the left on a large grass ledge.

1a) 5, 50m. The left-hand lower groove, and the right-hand upper groove, offer a slightly easier variation.

2) 5+, 45m. Trend right up corners and flakes, avoiding any temptation to traverse too far right under the overlaps. Step out left to a thin flake (peg) on a smooth face, then continue up right and then back left to a comfortable stance in a right-slanting corner.

3) 5, 50m. Walk right across a wide sloping ledge, then move up, traverse back left to join *Famous Grouse*, and follow this up the groove to a ledge and belay on the right.

4) 3, 25m. Climb easily rightwards up cracks in the slab to a stance on top of a big block.

5) 5+, 40m. Climb rightwards to a ledge then move left and climb the tricky crack, then the groove on the left, to another good ledge on the left below the final big groove. The groove left of the crack is an easier variation (**5**) if needed.

6) 5+, 35m. Layback and jam the huge upper corner system to its top - a good pitch.

7) 2, 20m. Finish up the grassy corner on the left to the summit.
FA. Arild Meyer, Finn Tore Bjørnstad, Hans Bjørnstad 8.1977. Finn Tore was singing a line from a popular political song called 'Rom and Cola', by the Swedish rock group, Norrbottens Järn, which went something like, "We're drinking rum and cola, laying in the sun, with no worries about tomorrow." The singing stopped when the heavy rain started, on the last pitch.

❺ Sex on the Beach . . . . . 🗒️ 🖉 [ ] 7 *A1*
About 250m. A direct and logical line, crossing the easier routes that follow the major right-trending lines on the crag, aiming for the attractive groove high on the left. A detailed description is lacking though the line is clear enough.

Follow the first pitch of *Rom and Cola*. Then continue up past the stance to belay on the big ledge of *Famous Grouse* - **5** to here. Climb across to cracks in the left wall and climb these to pass the arete and gain the upper slab and a belay at the base of the groove (**7** *A1*). Follow the groove for two pitches (**6+**, then **6**) then the arete and face (three pitches **5, 5, 4+**) to join *Famous Grouse*. Finish up this (**6+**), or escape left up loose ground and Descent 2.
FA. Oskar Alexanderson, Jonas Dahlstup 30.7.2004

❻ Gin Fizz . . . . 🗒️ 🖉 [ ] 5+
This two pitch variation finish follows the curving crack up the top, right-hand edge of the face, right of the final groove of *Rom and Cola*. Well-protected jamming and very exposed on the final wall.

6a) 5+, 40m. From the belay ledge, traverse right across a good ledge, then follow the right-slanting crack up the steep wall to a nice belay ledge on the left.

7a) 5-, 40m. Climb a corner on the left to a ledge, then jam up a crack on the right to another ledge. Traverse off to the right to finish, or climb the easy arete above to reach the usual top of *Rom and Cola*.
FA. Ed Webster, Sander Koetsier 21.7.1993

Descents - For all routes that go to the top of the cliff there is a choice of descents:
1) From the ridge crest above *Rom and Cola*, there is a small shoulder below the actual summit of the peak. Abseil 15m to the east, from a fixed sling anchor, then scramble farther east along the ridge (toward Litlkallen) to the green gully right of the face - this is the descent route. Abseil down the gully from fixed anchors using double ropes (2 x 50m) is better. With a single rope you need 5 x 25m abseils to reach the base of the wall.
2) From the final ledge of *Rom and Cola*, move left and descend the gullies and grassy ramps to a tree. Make a 35m abseil from this to the lower ledges, then follow these rightwards (looking out) until it is possible to drop into the back of the valley and loop back round to the base of the cliff.

The West

Henningsvær

Kalle

Kabelvåg

Svolvær

Trolltindan

Walking Peaks

Bouldering

Flua på veggen

This is the most prominent of the crack systems on the upper right-hand side of the large granite wall or steep slab which forms Litlkallen's south face. The main pitch is the big left-curving crack.

Approach - From Kallevatnet, walk towards the cliff base, then head up rightwards along diagonal vegetated ledges into a gully near the route's start.

❶ Flua på veggen. . . . . ☐ 6

100m. *(Fly on the Wall)* The exact line and the precise positions of the stances are uncertain - treat this information with care.

1) 4, 40m. Climb a loose rotten chimney, until it is possible to traverse out left onto a big ledge.

2) 6 30m. Head up the crack which widens before reaching a flake. Undercut around the flake, moving right into another crack and up to a stance.

3) 4, 30m. Follow an easy off-width crack to the top.

FA. Edly Grape took a serious leader fall attempting the crux pitch in 1981 - and rope-burned the mouth of his partner, Ivar Olsen, who held him. Olsen returned with Bent Svinnung and completed route on 20.5.1982

At least 2 other routes have been climbed up Litlkallen's large slabs to the left of Flua på veggen, but no precise details are known.

Breidtinden East Top (left),
Kallebordet and Lille Vågakallen
(right) seen from Øvredalen

Lille Vågakallen (498m)   Alkoholveggen   Litlkallen

Småkallanryggen

(Small Men's Ridge) Originally named by Arne Randers Heen, these impressive rocky tops are the largest peaks on the multi-summited ridge to the north of Vågakallen. Together they form the northwestern side of the steep-walled valley of Øvredalen. Located high upon this ridge is the bizarre geologic feature of Kallebordet *(the Kalle Table)* a huge flat plate of granite precariously perched on top of a section of the ridge just west of Lille Vågakallen. To climb Kallebordet, fall across a gap on its upper side, grab the edge, and mantelshelf.

❷ Småkallanryggen . . . . 🔲 4

A great outing - long, exposed and committing but nowhere very difficult. Nowadays the ridge is normally done south to north. From Kallevatnet, head up the grassy ramps to the seaward end of the ridge then follow it northwards - technically easy but parts of the ridge are extremely exposed with sheer walls falling away on both sides and escape would be problematic.

Either descend vague paths into Trolldalen then head down the valley - around 5 hours. Alternatively continue over Lille Vågakallen and up Vågakallen North Ridge for a really big day out.

FA. Nearly all of this spectacular ridge was traversed for the first time in the summer of 1933 (after a previous attempt the year before) by Arne Randers Heen and his cousin Eirik Heen. The pair started in Trolldalen, climbed a gully up onto the ridge crest, and then ascended in turn Lille Vågakallen, Kallebordet and Litlkallen before descending to Kalle.

Vågakallen

Lille Vågakallen   Kallebordet   Breitinden (582m)

Descent

Trollfestningen

Småkallanryggen seen from the east

The drive to the parking for Paradiset passes the superb sandy beach at Kallebukta, an excellent spot for chilling, paddling and exploring. Above the beach are two small crags - Honnikornsvaet, the smooth, short slab on the left split by two finger-cracks; and Cornflakesveggen, the much steeper cliff away to the right.

Approach   See main map on page 197

From the E10 to the east of Kabelvåg, turn south on Våganveien (also called Hopsveien) at signs for Hopen and Kalle Rorbu. Drive south then in a dip at 0.8km, turn right onto a dirt road that leads over a stone causeway across the estuary. Drive 2.7km to the fishing village of Kalle, then turn right, still on a dirt road, up a short, steep bumpy hill. Just over the brow is a public beach and grassy camping area by the beach at Kallebukta.

Camping Area

The grassy meadow that backs the beach has long been maintained as a free camping area by the commune, and it is an idyllic spot to camp. There are camping tables, rubbish bins, a couple of taps and a pit toilet. It can get very busy at times, which rather detracts from the whole experience, and the toilet becomes an unsavoury venue as the season progresses. There maybe moves afoot to make a more permanent solution with possibly the charging of a small fee to help maintain the area. Please keep the area tidy, leave it at least as neat as you found it, avoid creating new fire circles and use the toilet rather than the woods.

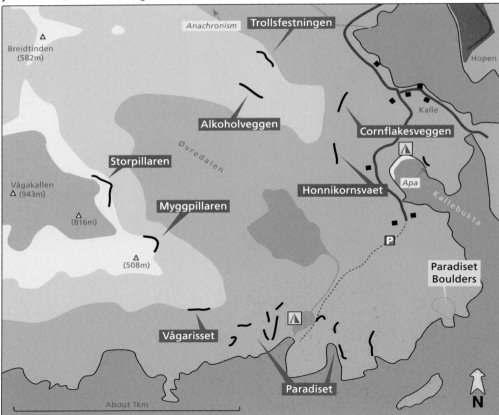

The West

Henningsvær

Kalle

Kabelvåg

Svolvær

Trolltindan

Walking Peaks

Bouldering

Kallebukta

Cornflakesveggen

Honnikornsvaet

The West

Henningsvær

Kalle

Kabelvåg

Svolvær

Trolltindan

Walking Peaks

Bouldering

Sherri Davy wading back to the car from *Apa* with the twin crags of
Honnikornsvàet and Cornflakesveggen visible in the shade.

The West

Henningsvær

Kalle

Kabelvåg

Svolvær

Trolltindan

Walking Peaks

Bouldering

Honnikornsvaet

The slabby wall of Honnikornsvaet has two prominent finger-cracks, the left-hand one fizzles out, but the right-hand one gives an excellent climb.

Approach - From parking, follow vague tracks leftwards through the trees, ferns and boulders to reach the base of the cliff in less than 10 minutes.

| Morning | 10 min | Sheltered |

Descent - scramble down the gully

1 Left-hand Crack . . . ⬚ 🪢 💭 ☐ 6

35m. The left-hand crack. Start in a vegetated bay below and left of the cracks (which can't be seen from below) with a flake-crack on its right-hand side. From the initial ledges, head up and left to reach the base of the crack and climb it to grassy ledges and a belay. Descend by abseil.

Colin Binks on the superb second pitch of *Puffrisset* (5+) - Yosemite by the seaside.

The West

Henningsvær

Kalle

Kabelvåg

Svolvær

Trolltindan

Walking Peaks

Bouldering

② Puffrisset . . . . . . [Top 50] 🧗 🐾 [   ] **5+**

110m. *(The Puff Crack)* The right-hand crack is excellent. Where the crack runs out, the route continues up the poorly-protected slabs above. Start as for the previous route in a vegetated bay below and left of the cracks (which can't be seen from below) with a flake-crack on its right-hand side. *Photo on this page and page 50.*

1) 5, 30m. Climb the flake then move right to ledges and continue up flakes and cracks to a small stance at the foot of the main crack.

2) 5+, 30m. Continue up the finger-jamming crack that splits the clean white slab to a ramp at the top of the crack and a small stance. A superb, sustained and well-protected pitch.

3) 5+, 30m. Traverse to the right, across several ledges, and up a flake then climb the slab to the right of a black streak - poor protection - to reach the large bushy ledge above. Move left to a tree belay in the corner.

4) 5-, 20m. Climb a short ramp then move out left to access the final crack and climb this, which eventually becomes vegetated at the top.

FA. Bjørn Braathen and partner climbed the main finger-crack 6.1981. Anders Bergwall, Mark Diggins, Johan Arnegård, Dick Johansson, Anders Swensson, Stefan Palm made the first complete ascent of the route during a guide assessment for the Swedish Mountain Guides Organization in 8.1992

Cornflakesveggen

This is the steep, accessible and largely neglected crag up and to the right of the tourist toilet and water tap at Kallebukta beach. It is reached by a rough 10 minute scramble to the base.

❶ **Shivering Dick** 6

40m. Two clean left-facing corners on the cliff's upper left-hand side. There is some loose rock towards the top of the climb. Scramble up left to a ledge at the route's base. Jam, layback and bridge up two short off-set corners to a stance at the base of the upper crack system. Climb up the left-hand crack, traverse right across several stacked cornflakes to the right-hand crack, and finish at a bushy ledge. Abseil off a big tree a little higher above.
FA. Dick Johansson, Anders Bergwall 8.1992

❷ **Ormen Lange** . . . . . 7+

60m. *(A Viking Longship)* Originally an aid climb, this is now a high quality and hard free route. The route heads towards the large orange section of rock near the cliff's centre before trending left. Take plenty of small cams.

1) 7-, 30m. Climb the crack in the prominent right-facing corner past an old bolt, then move left through the roof. From the ledge above the roof, go right and follow a good crack to a double-bolt belay. Sustained and technical.

Ormen Lange continued...
2) 7+, 15m. Traverse left then climb the crack which takes you to a prominent steep groove. Bolt belay at a sloping ledge.
3) 7-, 15m. Continue up a small groove, then up cracks for 15m to reach a belay bolt.
Descent - Abseil 50m to the ground.
FA. Odd-Roar Wiik, Niels Poulsen, Anders Jacobsson 4.1993
FFA. Gustaf Leijontufrud, Joachim Vagner 15.8.2003

❸ **Disco Volante** A3

60m. *(A ship in the film Thunderball)* A direct aid climb up the centre of the face. Start up the prominent right-facing groove of *Ormen Lange.*

1) A3, 30m. Start (free or clean aid) up *Ormen Lange* but transfer to the thin seam on the right of the groove and follow this to the roof - the final section is very thin, copperheads needed. Move left and follow the good crack through the overhang to the first stance on *Ormen Lange.*

2) A2+, 30m. Aid easily rightwards then head up the thin seam that leads towards the hole (some loose rock) and a three-bolt ladder. Continue up the crack until a couple of bolts point the way rightwards to a bolt belay. Abseil descent.
FA. Fredrik Rapp, Mathias Sjöberg 11.1999

Apa

A strenuous pair of routes is hidden on the seaward side of a large boulder on the eastern shore of the Kallebukta, the delightful bay in front of the sandy beach in Kalle.

Approach - Walk over the sand (or paddle at high tide) to the far side of the bay. It is also possible to follow various small paths around the landward side of the boulder.

❹ Baboon . . . .  6+

16m. *(The Baboon)* Climb the wall to the slippery break then move left under the roof to the arete. A hold on the lip allows a desperate mantelshelf move to be made to reach easy ground.
FA. Tony Whitehouse, Sarah Whitehouse 2000

❺ Apa 6

16m. *(The Ape)* The right-slanting crack steepens as it rises eventually reaching a good rest. The crack then widens and becomes tricky, with the odd layback move and an awkward exit.
FA. Ben Campbell-Kelly. Kjell Skog 1976. Campbell-Kelly, an Englishman, had climbed extensively in Yosemite Valley in California and, "with this climb introduced us to harder jam cracks that had a much higher pain threshold," said Kjell Skog.

Colin Binks demonstrating that *Apa* is "only gritstone HVS".

The West
Henningsvær
Kalle
Kabelvåg
Svolvær
Trolltindan
Walking Peaks
Bouldering

Trollfestningen

The West

Henningsvær

Kalle

Kabelvåg

Svolvær

Trollfjorden

Walking Peaks

Bouldering

The second pitch of *Spurven* (6+) - *page 248* - on the Trollfestningen. The outward view is almost as good as the cliff.

The West

Henningsvær

Kalle

Kabelvåg

Svolvær

Trolltindan

Walking Peaks

Bouldering

Easily seen when driving towards Kalle from the E10, the Trolls' Fortress is a big shady crag sat high on the south side of Trolldalen, the valley that runs parallel to Øvredalen over on the opposite side of the ridge. The main buttress of Trollfestningen is split in two by a grassy ledge at half height. The lower section only has a couple of lines which need to be followed to gain the ledge. Above this, the upper section is formed from massive sheets of granite and has remarkably few natural lines, although the corner of *Odin's Bue* is one very obvious feature. By far the most popular route here is the long line of *Colibrien* which can get congested since the lower pitches are also the common access pitches for the upper routes. Nipping up the crack of *Fingerrisset* is a useful distraction, and *Spurven* and *Havørnen* make worthwhile alternatives albeit at a more difficult grade.

Also covered in this section are three outlying climbs on the other quality rock faces in Trolldalen.

Approach   See map on page 234

Park at a choice of lay-bys 2.2km from the E10 (snowplough sometimes in-situ) opposite the small black and white 'sighting house'. Follow the path which starts just left (south) of the Trolldalsvatnet stream. From a rocky knoll and clearing in front of the cliff, turn left and scramble up to the base of low-angled slabs under the cliff. Scramble up these, or the gully to the right, to ledges at the foot of the face - about 30 minutes from the car.

Conditions

North facing and with a remote and rather sinister feel about it, the crag is at its best after a few dry days. It makes a good hot weather retreat. The aspect makes it rather slow to dry, though the rough rock means that the odd damp streak shouldn't spoil things to much.

❶ Trolltrappen

. . . . . 〰 ✦ ⛰ ☐   **7+**

About 80m. *(Troll's Ladder)* A solitary route up the overlapping slabs high on the valley side, reached by scrambling towards the foot of the face then using the gully on the right to access the ledge at the foot of the cliff. The first pitch **(7)** goes up easy cracks leftwards then powers through the big roof crack left of the major groove. Pitch 2 **(7+)** traverses right as far as a big rock scar then follows the superb crack up the face with moves left at half height.

Descent - Make two abseils down the gully to the right.

FA. Jonatan Rask, Jonas Dahlstrup (as an aid route, because they forgot their rock shoes) 12.8.2005. FFA. Erik Grunnesjø, Jonas Dahlstrup 2007

Lo-Profile - Jonas Dahlstrup

I come from the great mountainous nation of Denmark and I work as a guide for Nord Norsk Klatreskole.

My Lofoten: I came to Lofoten in 2002 with no clue about the climbing. Got pretty stoked and have been ever since.

My climbs: All-time favourite climb is *Gandalf* - no climb has given me so many beautiful moments. First climb to be done in the spring, the last in the autumn. Other beautiful climbs: *Vestpillaren,* climb it fast, climb it slow, great fun no matter. *Storpillaren,* a big route with amazing pitches. And so many more...

My story: A friend and I planned to climb the north ridge of Rulten. We got up very early and jumped in a borrowed boat, fired up the engine, put it in reverse and set out. But it turned out the engine only wanted to be in reverse and the wheel was jammed in one position. After circling around in the harbour for half an hour we finally managed to get back to port. Must have been quite a sight. Realising that Rulten had to wait, we quickly repacked and ran for the bus, only to find out we had no money. The kind driver accepted payment for 1 child fare. We got to Kalle, spotted a new route and off we went. The approach took us one hour up steep grass. Unpacking our pack we realised neither of us had climbing shoes. Pretty frustrated by now we went for it on aid. Two long pitches of beautiful crack climbing led to the top. A typical day out in Lofoten!

The West · Henningsvær · Kalle · Kabelvåg · Svolvær · Trolltindan · Walking Peaks · Bouldering

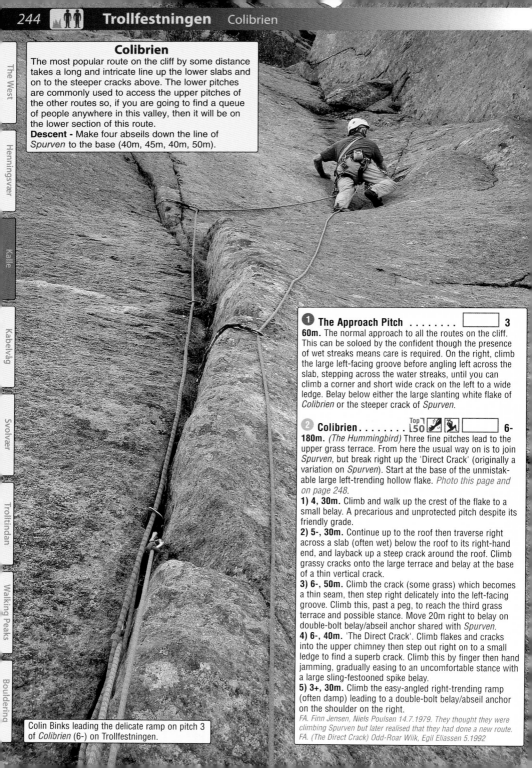

Colibrien

The most popular route on the cliff by some distance takes a long and intricate line up the lower slabs and on to the steeper cracks above. The lower pitches are commonly used to access the upper pitches of the other routes so, if you are going to find a queue of people anywhere in this valley, then it will be on the lower section of this route.

Descent - Make four abseils down the line of *Spurven* to the base (40m, 45m, 40m, 50m).

❶ **The Approach Pitch** . . . . ☐ 3
60m. The normal approach to all the routes on the cliff. This can be soloed by the confident though the presence of wet streaks means care is required. On the right, climb the large left-facing groove before angling left across the slab, stepping across the water streaks, until you can climb a corner and short wide crack on the left to a wide ledge. Belay below either the large slanting white flake of *Colibrien* or the steeper crack of *Spurven*.

❷ **Colibrien** . . . . ⌐50⌐ 🔁 🏃 ☐ 6-
180m. *(The Hummingbird)* Three fine pitches lead to the upper grass terrace. From here the usual way on is to join *Spurven*, but break right up the 'Direct Crack' (originally a variation on *Spurven*). Start at the base of the unmistakable large left-trending hollow flake. *Photo this page and on page 248.*

1) 4, 30m. Climb and walk up the crest of the flake to a small belay. A precarious and unprotected pitch despite its friendly grade.

2) 5-, 30m. Continue up to the roof then traverse right across a slab (often wet) below the roof to its right-hand end, and layback up a steep crack around the roof. Climb grassy cracks onto the large terrace and belay at the base of a thin vertical crack.

3) 6-, 50m. Climb the crack (some grass) which becomes a thin seam, then step right delicately into the left-facing groove. Climb this, past a peg, to reach the third grass terrace and possible stance. Move 20m right to belay on double-bolt belay/abseil anchor shared with *Spurven*.

4) 6-, 40m. 'The Direct Crack'. Climb flakes and cracks into the upper chimney then step out right on to a small ledge to find a superb crack. Climb this by finger then hand jamming, gradually easing to an uncomfortable stance with a large sling-festooned spike belay.

5) 3+, 30m. Climb the easy-angled right-trending ramp (often damp) leading to a double-bolt belay/abseil anchor on the shoulder on the right.

FA. Finn Jensen, Niels Poulsen 14.7.1979. They thought they were climbing Spurven but later realised that they had done a new route.
FA. (The Direct Crack) Odd-Roar Wiik, Egil Eliassen 5.1992

Colin Binks leading the delicate ramp on pitch 3 of *Colibrien* (6-) on Trollfestningen.

The West
Henningsvær
Kalle
Kabelvåg
Svolvær
Trolltindan
Walking Peaks
Bouldering

Not much sun

30 min

Descent from
routes 3 to 7

Close-up of this
section on page 249

The West

Henningsvær

Kalle

Kabelvåg

Svolvær

Trolltindan

Walking Peaks

Bouldering

Descent

Not much sun
30 min

The West

Henningsvær

Kabelvåg

Kabelvåg

Svolvær

Trolltindan

Walking Peaks

Bouldering

A

7

6

5

4

3

2

8

It is possible to scramble up the gully but it is hard work and messy

Odins bue

The upper left-hand side of the main bulk of Trollfestningen is dominated by some striking cracks and grooves beneath a huge capping roof high on the wall. The left-arching groove system is the classic *Odins Bue* which is the major tick on the wall. *Fingerrisset* is also popular, whereas the other routes here see little action.

Approach Pitches - The routes start on the mid-height ledge which is best reached by doing the first 2 pitches of *Colibrien* (page 244) or *Spurven* (page 248). Then scramble about 50m to the left to gain the ledge.

Descent - Cross the top of the cliff then head down very exposed grassy ledges to the right (northwest), finally climbing down to the top bolt station on *Spurven*. Four abseils lead down *Spurven* to the base (40m, 45m, 40m, 50m) - see topo on page 248.

❸ Swedish Highway Blues 🗒️🪣 ⬜ 6+ *A1*

210m. The left-hand arete of the crag in five long pitches. The exact line is uncertain, and some aid is needed - four blade pegs should cover it. Start on the left-hand end of the ledge below the upper part of the buttress

1) 6+ *A1*, **35m.** From a perched block, climb slabs and grooves (a little aid in the upper groove) to reach a crack. Up this then trend left across the slab to a bolt belay.

2) 5+ *A1*, **35m.** Climb left to the arete, crossing to the left-hand side to outflank the overhang (some aid). Back on the right-hand side, climb a long crack (loose block to the right) to a ledge. Peg and bolt belay.

3) 6-, 45m. Climb a short crack then traverse the slab rightwards under the overhang to reach a crack splitting its right-hand side. Climb this to a ledge with peg belays.

4) 5, 45m. Climb rightwards to reach a crack on the right-hand side of the arete and follow this as it widens to a stone-filled gully. Up this to a belay in the base of the huge chimney on *Odins bue*.

5) 4, 50m. Walk into the back of the chimney and climb to a ledge at its top.

FA. V.Šatava, M.Vrkoslav 16.7.1999

❹ Fingerrisset ...... Top🪣 🪣🪣 ⬜ 6-

40m. *(The Finger-crack)* A fine finger-crack splitting the big slab left of the *Odin's Bue* overlaps gives sustained and well-protected finger-jamming, and is worth the rather arduous approach. Start up the groove on the right then follow flakes leftwards until a move up right across a short face gains the main crack. Up this with sustained interest to reach a small stance with multiple fixed wires. Descend by abseil.

FA. Helge Stokstad, Rune Thrap-Meyer 1982

❺ Odins bue .... Top🪣 50 🪣 ⬜ 7

200m. *(Odin's Bow)* One of Lofoten's most sought-after hard climbs, ascending the large, left-facing arch on the cliff's left-hand side. It features masses of laybacking and undercutting. Although the rock is beautiful clean granite, some persistent wet streaks mean the route should only be attempted after a long dry spell. Carry a good rack including micro wires and duplicate cams in the mid ranges plus some larger ones. Start at the base of the large, left-facing, Yosemite-like groove.

1) 7-, 30m. Layback up the left-facing overlap, using some extremely thin jams, moving around an overhang to a hanging belay at a foothold.

2) 7, 25m. Continue laybacking and jamming up the unrelentingly steep groove to a tiny stance on the left.

Odins bue continued...

3) 7, 25m. Two bolts protect hard moves to pass the overlap on the right to reach the higher arch. Layback left up this (often wet) past a peg and a wide section continuing with more difficulty to a hanging belay at a peg.

4) 7, 30m. Traverse up and left, undercutting along the arch in a spectacular position. When the crack thins out, undercut left before making a very thin move to better jams and a small belay stance at a flake on the left.

5) 6+, 40m. Climb a small corner to a hollow flake and the base of a thin vertical crack in the upper slab. Climb the crack to the base of a groove then make a heroic move escaping out left to gain and climb a slabby corner to the base of the grim cleft of the 'Troll's Chimney'.

6) 4, 50m. Walk into the back of the chimney and climb to a ledge at its top.

FA. Ivar Olsen and Edly Grape climbed the first 2 pitches and the overlap start of pitch 3 on aid in 1981. Arild Meyer and Ed Webster free climbed the first 2 pitches on 23.7.1993 but were thwarted by the pitch 3 overlap. Returning on 4.8.1993, after a start up Fingerrrisset, Meyer and Webster placed one bolt each on aid on the overlap. The pitch 3 arch above was dripping wet; Webster led it almost entirely on aid, but Meyer followed it free except for the 2 aid bolts! These were eliminated by Jonas Tetlie, Andras Christiansen, Knut Storvik in the summer of 1998.

❻ Cmelák .... 🗒️ 🪣 ⬜ A3

180m. *(The Bumble Bee)* A major route up the soaring buttress to the right of *Odins Bue*. Carry a big aid rack including a full set of cams, two sets of wires, 10 knifeblades, 5 angles, 3 rurps, cam hooks and a range of regular hooks. Start at the left-facing groove right of *Odins Bue*.

1) *A2+*, **30m.** Climb the groove (rurps and birdbeaks early on) to reach a poor double-bolt belay.

2) *A2*, **40m.** Continue aid climbing up the groove and crack to reach a niche with a peg and strange bolt belay. This is just above the bolts on pitch 3 of *Odins Bue*.

3) 5, 30m. Exit rightwards then climb the slab passing some loose flakes to a stance (bolt belay) under the huge roof.

4) *A3*, **15m.** The "Be as a Butterfly" pitch. Wild climbing over the roof and up the open groove, passing some loose rock, to reach a small stance on the left.

5) 5- *A2*, **25m.** Continue up the right-trending groove to reach the hanging slab above then move left to a stance on the edge.

6) 5, 40m. Make an exposed traverse left to reach a crack, then climb this and the continuation off-width to reach a ledge. Easy ground leads to the crest of the buttress.

FA. Dalibar Mlejnek, Roman Kalpárek (Czech Republic) 13/14.7.1999

❼ Nemesis trollkirka .... 🗒️ 🪣 ⬜ A3+

110m. *(Nemesis of the Troll Church)* An good aid climb up the centre of the big smooth wall in the centre of the cliff. This is one of the hardest aid climbs on Lofoten and is a major undertaking. The required rack includes small-to-mid cams, 3 knifeblades, 5 lost arrows, 4 rurps, a birdbeak, many micro wires, plenty of small wires, plus assorted copperheads. Start under the blank wall split by a single thin vertical crack.

1) *A3+*, **35m.** 'The Dream of Two Wings Pitch'. Climb a short crack to a ladder of 5 bolts then aid a thin vertical crack up the face on rurps and copperheads to a flake. Then up another thin crack to a hanging belay at 2 bolts.

2) *A3+*, **25m.** 'The Golden Parachute Pitch'. Start with a traverse left on copperheads and micro wires, then aid easier cracks to a good belay - half-hanging - at 2 bolts. Abseil off from here, or continue.....

3 and 4) 6-, 50m. Up cracks for two more pitches to the top.

FA. Odd-Roar Wiik, Niels Poulsen 11.1993. They abseiled off at the top of pitch 2.

The West
Henningsvær
Kalle
Kabelvåg
Svolvær
Trolltindan
Walking Peaks
Bouldering

Spurven

This series of variation pitches actually includes the original route of the buttress - *Spurven*. Today's most popular attraction of *Colibrien* is described on page 244. **Descent** - Four abseils lead down *Spurven* to the base (40m, 45m, 40m, 50m).

8 Spurven...... 6+

170m. *(The Sparrow)* The first route on Trollfestningen and an excellent outing though the line involves a poorly-protected wide crack and serious traverse (pitch 3). As a result, it sees less attention than it deserves. *Photo on page 240.*

1) 5+, 30m. Climb right and left to reach a crack then head up this, past some technical grass climbing, and a tough wide section (laybacked or thrutched - often wet) to a restricted stance.

2) 5, 30m. Continue up the easier crack above to reach the right-hand end of the second grass terrace. There is a double-bolt belay/abseil anchor on the right.

3) 6+, 40m. On the far right above the ledge is a wide crack in a corner (the crack above the stance is a top-rope pitch (**6+**) the crack to the left is pitch 3 of *Havørnen*). Climb this - strenuous and awkward to protect - then make a poorly-protected traverse to the right across the slabby face to ledges. Now scramble up and left to the double-bolt belay shared with *Colibrien*.

4) 5+, 40m. Step right and climb the jamming crack into the deep groove then continue up into a chimney on the left side of a tall flake. Climb the chimney, almost to its top, then make an awkward escape out right to reach the upper crack system. Belay at a restricted stance, a little higher, at a rock spike with slings.

5) 3+, 30m. Climb the easy-angled right-trending ramp (often damp) leading to a double-bolt belay on the shoulder on the right. *FA. Arild Meyer, Kjell Skog 7.1977*

9 Spurven/Colibrien....... 5+

200m. A devious but popular combination that avoids the wide crack on *Spurven* by a long loop out to the left. Included here so you have something to tick if you do it! Climb the 1st and 2nd pitches of *Spurven* then traverse 20m left along the ledge. Continue up the 3rd pitch of *Colibrien*, before traversing back right for the 4th and 5th pitches of *Spurven*.

10 Havørnen.......... 6+

170m. *(The Sea Eagle)* A link-up of several strenuous cracks gives a worthwhile combination.

1) 2) 5- or 5+, 60m. Climb the first two pitches of either *Spurven* or *Colibrien*.

3) 6+, 40m. Climb the left-hand of the two finger-cracks in the steep wall behind the ledge - sustained with several thin moves. At the end of the crack, climb across to the left then move up onto the third grass terrace. Traverse right along this to the double-bolt belay/abseil anchor on *Spurven*.

4) 6+, 25m. Jam to, and over, a small overhang directly above the belay, then continue up the strenuous crack to a flake. Step right and belay on top of a large block on the right.

5) 6-, 25m. From the block, traverse right into the chimney. Climb this, making an awkward exit to the right at its top around a flake. Move right into *Spurven's* upper crack system and continue up to the spike belay on *Spurven*.

6) 6, 20m. Strenuous jamming leads up the rough crack ('Thorbjørnsrisset') on the steep left-hand wall above. Climb all the way up the crack, past the left side of a chockstone, and up to a good belay ledge with a double-bolt belay.

FA. Thorbjørn Enevold first top-roped pitch 3. Arild Meyer and Kjell Skog first climbed pitch 5 during the first ascent of Spurven in 7.1977. Pitch 6 - Thorbjørnsrisset - was first climbed by Thorbjørn Enevold and NNKS students in the summer of 1989. Ed Webster and Leif Henriksen climbed the complete route described on 29.7.1998

Tim Wilkinson pulling into the Direct Crack on *Colibrien* (6-)
- *page 244* - on the Trollfestningen. Photo: Ali Kennedy

Not much sun 30 min

See page 245 for another topo of lower pitches of *Spurven*

The West

Henningsvær

Kalle

Kabelvåg

Svolvær

Trolltindan

Walking Peaks

Bouldering

The West

Henningsvær

Kalle

Kabelvåg

Svolvær

Trolltindan

Walking Peaks

Bouldering

Abseil Descents

It's easier to have an accident abseiling than at any other time during a long climbing day. All it takes is one error: you don't put your abseil device on right; you put it on right but on the wrong rope; you don't realise how far you've gone and abseil straight off the end of the rope. There are many ways to get it wrong and almost every one of them will kill you. When added to that the fact that you are probably tired, it may have started raining and you could be shivering with cold, then you should begin to realise how important it is to double check everything at every stage when abseiling.

Use an auto-locking abseil device, or a backup prusik, and you won't fall if you get hit by loose rock, or lose control of the rope for some reason. It will also allow you to use both hands if you have to sort out tangles in the rope on the way down. If you don't have a locking system in place, you can free both hands by wrapping the rope a couple of times around your leg, but it is just as quick and invariably safer to use a prusik.

Tying an overhand knot near the bottom of the ropes will stop you abseiling off the end. You can tie knots separately in each rope or tie both ropes in one knot. The former method is less prone to tangling but the latter has the advantage that all is not lost if you forget to untie the knot before pulling the rope. One way of minimising rope snags when dropping the ropes is to hurl the ropes upwards and outwards, away from the cliff face, to ensure they fall more freely out of the way of any trees or rock spikes. On short vertical abseils you may want to avoid knots altogether.

One of your main concerns should be finding the next place to abseil from. Sometimes even fixed belay points are hard to spot, particularly if it is getting dark, and you won't want to go past as it can be hard and slow having to prusik back up again. If it isn't steep you can swing a few metres to either side to get a better look, and if you're descending the route you climbed you may be able to remember important details like traverse sections.

Another big risk in multiple abseils is getting the rope stuck. If it is a long abseil, the sheer weight of hanging rope will mean it isn't easy to pull, so minimising additional friction can be critical. Using a maillon, or a karabiner, instead of threading nylon directly will help reduce the drag. If you use an overhand knot to join your ropes together the knot will have a tendency to roll around any edges it meets rather than butt up against them.

If you are not sure whether the rope will pull okay, get the first person down to try and pull it, while there is still time to make changes. Another good idea to speed up the descent is the first person down can begin threading the next belay while the second is abseiling - make sure you thread the rope you are going to pull though. The last person down can often help further by stopping on a ledge a short way down and pulling one rope through until the knot clears any edge near the belay. Note that this should only be considered if the rope is attached via a maillon or a krab, as pulling rope directly through a nylon belay can seriously reduce its strength.

Based on text from the *Multi-pitching* chapter of *Trad Climbing+* by Adrian Berry and John Arran, published by Rockfax 2007 - see back cover flap

The West

Henningsvær

Kalle

Kabelvåg

Svolvær

Trolltindan

Walking Peaks

Bouldering

Abseiling off *Bare blåbær* (5-) - *page 116* - in Djupfjord.

The West

Henningsvær

Kalle

Kabelvåg

Svolvær

Trolltindan

Walking Peaks

Bouldering

❶ Tranedansen . . . . [ ] **5** *A2*

(The Crane Dance) This five pitch route is on a smaller cliff to the right (northwest) of Trollfestingen. The start of the route is at the same height as the finish of *Spurven* and little is known about it other than the description given by the first ascensionists - treat the information with caution. The first ascent team used several skyhook moves, but this aid section might go free with effort and modern gear.

"Hike up the Trolldalen path almost to Trolldalsvatnet (the Kalle reservoir), then bushwack up the hillside to the right of Trollfestningen to a grassy ramp that slants up and left to the cliff base. Begin below an inviting looking V-groove which is up and right of a block near the centre of the cliff.
1) 4, 10m. *Below the block, a short traverse right leads to a belay at the base of the corner.*
2) 5-, ?m. *Climb the corner, then move slightly right and up easier weaknesses past a block to a belay.*
3) ?, ?m. *Step left, then head up and right along a grassy ledge into a deep chimney behind a big block. Belay on top of the block.*
4) 5 A2, ?m. *Traverse right across a short wall into a small corner (A2, six points of aid) followed to a steep slab with a faint crack. When the crack ends, skyhook right for 4 moves to easier ground. Climb a slab and a left-slanting corner to the belay.*
5) *An easy slab and a chimney gain the top."*
FA. Arild Meyer, Finn Tore Bjørnstad 8.1977

Outlying

The extensive rock in the upper part of Trollsdalen only has two routes at present. A lone route on the walls immediately to the right of Trollfestningen, and an attractive clean white slab, tucked under the southern flanks of Glåmtinden.

Approach - Both routes are reached by walking along the base of the valley and around the left-hand side of the lake of Trollsdalvatnet and under Trollsfestningen. Continue to the end of Trollsdalen for *Anachronism*.

❷ Anachronism . . ⬚ 🦅 [ ] **7-**

55m. Start right of the toe of the buttress.
1) 6, 20m. Climb cracks and flakes to a bulge. Move left across this to a tiny stance.
2) 7-, 35m. Climb up just left of the pale streaks to reach a ramp. Finish leftwards up this.
Descent - Abseil back down the route.
FA. Arild Meyer 2006

Vågakallen (916m)

Trollsfestningen

Tranedansen

1

Glåmtinden (419m)

Trollsdalvatnet

The West

Henningsvær

Kalle

Kabelvåg

Svolvær

Trolltindan

Walking Peaks

Bouldering

Lots of sun

30 min

Sheltered

A

2

The West

Henningsvær

Kalle

Kabelvåg

Svolvær

Trolltindan

Walking Peaks

Bouldering

Colin Binks and Chris Craggs on the second pitch of
Ørneryggen (5+) - *page 257* - Glåmtinden. Photo: Sherri Davy

Glåmtinden

Popular with the locals and visitors alike, this small but classy mountain affords an easy hike taking no more than a couple of hours. On a clear day the view from the summit ridge is a truly fantastic panorama of sea and mountains on both nearby Lofoten and beyond. Currently it is home to just two climbs, and only one of these sees much attention.

Conditions

This is a high mountain crag with a prominent summit that catches all the wind that's going. The rock drys quickly and both routes get loads of sunshine. There is some loose rock up here both gritty granite and bigger blocks and flakes - care needed.

Glåmtinden (419m)
1
E10
P On the old road

Approach   See map on page 197
The normal route of ascent starts at an extensive lay-by at the base of the old Route 19, 0.65 km east of the Rørvika junction (E10 and 816). A steady 1.65 km leads up the old road (this is the dirt road that was the only way south before the tunnel was built) to the col then head right towards the peak up steeper terrain, to a leveller area. The final section is an easy scramble up the rocky ridge to the summit. An alternative ascent is via the rocky ridge that runs east/west from the causeway across Hopen/Hopspollen - see page 299 for summit walks.

The West
Henningsvær
Kalle
Kabelvåg
Svolvær
Trolltindan
Walking Peaks
Bouldering

The West

Henningsvær

Kalle

Kabelvåg

Svolvær

Trolltindan

Walking Peaks

Bouldering

Southwest Face

There is a solitary route up the arete that bounds the Southwest Face of the mountain, the relatively popular outing of *Ørneryggen (Eagle Ridge)*.

Approach - Walk up the normal Glåmtinden path until just below a final steep section of the peak, where a vague path branches horizontally to the right (west). Follow this for a few minutes to a sandy col. Look around the corner to your left, and you will see the ridge of *Ørneryggen*, on the cliff's left side. Cross steep ground to its base.

Descent - Follow the normal walking path down the north ridge of the mountain, scrambling at first, then easy.

❶ Ørneryggen ..... 🗒️ 🅱️ 🔲 5+

100m. *(Eagle Ridge)* An interesting climb with an exciting finish plus the bonus of a nice summit. Protection is generally good, but there is some crumbly rock on the first pitch. *Photo on page 254.*

1) 5, 38m. Begin under the steep section of the ridge, in a sandy gully. Head straight up a steep groove to a crack on the right side of the ridge. Alternatively (easier) reach the start of the crack by traversing left under a roof. Both starts have some poor rock and loose flakes, though it doesn't detract too much from the climbing. Jam the crack, step out onto the steep left-hand wall and move up right to a small stance on the arete.

2) 5+, 32m. Step right into an easy crack and climb to its top. Traverse left and follow another vertical crack to an exposed ledge on the left, under a leaning wall, which fortunately is equipped with huge holds. Sprint up this to an excellent belay ledge. The loose groove to the right is an oft-climbed (poor) variation that isn't any easier.

3) 30m. Walk right on the ledge, then move up and back left (one awkward move up a corner) to reach the flat summit of Glåmtinden complete with summit log.
FA. Thorbjørn Enevold, Brynjar Østgaard, Odd-Birger Hanssen 11.6.1993

❷ Direkte-Innsteget .... 🗒️ 🔲 4

1) 4, 40m. *(The Direct Start)* An interesting pitch up the slab and a short crack below the usual start makes the climb one pitch longer. This bit is only 4 but the rest is **5+**.

Southeast Face

The southwest face also only has a single route at the moment, through there is certainly scope for more. Few details are known about the climb.

Approach - Walk up the normal Glåmtinden path until just below final steep section of the peak, then head left to the shoulder. Cross this then descend grass before traversing west under the face to locate a right-trending grooveline (the left-hand of a pair) just before the steep grassy gully that runs up the ridge between the two faces.

Descent - Climb the short distance to the summit then follow the normal walking path down the north ridge, scrambling at first then easy.

❸ Herman Hedning ..... 🗒️ 🖊️ 🔲 6-

The route follows corners and cracks before trending out left to gain a crack system in the ridge. It has three long pitches and is reported to have good belays.
FA. Andreas Christiansen, Ragnar Ekker 6.1998.

The West · Henningsvær · Kalle · Kabelvåg · Svolvær · Trolltindan · Walking Peaks · Bouldering

The West

Henningsvær

Kalle

Kabelvåg

Svolvær

Trolltindan

Walking Peaks

Bouldering

The steep lower section of *Snykov* (8-) - *page 261* - at Sandvika,
leads to a poor rest in the groove and taxing moves to pass the roof.

Kabelvåg

The West

Henningsvær

Kalle

Kabelvåg

Svolvær

Trolltindan

Walking Peaks

Bouldering

The West

Henningsvær

Kalle

Kabelvåg

Svolvær

Trolltindan

Walking Peaks

A collection of short sport routes, in a secluded setting, close to the Sandvika campground. The routes tend to be steep powerful and hard - there is no fancy slab climbing available here and a few hours activity should ensure a good workout.

Approach
Drive into the Ørsvågvær/Sandvika campsite complex and keep left. Drive past the reception and turn left up a side track, park sensibly here. An old track branches left again, walk up this to where it flattens out then scramble awkwardly rightwards to the ledges below the face.

Conditions
The crag faces southeast and gets the sun in the morning. Much of the rock is steep enough to stay dry in the rain, though some areas do seep and sea mist can make the cliff damp at times. There are some patches of loose rock and progress along the cliff base is awkward and exposed - take care.

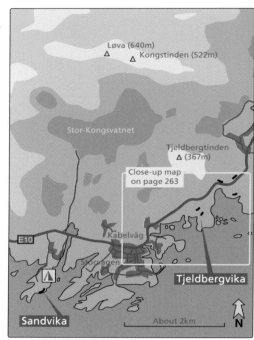

Løva (640m) △
Kongstinden (522m) △
Stor-Kongsvatnet
Tjeldbergtinden △ (367m)
Close-up map on page 263
E10
Kabelvåg
Storvågen
Tjeldbergvika
Sandvika
About 2km
N

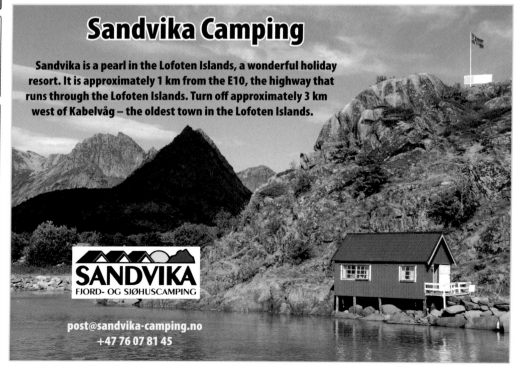

The left-most routes start from a sloping ramp which is reached by an exposed scramble from the right, up juggy rock right under the steeper walls

1 Ridderne av Niih. . . . . 🏷️ 7-
6m. (*The Knights who Say Niih* - Monty Python fans will understand). The tiny leaning rib on the left has two bolt runners.
FA. Knut Storvik 4.2002

2 Ridderne av det runde bord . 🏷️ 6-
6m. (*Knights' of the Round Table*) The short hanging groove just to the right has a steep entry (good wires) and leads smartly to a lower-off on the ledge above.
FA. Knut Storvik, Eivind Storvik 9. 2001

3 Power of the Dragonflame . . 🏷️ 8-/8
10m. The smooth undercut wall has a couple of desperate moves to start and fingery climbing above.
FA. Eivind Storvik 2002

4 Crusaders of the Metal Blade
. . . . 🏷️ 6-
12m. A worthwhile easier climb up the orange flakes to a lower-off on the edge of the wall. Pity it isn't three times longer.
FA. Eivind Storvik 4.2002

5 Dødsballe . . . . 🏷️ 8-
12m. (*Dead Ball*) From a small pillar of bubbly rock, climb the smooth leaning wall with difficulty.
FA. Knut Storvik 2002

6 Slogpojken. . . . . . . 🏷️ 5+
20m. (*Fish Guts Boy* - I bet you are glad you asked) A trad line that follows the right-trending ramps and niches and the big bird-limed flake, past the lower-off of *Rage of Honour*, to reach the one above *Stressless.*
FA. Knut Storvik, Andreas Christiansen 2002

7 Turistens klagan . . . . . . 🏷️ 8
20m. (*Tourists' Complaint*) Start up the groove of *Rage of Honor*, but move left to a ledge after the second bolt. Climb the wall with difficulty then follow the undercut cracks rightwards until it is possible to break through the overlap to a lower-off just above.
FA. Andreas Christiansen 2003

8 Rage of Honor . . . . 🏷️ 7-
16m. Steep climbing on generous holds though some of them feel a bit creaky, especially the big flake at half height - care required. Start up the groove then gallop up the juggy rib to reach easier-angled ground.
FA. Knut Storvik 2002

9 Stressless . . . . 🏷️ 8-
18m. Start up *Rage of Honor* until it eases then move left and continue up the wall to join the last few moves of *Turists Klagan.*
FA. Knut Storvik 2002

10 Revenge of the Niña . . . 🏷️ 8
18m. Climb the centre of the steep wall heading for the left-hand of the stepped roofs. Difficulties are sustained and considerable - one of the best routes here.
FA. Andreas Christiansen 2002

11 Snykov . . . . . . 🏷️ 8-
18m. (*Blizzard*) Climb the lower wall into the black hanging corner and exit from this with difficulty by using disappointing holds over the lip of the roof. Another great outing. *Photo on page 258.*
FA. Knut Storvik, Andreas Christiansen 2002

The West
Henningsvær
Kalle
Kabelvåg
Svolvær
Trolltindan
Walking Peaks
Bouldering

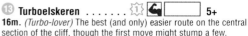

13 Turboelskeren . . . . 🌀 ⛰ ▭ 5+
16m. *(Turbo-lover)* The best (and only) easier route on the central section of the cliff, though the first move might stump a few. A powerful slap gains the start of the black ramp, follow this steeply to the lower-off in the wall above.
FA. Eivind Storvik, Knut Storvik 2002

14 Bestillingsoppdraget . . . . . . 🗺 ▭ 6
6m. *(Contract Mission)* A tiny route up the short and severely undercut pocketed rib. Failure to clip the first bolt may result in a fall that is longer than the size of the route!
FA. Andreas Christiansen 2002

To the right a solitary low bolt marks the start of an abandoned project. Right again a large boulder lies on the floor of an alcove formed by a curving overhang. The next two routes start out of this alcove.

15 Camping vogna . . . 🌀 ⛰ 📷 ▭ 7+
14m. *(Caravan)* Start from the left edge of the boulder and climb the short leaning wall then the smooth-looking slab above.
FA. Knut Storvik 4.2002

16 Power of the Locals . . . 🌀 ⛰ ▭ 8+
10m. Climb out of the right-hand side of the recess and continue up the severely tilted rock above. Power indeed!
FA. Knut Storvik, H. Sømme 15 .8.004

17 Skrova festivalen . . . . . 🌀 ⛰ ▭ 7
8m. Climb the left edge of a patch of black 'crazy-paving' to a lower-off on the edge of the wall.
FA. Andreas Christiansen 5.6.2003

18 Cobra . . . . 🌀 ▭ 6+
8m. The right edge of the black rock is the last route on the cliff - another short and sharp offering passing three bolts.
FA. Knut Storvik 7.2002

The wall continues rightwards, steepening up to give some hard routes up a shorter leaning wall.

12 Bære baill . . . . . . 🌀 📷 ⛰ ▭ 7+/8-
16m. *(A Mess)* Climb the central section of the face, heading for the hanging niche. Once established in this the lower-off is not too far away.
FA. Jonas Tetlie 2002

Along the coast from the town of Kabelvåg are three small crags around the bay of Tjeldbergvika which have been mainly developed with sport routes. **Urdstabben** has a nice set of sport routes in a surprisingly quiet setting, but is secluded and hard to find considering it is only a few hundred metres from the main road. **Tjeldbergvika** consists of a pair of cliffs above the E10 which are easy to reach. They offer some trad routes and a few semi-sport routes in a pleasant south-facing location. The final location is **Finnvika** - a fine block of glaciated granite which looks like a huge boulder (or a beached whale) and offers a small selection of fine face routes that tend to be delicate and technical.

Approaches   See main map on page 260

The crags are approached from a trio of parking spots on the south side of the E10 - see map. The westerly one is signed Ådvika, the central one is where a red and white barrier blocks access to a fish farm, and the easterly one is below Tjeldbergvika. In all three places parking is by the cycleway. Please park sensibly.

Urdstabben - The approach track starts at the Svolvær end of a short section of crash barrier beside the cycle path. Descend the slope and head into the trees. Bear left at a rock barrier after 15m, cross a mossy slab then descend into the valley bottom. The improving path leads gently downhill, past a damp section and out into a flat area. Avoid a left turn (which leads to a tiny and pleasant beach) the path then starts to climb into a narrow rocky canyon. Exit left out of this and continue up to a shoulder, where the crag is visible for the first time. Cross the boulder slope to the Urrisse Wall, or head down the gully and loop round to reach the Martha Wall.

Tjeldbergvika - Both crags are easily reached above the road by short scrambles.

Finnvika - This is best approached from the parking below Tkelbergvika Hjørnet. Follow an improving track down a little valley towards the sea. After less than five minutes the boulder beach appears and the crag can be seen away to the right.

Conditions

The various buttresses generally face south and so are nice and sunny, except for the South Wall at Urdstabben. All the crags dry quickly and are relatively sheltered. More details are given with the individual buttresses.

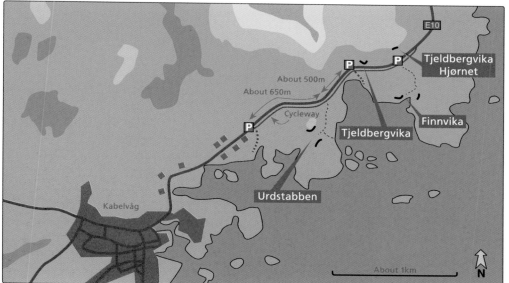

The West

Henningsvær

Kalle

Kabelvåg

Svolvær

Trolltindan

Walking Peaks

Bouldering

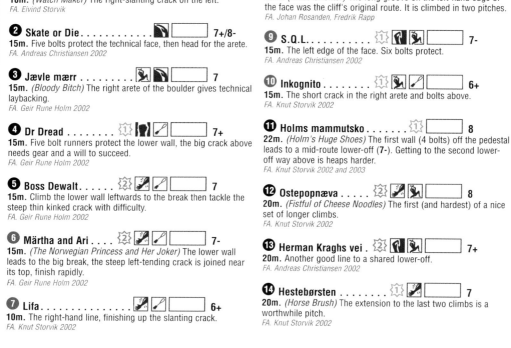

Martha and Ari Wall

This small wall is situated on the left (northwest facing) side of the wide bouldery canyon. The routes mostly follow cracks and are trad in style.

Approach - See page 263.

Conditions - The crag faces northwest and gets the sun late in the afternoon. It dries quickly and is reasonably sheltered. There is quite a lot of moss and lichen on some areas, these retain the damp longer.

① Urmakeren 6-
10m. *(Watch Maker)* The right-slanting crack on the left.
FA. Eivind Storvik

② Skate or Die . . . . 7+/8-
15m. Five bolts protect the technical face, then head for the arete.
FA. Andreas Christiansen 2002

③ Jævle mærr 7
15m. *(Bloody Bitch)* The right arete of the boulder gives technical laybacking.
FA. Geir Rune Holm 2002

④ Dr Dread . . . . 7+
15m. Five bolt runners protect the lower wall, the big crack above needs gear and a will to succeed.
FA. Geir Rune Holm 2002

⑤ Boss Dewalt 7
15m. Climb the lower wall leftwards to the break then tackle the steep thin kinked crack with difficulty.
FA. Geir Rune Holm 2002

⑥ Märtha and Ari 7-
15m. *(The Norwegian Princess and Her Joker)* The lower wall leads to the big break, the steep left-tending crack is joined near its top, finish rapidly.
FA. Geir Rune Holm 2002

⑦ Lifa . . . . 6+
10m. The right-hand line, finishing up the slanting crack.
FA. Knut Storvik 2002

Urrisse Wall

The rest of the routes are on the tall red southeast-facing wall, on the right-hand side of the blocky gully. There are two tall (10 bolt runners) projects over on the left.

⑧ Moss orienteraren 6
40m. *(Moss Orienter)* The long groove on the left-hand edge of the face was the cliff's original route. It is climbed in two pitches.
FA. Johan Rosanden, Fredrik Rapp

⑨ S.Q.L. 7-
15m. The left edge of the face. Six bolts protect.
FA. Andreas Christiansen 2002

⑩ Inkognito . . . . 6+
15m. The short crack in the right arete and bolts above.
FA. Knut Storvik 2002

⑪ Holms mammutsko 8
22m. *(Holm's Huge Shoes)* The first wall (4 bolts) off the pedestal leads to a mid-route lower-off (7-). Getting to the second lower-off way above is heaps harder.
FA. Knut Storvik 2002 and 2003

⑫ Ostepopnæva 8
20m. *(Fistful of Cheese Noodles)* The first (and hardest) of a nice set of longer climbs.
FA. Knut Storvik 2002

⑬ Herman Kraghs vei . 7+
20m. Another good line to a shared lower-off.
FA. Andreas Christiansen 2002

⑭ Hestebørsten 7
20m. *(Horse Brush)* The extension to the last two climbs is a worthwhile pitch.
FA. Knut Storvik 2002

The West
Henningsvær
Kalle
Kabelvåg
Svolvær
Trolltindan
Walking Peaks

Urrisse Wall

This tall face has some excellent sport routes in a glorious setting.
Approach - See page 263.
Conditions - The crag faces southeast and gets the sun until mid afternoon. It dries quickly and is reasonably sheltered.

10m to right

The West

Henningsvær

Kalle

Kabelvåg

Svolvær

Trolltindan

Walking Peaks

Bouldering

⑮ Änglamarken . . . . . ⚐ 🧗 ▭ 6+
20m. *(Angels's Field)* The left-hand of the trio of face climbs left of the crack.
FA. Andreas Christiansen 2002

⑯ Urmannen . . . . ⚐ 🧗 ▭ 7-
20m. *(The Cave Man)* The middle one of the trio shares the lower-off.
FA. Knut Storvik 2002

⑰ Sponsoren . . . . . . ⚐ 🧗 ▭ 7-
20m. The right-hand climb, just left of the crack.
FA. Knut Storvik 2002

⑱ Urrisse . . . . ⚐ 🧗 ▭ 6+
20m. *(Boulder Crack)* Follow the long 'pseudo-crack', and bring some runners.
FA. Knut Storvik 2002

⑲ Svettpeisen . . . . ⚐ 🧗 ▭ 6+
25m. *(Sweaty Knob)* - hope Hendrik changes his underwear regularly). A fine climb that weaves up the wall to the right of the crack. The longest pitch here - eleven bolts.
FA. Hendrik Bollingmo 2002

⑳ Jann's Adventure . . . . ⚐ ▭ 4+
12m. The easiest route here with a steep start - six bolts.
FA. Lofoten Tindeklubb 2006

Left

The left-hand crag has a small set of old trad routes. It has quite a bit of potential though a fair amount of cleaning may be needed.

Approach (see map on page 263) - The crag is easily reached in five minutes from parking by an access gap for the fish farm - park carefully or you might get a ticket.

❶ Risset 5
22m. The groove and continuation crack starting from a ledge with some big blocks.
FA. Jonas Tetlie, Eirik Skjeseth, Kenneth Jensen, 1996

❷ Diederet 6
20m. The groove to the right of the protruding buttress leads to a tough finish up the crack splitting the slab.
FA. Jonas Tetlie, Knut Stornvik, Ragnar Ekker (aid) 1996.
FFA. Andreas Christansen, Knut Storvik 1998

❸ RUSS 96 6
36m. (*School Finishers of 1996*) A three pitch outing (quite short pitches though) up the centre of the cliff, with a stance under the overhangs and one out on the nice ledge on the right. The first pitch is **5-**, the others **6**.
FA. Jonas Tetlie, Andreas Christansen 1996

❹ Fast Food . . . . 5+
18m. Start round to the right and climb a steep groove before moving out left to the stance and finish of the previous climb.
FA. Andreas Christansen, Runar Eilertsen 1997

Tjeldbergvika Hjørnet
On the left a solitary bolt marks a project that will be a variation start to the other routes, it is supposed to be about 8- and reachy.

❺ Sko and garn . . . . . 6+
18m. (*Shoes and Yarn*) The cracks and groove in the centre of the face (bolts) are climbed until it is possible to head right into *Ninjarisset* to finish - gear required.
FA. Andreas Christansen 2002

❻ Fu Manchu 7
18m. A more direct finish to *Sko and garn* heads slightly left up the face.
FA. Andreas Christansen 2002

❼ Ninjarisset 7
18m. The superb thin crack splitting the right-hand side of the face gives a fine, and hard, piece of finger-jamming.
FA. The route was an aid climb back in the 1980s. The FFA was by Petter Restorp in 2000 though it had been top-roped the previous year.

Tjeldbergvika Hjørnet

The right-hand crag, Tjeldbergvika Hjørnet is the tall imposing buttress opposite the parking for Finnvika. There are only three routes here at the moment though there is considerable potential. The current routes are on the clean left-hand face.

Approach (see map on page 263) - The crag is easily reached in five minutes from parking. Scramble up from the right to the routes.

Lo-Profile - Knut Fausa Storvik

I was born in 1970 and I come from Kabelvåg, currently I am studying nursing in Trondheim.

My Lofoten: I grew up in Kabelvåg, my father introduced me to climbing, though I started climbing by myself at the age 13. I did mostly trad climbing the first years.

Favourite climbs: *Vestpillaren* of course, but I also enjoy sport climbing and bouldering. Eggum is my favourite spot especially the routes *Gullfaks*, *Commando* and *Full Belastning*. The long 6a bouldering traverse beneath Presten is probably my all time favourite in Lofoten.

My story: We aid climbed *Storpillaren* when I was 18. After 20 hours I was sleeping underneath the steep and serious grass gully near the summit. My friends Andreas and Jonas discussed who was about to do this pitch. They woke me up and asked if I could do it to which I answered yes, and then immediately fell asleep again. They put the rack on me and sent me up the pitch, though I couldn't remember much about it afterwards!

Finnvika

A fine buttress of excellent rock, in a sunny situation and only a short distance from the road. The routes are all sport climbs (bar the original line of the cliff) and tend to be fingery and balancy rather than particularly strenuous.

Approach (see map on page 263)
The crag is hidden in a secluded spot. The tall crag of Tjeldbergvika Hjørnet above the road is a good marker. Park sensibly in the access road to the cycleway and follow an improving track (damp near the start) as it heads down a little valley towards the sea. After less than five minutes the boulder beach appears and the crag can be seen away to the right.

Conditions - The crag faces southeast and gets the sun in the morning. The rock takes no drainage and so dries rapidly after rain. The approach is non-tidal, though big seas and a high tide might make things tricky.

1 Tante Bente . . . . 🔭 ⬜ **6-**
10m. *(Aunty Bente)* A short line with a fingery start.
FA. Knut Storvik, Andreas Christiansen 2005

2 Oves kvalbiff . . . . 🔭 🐾 ⬜ **6-**
10m. *(Ove's Whale Beef)* A tricky start up a blank groove.
FA. Knut Storvik, Andreas Christiansen 2005

3 Hardt klientell . . . . 🔭 ✏️ ⬜ **7**
30m. *(Hard Customers)* This two pitch outing follows the line just above the curving overlap. Pitch 1 is **7** and pitch 2, continuing the traverse until a vertical crack leads to the top, is **5+**.
FA. Andreas Christiansen, Eivind Storvik, Jonas Tetlie 1996. The original route on the cliff by quite a few years.

4 Svinluggen. . . . . 🔭 🐾 🦶 ✏️ ⬜ **8-**
20m. *(Pig's Forelock - a north Norwegian insult)* Start along *Hard Klientell* (gear) but take the boltline that runs up the steep shallow groove and onto the face above.
FA. Knut Storvik 2005

5 Langbeins svaparadise . 🔭 🐾 ⬜ **6+**
20m. *(Goofy's Slab Paradise)* The rib with a prominent pothole is harder than it looks.
FA. Knut Storvik 2002

6 Fjell og vidde klatring . . 🔭 🦅 ⬜ **5+**
16m. *(Mountain and Moor Climbing)* Start up a groove, trend left to reach a short right-trending flake with the lower-off at the top.
FA. Ragnar Ekker, Knut Storvik 2004

7 Gravitasjon . . . . . . 🔭 🐾 🦅 ⬜ **7-**
20m. Start up the groove of *Fjell og vidde klatring* and pull over the roof. Continue up the wall with escalating difficulties.
FA. Andreas Christiansen 2006

8 Drømmen om Michaela 🔭50 🐾 ⬜ **6**
20m. *(Michaela's Dream)* Excellent fingery climbing. Climb the flake-crack to its top then head up the scooped wall until a tricky move can be made up and right to reach the lower-off.
FA. Robert Caspersen with NNKS students - Marius, Piter, Erika, Ilse, Olav and Øyvind 2003

9 Bormeister Fausa . . 🔭 🐾 ✏️ ⬜ **6**
20m. *(Drill Master Fausa)* Another great climb. Start behind the huge block and climb the boltline right of the crack.
FA. Hendrik Bollingmo 2002

Colin Binks zipping up *Drømmen om Michaela* (6)
possibly the best route on the cliff.

269

The West

Henningsvær

Kalle

Kabelvåg

Svolvær

Trollitindan

Walking Peaks

Bouldering

⑩ Surprise Cafe. . . . . �"2 🖾 🖾 ☐ **6+**
20m. From the start of *Bormeister Fausa*, follow the flakes out
right (more holds than it looks) then head straight up the face.
FA. Andreas Christiansen 2004

⑪ Lukket prosjekt . . . . ☐
22m. The right-hand line is a closed project.
Bolted by Andreas Christiansen 2006

*On the other side of the bay (left of the approach path) is a wall
known as Haikjeften, with a steep overhang and a single route.*

⑫ Håkjaerringa . . . . . �"2 🖾 🖾 ☐ **8+**
20m. *(Greenland Shark)* The line of bolts also needs a selection of cams. Worth seeking out, if you are up to it.
FA. Knut Storvik 2006

The West

Henningsvær

Kalle

Kabelvåg

Svolvær

Trolltindan

Walking Peaks

Bouldering

Svolvær

The enigmatic statue of the fisherman's wife waves farewell from Svolvær's
harbour as the small boats head towards the Vesfjorden and the fishing ground.

Theis.
Henningsvaer
Kalle
Kabelvåg
Svolvær
Trolltindan
Walking Peaks
Bouldering

Blåtinden (621m)

Fløya (590m)

The Frog

1

2

Geita

1 Skårungens hevn . . . . 🏆 ☐ **6** *A1*

About 200m. *(Fisher Apprentice's Revenge)* A six pitch route on the south face of Blåtinden which uses a little aid. The team tried the route a number of times before eventual success. There is some good climbing on the route, though the crag is rather mossy. Start up a slab to the left of a long sharp arete that bounds the left-hand side of a deep reccess.

Descent - Traverse right and scramble down and across exposed grass ledges to reach the open hillside, or continue scrambling up to the top. From here descend the well-trodden normal way to this popular summit - see page 304.
FA. Arild Meyer, Odd-Roar Wiik 9.1995

Lots of sun | 60 min | Bad weather

2 Frosken. . . . . ☐ **5**

About 100m. *(The Frog)* The conspicious 'blip' on the ridge near the low point on the Blåtind/Fløya ridge is known as 'the Frog'. It has a single route of three pitches all believed to be grade **5**. Nothing else is known about the climb. The substantial approach means it probably hasn't had a second ascent.
FA. Arild Meyer 1980s

1

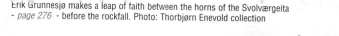
Erik Grunnesjø makes a leap of faith between the horns of the Svolværgeita
- *page 276* - before the rockfall. Photo: Thorbjørn Enevold collection

The West

Henningsvær

Kalle

Kabelvåg

Svolvær

Trolltindan

Walking Peaks

Bouldering

Svolværgeita

High above north Lofoten's main town, is the Svolværgeita (usually known simply as 'The Goat', with the two giant blocks of the horns balanced on its crest and, if you visit Lofoten and you consider yourself any kind of climber, at least one ascent of The Goat is mandatory! The first ascent of The Goat in 1910 was a seminal point in the history of Norwegian climbing. In a two week period the same team made the first ascent of Stetind on the mainland (after sailing up the fjord to reach it), as well as *Trakta*, and *Store Klokktinden* on Lofoten. It has long been traditional to jump the gap between the horns, though fortunately this has never actually been compulsory! Sadly in the winter of 2006/7 a chunk of the inner edge the Lillehorn (the smaller of the two horns) fell away, meaning that the jump is now wider and the landing platform is smaller. The jump is no longer recommended and the local guides now decline to take clients there.

Approach

From the roundabout in Svolvær, turn left (signed E10/Fiskebøl) and follow this for 1.1km to a left turn just beyond the fire station (which is on the right) into Nyveien (signed to Melkerdalen/Nybyen). Follow the loop right, and right again, then turn left into Blåtindveien. Park sensibly on the left by the nursery school/playing field. Take a left turn towards a quarry then almost immediately branch right on a path signed STI TRACK. Follow the path up a slab and through the boulders into the steep gully. The path weaves up this then emerges onto a shoulder, at this point bear right towards The Goat, passing a perennial stream. Either scramble to the col or cut diagonally across the steep grass slope to the base of *Forsida* - 30-40 mins from the parking, care required in the wet.

The old approach to The Goat has long been up the eastern gully but this is steep(er) and loose(r) and is best avoided.

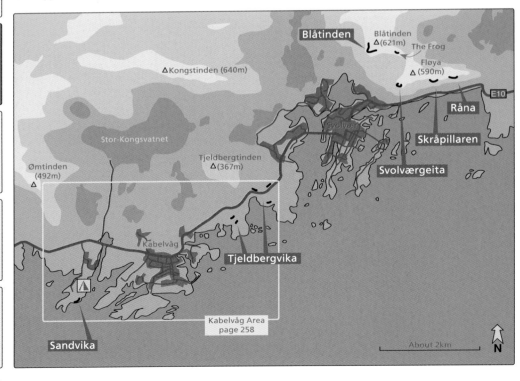

The West

Henningsvær

Kalle

Kabelvåg

Svolvær

Trolltindan

Walking Peaks

Bouldering

❶ Kirkegårdsrisset... 🏔 🤚 👤☐ 8-
27m. *(Churchyard Crack)* In the huge boulderfield that
lies between the church and The Goat is a compelling
crackline, easily spotted from the road.
1) 5, 12m. Climb a groove to the ledge and a stance.
2) 8-, 15m. The large roof crack and its continuation are
the real challenge. Carry medium to large cams.
Descent - Make a short abseil off the back of the block
FA. Kjell Arne Andreassen 1980s. FFA. Robert Caspersen 2003

The Svolværgeita, with its spectacular horns,
towering 300m above Svolvær chuch and graveyard.

Not much sun

40 min

The West

Henningsvær

Kalle

Kabelvåg

Svolvær

Trolltindan

Walking Peaks

Bouldering

North Face

The broad col behind the Svolværgeita is the usual base for attempts on routes on the short side of the tower. It is a shady, cold and rather unfriendly spot, the atmosphere can be quite intimidating. Scrambling up the path opposite the tower should guarantee spectacular photographs of the ascent team in action.

Caution - This path is steep and a bit loose, it does NOT go to the top of Fløya, care is needed as there have been fatalities here.

Descent - From the Lillehorn, reach back and use bolts in the Storhorn to abseil into the notch (tricky take-off) reaching ledges and a second set of chains - 15m. From here make a 28m abseil to the grassy col behind the tower.

West Gully approach route

East Gully approach route

The West

Henningsvær

Kalle

Kabelvåg

Svolvær

Trolltindan

Walking Peaks

Bouldering

① Rapellruta 5

48m. Fine climbing up the line of the abseil descent, steep and juggy after a surprisingly tough start.

1) 5, 28m. Struggle up the leaning groove to reach a resting ledge then step out onto the steep face on the left and plough up the ladder of jugs following a crackline to reach a ledge and double-bolt belay. Exhilarating climbing

2) 4+, 20m. Finish as for *1910 ruta*.

② 1910 ruta . . . . Top 50 4+

56m. A great route and an astounding effort for its day. The climb remains steep and intimidating, with a great atmosphere and a spectacular finale.

1) 4+, 22m. A steep start up the right-hand groove (easier just to the left) leads to ledges, continue up a flake on the left and a steep juggy groove/chimney to a stance on the right with spike belays.

2) 4+, 14m. 'The Rubenson Traverse'. Trend diagonally left across the steep and exposed wall, on a line of superb jugs, passing a couple of pegs. Make an exposed move round the arete to a good stance and double-bolt belay.

1910 ruta continued...

3) 4+, 20m. Continue up the deep groove system on the left to reach the notch between the horns (view). Traverse right across the inner face past flakes (exposed) to reach the western arete of the Storhorn and climb this to the top. Cross the gap to a belay on gear on the Lillehorn. Take care with rope work on this pitch.
FA. C.W.Rubenson, A.B.Bryn, F.Shcjelderup 1910

③ Baksida . . . . 5+

44m. A combination of good pitches makes for a popular outing. Also known, for obvious reasons, as *The Spiral Route*.

1) 4+, 24m. Start as for the *1910 Ruta* but keep right up a flake, then follow the groove to the shoulder and a good stance.

2) 5+, 20m. The diagonal crack splitting the front face of The Goat is 'The West Wall Finish' to *Forsida*. Make a hard start then continue to the notch between the horns and a possible stance at a fat old peg. Traverse the slab leftwards to gain the western arete and finish up this to the top of the Storhorn. Cross the gap to belay on the Lillehorn. The rockfall from the Lillehorn may have damaged the start of this pitch making it even harder than it used to be.
FA. (P1) G.Santesson, E.Tjerneld 1938. (P2) Bjørn Bommen, B.Lyche 1928

The West

Henningsvær

Kalle

Kabelvåg

Svolvær

Trollfjorden

Walking Peaks

Bouldering

West Face

The West Face is clearly visible on the usual approach, giving a good chance to spy out the lines of the various routes. The narrow path leading across the steep grass slope to the start of *Forsida* is exposed - care is needed, especially if wet.

Descent - By abseil, see page 277.

Sofen - 'The Sofa'

4 Englevinger . . . . . . Top L50 🔲📷 🍴 ⬜ **6+**

85m. A good hard route which gives some great jamming up a strong line. Opinions vary on the grade. Bring a good range of cams including a few big ones. Start down and right of the col at a clean area reached by an exposed scramble.

1) 6, 30m. Traverse right (bolt) and climb the thin crack before moving back left then head direct to a good stance.

2) 6+, 35m. The thin crack in the steep groove leads to an overhang, power over this and continue to the shoulder.

3) 6+, 20m. Descend left to the foot of a steep crack, climb this, gradually widening, to an action-packed finish.

FA. Ed Webster, Arild Meyer, Odd-Roar Wiik 1993

5 Forsida . . . . Top L50 🔲📷 ⬜ **5+**

128m. *(The Outside Route)* A great climb and by far the best way up The Goat - if you are on the island make the effort to get this one done. The famous jump is now more difficult and dangerous than it used to be due to the wider gap and smaller landing area - it makes MUCH more sense to climb across. *Photo on page 8.*

1) 3+, 34m. Start at a worn area below the southwest arete of The Goat. Climb a short steep wall then slant left up a rib (or the easier groove on the right) to easy ground. Follow a horizontal crack out right and belay a little higher.

2) 4, 14m. The groove leads to a shoulder, then its continuation ends at a good stance.

3) 5, 30m. Trend left to the base of the prominent crack then jam this, before moving right then back left to exit onto a slab. A little higher, cross the ridge to reach the huge terrace of Sofen (the sofa) and a super-comfy stance.

4) 5, 30m. Climb over blocks to reach the diagonal cracks that split the face above. The initial wide section is awkward then easier climbing leads to the base of a thin section. Up this by finger-jamming to a stance on the shoulder.

Horny Tales

As might be expected, such a notable feature as the Svolværgeita has attracted the attention of thrill seekers over the years. Arne Randers Heen can take the blame for starting the ball rolling with his spectacular leap between the twin horns back in the 1930s. It became 'de rigueur' to do the leap as a rite of passage and even non-climbers came to Lofoten to do it.

In the early 1980s climbers from Svolvær spent a night in a tent on the summit of the Lillehorn, history doesn't record how well they slept though!

Going one better, in the 1990s someone made the local papers by dragging a kayak up onto the horns. Exactly why he did this, he never explained!

Also in the 1990s, a couple got married on the Abseil Ledge. In fresh snow they managed to drag a horrified priest up there to perform the act.

In 2004 Chris Craggs arrived in Svolvær after 40 years of dreaming, on seeing the Geita, Sherri Davy indicated that she wouldn't be heading up there! A guide was booked from NNKS and Thorbjørn Enevold turned up, intrigued by, "an Englishman interested in the *Forsida ruta*". The meeting eventually led to this guidebook. Chris declined to make the jump and crossed the gap by a reverse mantel, downhill hand-traverse and long stride, Thorbjørn commented that he had never seen anything like it!

5) 5+, 20m. The diagonal crack splitting the face is the 'West Wall Finish'. Make a hard start, then continue to the notch and a possible stance by a fat old peg. Traverse left across the slab to gain the western arete and finish up this to the tip of the Storhorn. Cross the gap to belay on the Lillehorn.

FA. W.Höyer, A.Krane 1947. FA. (West Wall Finish) B.Bommen, B.Lyche 1928

Colin Binks on the Storehorn after doing three of the classics in a day.

South Face

The 100m+ valley face of the Geita is tall and impressive though unfortunately most of it is heavily vegetated with a layer of moss and lichen. Two worthwhile climbs skirt the opposite edges of the face, the long central grooveline of the well-named *Vegetarianeren* being so overgrown as to be worthless, at least in summer.

Lots of sun · 40 min

5

Sofen - 'The Sofa'

West Gully (new approach)

7

5

6

East Gully (old approach)

The West · Henningsvær · Kalle · Kabelvåg · Svolvær · Trolltindan · Walking Peaks · Bouldering

Chris Craggs celebrates
(right) in 2006 and steers
clear (left) in 2007!

The West

Henningsvær

Kalle

Kabelvåg

Svolvær

Trolltindan

Walking Peaks

Bouldering

Before and After
Spot the difference. The two shots were taken a year apart, the change in the size of the gap between the two horns can clearly be seen.

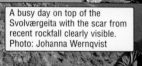

A busy day on top of the Svolværgeita with the scar from recent rockfall clearly visible.
Photo: Johanna Wernqvist

⑥ Vegetarianeren . . . . ☐ **5** *A1*
125m. *(The Vegetarian)* In the centre of the front side of The Goat is a prominent overgrown groove. It is seldom (if ever) climbed. A brief description is included for inspired botanists.
1) 5 *A1*, **40m.** From the base of the corner, climb out right on aid to a groove, then diagonally back left into the main corner. Up this before moving out right and up to a stance.
2) 4 *A1*, **35m.** Climb the main groove, then move out right on aid past a small roof. Step left again into the corner, and climb up a slab on the right to a stance.
3) 5-, 35m. Climb a crack, then head left up a ramp to the top of the main corner. Step around another roof then traverse left, and belay above a short chimney.
4) 15m. Scramble up to the right-hand end of Sofen. Finish up the 'West Wall Finish' of *Forsida*.
FA. The story goes that two Scottish climbers made the first ascent, in extremely bad weather, in the mid 1970s

⑦ Highway to Heaven. . . . 🏃 ☑ ☐ **7**
110m. Originally the cause of some controversy, this route involved a lot of highly visible cleaning. It ascends the prominent pale stripe up the upper right-hand face of The Goat's front face. Each of the main pitches has a short aid section at the start then some strenuous jamming. Carry a few blades and lost arrow pegs for the aid.
1) 30m. Climb steep exposed and scary grass and ferns to reach a ledge at the foot of the cleaned crack system.
2) 7, 45m. Climb the serious crack (the first 8m can be aided at **6+** *A2*) and continue up a thin vertical crack until a hollow flake can be free climbed to a possible stance. Belay or continue up the off-width above to easier cracks and a small stance on the right.
3) 6+ *A1*, **35m.** Aid up the smooth face on the right (two bolts) then free climb up the exposed and strenuous right-trending crack.
FA. Ed Webster, Odd-Roar Wiik 12.8.1991. This was after spending two days cleaning the route. They were met upon their descent after one day of cleaning by a local policeman and the Svolvær Mountain Rescue team. Their dislodging of loose rocks and warning shouts had prompted an elderly woman neighbour to telephone the police to say some climbers needed rescuing. This was duly reported the next day on the local radio and in Lofotposten. Øyvind Vadla free climbed part of pitch 2 on 2.7.1993

The West

Henningsvær

Kalle

Kabelvåg

Svolvær

Trolltindan

Walking Peaks

Bouldering

Fløya (590m)

Svolven (446m)

Skråpillaren

Råna

Descent

Geita

Descent

Svolvær

Descent

Skråpillaren

To the east of the Svolværgeita, towards the Svolvær Airport, several alpine-like cliffs including Skråpillaren and Råna rise steeply above the road. The first and most obvious cliff is the grey right-slanting Skråpillaren (Leaning Pillar), to the left of Råna.

Approach - Park on the road below the cliff 1.6km east of the Svolværgeita. Scramble up to the long diagonal ledge system to reach the base. The approach takes about 20 minutes from the road.

Descent - Scramble (grade 3 or 4) to the summit of Svolen (446m), then follow a ridge towards Fløya (590m) until you reach an easy-angled grassy gully that brings you back down to the road in about 45 minutes.

❶ Meyer/Wiik ruta .. ☆ 🪶 👊 ⬜ **6**

230m. The first (and still the only) route on the cliff featuring some fine crack-climbing in its upper reaches.

1) 4+, 35m. Scramble up the narrow ledge system to reach the ramp system which begins on the pillar's right-hand side. Climb the ramp for 20m, then continue past a big block on the left to a stance on a tiny ledge.

2) 5-, 30m. Climb a crack above the belay, up a left-facing groove, and through a small overhang to a large grassy ledge.

3) 6, 45m. Climb the wall to the base of a right-facing groove above. Up this for 5m, then continue straight up the face above to reach the next corner. Climb up this for 7m then make an unprotected traverse out right to the next belay.

4) 6, 40m. After a delicate start up a shallow groove, traverse right 5m to a grassy groove. Climb this past a bulge to a right-leaning jamming crack which leads to a stance.

5) 6, 35m. Ascend the impressive right-facing corner above the stance. After a 'wicked off-width' at the top of the pitch, belay on another good ledge on the right.

6) 4, 45m. From the right end of the ledge, climb a chimney leading to easier ground. Belay at the end of the steep section.

FA. Arild Meyer, Odd-Roar Wiik 8.5.1994

The West

Henningsvær

Kalle

Kabelvåg

Svolvær

Trolltindan

Walking Peaks

Bouldering

Råna

This is the right-hand of the faces rising above the E10, 2km east of the Svolværgeita. The route is one of Lofoten's older classics - a fine and lengthy expedition considering its roadside setting, featuring some complicated route finding. The route's reputation for loose rock has been overstated in the past and most of the loose stuff has long gone. Protection is good throughout, but carry several large cams to protect the top jamming crack.

Approach - Park on the right just before the sharp bend leading up to the Svolvær Airport Tunnel, 2km east of Svolværgeita. (From the Svolvær Post Office, it is 3.5km to the parking spot.) The cliff towers above the boulder slope that hangs over the road. From the road, walk back towards Svolvær for 200m then scramble up the scree and boulder slope and into the rocky gully on the left-hand side of Råna. Then head up and right by some very steep and insecure grass climbing (Grade 2, avoid if at all wet) to reach a bush-covered terrace below the base of two steep, left-facing grooves that identify the start of the route.

Descent - From the summit, follow a faint path heading east to a 15m abseil (sling on a block) to reach the forest below. Now descend a scree gully to the south back to the E10.

Descent

② **Råna** .... 🔁 🦶 📷 ▭ **6-**
335m. Begin just to the right of a small cave, or niche, below a sharp-edged, left-facing groove.
1) 4+, 35m. Climb up the short groove, then follow a crack system straight up to a large detached flake. Above are two grooves, climb either one and belay on a ledge.
2) 3+, 20m. A short pitch gains the huge bushy terrace above. Move left to belay below a steep wall. (DO NOT climb higher up on the terrace to your right, towards an old off-route peg.)
3) 5-, 35m. Step out left from the belay, past a small overhang, and onto the steep face above. Now climb cracks straight up the middle of the face, then move over another small overhang and climb up to a ledge with a tree belay. A good pitch.
4) 5- 40m. Continue up the crack system, with a hard move at the start. Move up then step left under a block and around an overhang, climb up a chimney to another bushy terrace. Step up to a good ledge at the base of the left-hand of two prominent corner cracks.
5) 5-, 45m. Climb the grooves and cracks into the route's upper chimney system, and continue up the chimney (loose rock) until a traverse out left gains a big ledge with a large belay spike. (The FA team traversed out of the chimney halfway up, and then climbed a parallel chimney on the left, which is less direct).
6) 5, 40m. Climb a vertical crack on the right, then step left and up to the bottom of the large prominent black slab on the left, which can be easily seen from the road. Traverse left at the bottom of the slab, then climb a vertical crack which splits its centre. Now traverse left along a ledge to an excellent belay ledge under the crucial groove with its wide crack.
6a) 4+, 50m. An easier variation; from the bottom of the slab, climb a terrace up and right, then go up an easy groove until a 15m horizontal traverse back to the left reaches the normal belay ledge.
7) 6-, 25m. A sustained pitch of wide jamming leads up the steep groove to the large belay ledge.
8) 4+, 45m. Climb the short arête on the right and finish easily up more broken rock to the summit.
FA. Arild Meyer, Finn Tore Bjørnstad 14.6.1978. It took them four and a half hours. They used one point of aid (for a rest) on pitch 7, but typically still gave the pitch a rating of 5+!

Lots of sun | 20 min | Bad weather

The West

Henningsvær

Kalle

Kabelvåg

Svolvær

Trolltindan

Walking Peaks

Bouldering

The West

Henningsvær

Kalle

Kabelvåg

Svolvær

Trolltindan

Walking Peaks

Bouldering

The view out from the slopes of Kongstinden towards the islands of Lillemolla and Skrova.

Trolltindan

Higravtindan (1146m)

Geitgaljen (1085m)

Rulten (1062m

The Trolltindan mountains seen from Blåtinden. Photo: Colin Binks

The West

Henningsvær

Kalle

Kabelvåg

Svolvær

Trolltindan

Walking Peaks

Bouldering

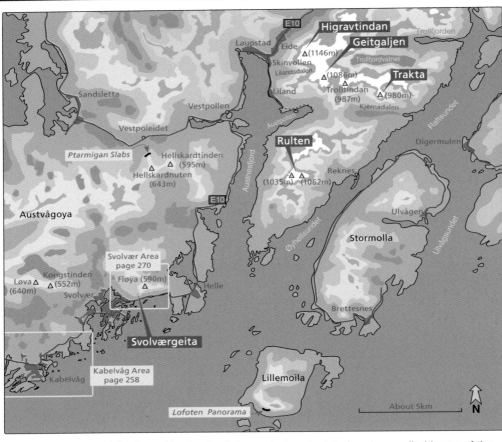

Located northeast of Svolvær, Nordre Austvågøya is the glaciated and unspoiled home of the Trolltindan Mountains. These wild and stark mountains, sandwiched between the fjords of the Austnesfjorden and Higravfjorden in the west, and Øyhellsundet and the Raftsundet in the east, include the renown rocky peak of Rulten (1,062m) - perhaps Lofoten's most beautiful summit, and the narrow, granite-walled Trollfjorden - one of Norway's most famous and spectacular fjords. Climbs in the Trolltindan have retained a well deserved reputation for their rugged, yet pristine wilderness and trips here are best considered as mini-expeditions requiring a multi-day stay and an experienced and self-sufficient team.

Approaches

If your goal is either Hilgravtindan or Geitgaljen, you can approach from the villages of Laupstad, Eide or Skinvollen north of Svolvær on the western side of the peninsula. Access to the remote interior peaks such as Rulten, Trakta (also known as Litlkornestinden) or Trolltindan is considerably more awkward and must be made by boat, requiring a drop-off at one of the local farms on the western shore of the Raftsundet. Boat rentals, drop-offs, and sightseeing trips to Trollfjorden (well worth considering) are all easily arranged at the Destination Lofoten tourist information office in Svolvær near the ferry terminal.

Ptarmigan Slabs

Ptarmigan Slabs offers a mountain day with easy climbing on perfect rock, which can include the bagging a subsidiary peak, part of Hellskardnuten. The route follows a line to the left of the overlapping slabs where the overlaps are less fierce. The wall is northwest facing but slabby hence it can catch plenty of late afternoon and evening sun depending on the time of year.

Approach - The slabs are located on the left wing of a large north-facing corner south of the road from Vestpollen to Sandsletta and can be seen from Vestpolleidet. Park at Vestpolleidet and bushwack between small lakes and continue up to the crag.

Hellskardnuten (643m)

Photo: Roger Brown (on his phone camera)

❶ **Ptarmigan Slabs**. . . 1   **4+**

"In the centre of the slabby northwest facing section is an extensive area of overlaps above a step in the slabs. The climbing is mainly grade 3 with occasional moves of 4 or 4+, but even these can most probably be avoided by careful choice of line. All stances can be protected but the slab pitches themselves tend to be a little run out. Start up the arete where the slabs drop down. Climb up to a small tree then take a rising traverse moving to the left of the overlapping slabs, wherever appropriate. 10 to 11 pitches of pleasant slab climbing eventually lead to a finish on a shoulder high on the left side of the hill, and only a short walk from the top of the nearby peak - Hellskardnuten.

Descent - Drop down the shoulder until the left-hand side of the slabs permits easy scrambling."

FA. John Holden, Roger Brown 4.8.1998

The information and the topo photo for this route are as supplied by the first ascensionists. Unfortunately our man on the scene photographed the wrong cliff! The hillside in the backdrop is in the same valley but a little further east. It does however seem to have plenty of potential for new routes.

The West

Henningsvær

Kalle

Kabelvåg

Svolvær

Trolltindan

Walking Peaks

Bouldering

Higravtindan (1146m)

Geitgaljen (1085

Lilandsdalen

3

1

2 3

Liland

Higravtindan

The highest peak on Lofoten is the west-most of the major peaks in the Trolltindan area, and is situated just to the east of the village of Eide on the E10, 20km northeast of Svolvær.

❶ Vestveggen . . . .

(West Face) The easiest way up the mountain starts in Eide, at the junction of the E10 and the small road leading south to Skinvollen. Climb directly up the slopes, up a slight gully at the start, heading east to the summit.
Time - 4-6 hours round trip.

❷ Sørvest ryggen. . . . .

(Southwest Ridge) This is the original route up the mountain. The ridge can be reached from part way up the valley of Lilandsdalen, east of Skinvollen, or from the col at the head of Lilandsdalen, between Geitgaljen and Higravtindan. No rope is needed. Climb east up a wide grassy ridge until it narrows. Continue up slabs and traverse left into a wide gully just north of the ridge. Follow the gully to its top, where it meets a ridge, just to the left of a small rock tower. Traverse across the col and head towards another col 100m further east. Just before reaching this, turn north, then west, up slopes and gullies which gain the main southwest ridge. Walk over the summit of another tower, separated from the main peak (only 20m away) by the Jordan Gap. Descend into the gap, then head north about 20m along a broad ledge until east of the summit. Climb past a crack with a flake wedged at its base, then step left over a block to the bottom of the last obstacle - a 25m chimney filled with blocks, forming a staircase.
Time - 4 hours up, 2 hours down.
Descent - Reverse the route.
FA. Prof.J.Norman Collie, G.Hastings, H.Priestman, H.Woolley, E.Hogrenning 4.8.1901

Geitgaljen

An enjoyable and popular peak, easily accessible from Skinvollen, just south of Eide and the E10.

❸ Nordvest ryggen. . . . .

(Northwest Ridge) A long easy route starting in the village of Skinvollen heading east up Lilandsdalen to reach the ridge near Hivgravtinden. It then crosses two smaller peaks to reach the top. Descend the same way or direct down into Lilandsdalen.
FA. Alf B.Bryn, Carl Wilhelm Rubenson, Ferdinand Schjelderup 1910

❹ The Italian Route 7- A2

A difficult route on the vertical granite wall of the southeast face. Eight pitches were climbed, the line is marked by their belay/abseil bolts. The first ascent team had to abandon the climb only 20m from the top of the face. It hasn't yet been completed.
FA. A strong Italian team, summer 1992

❺ Nordøst ryggen . . . .

(Northeast Ridge) From the head of the inlet of Austpollen, climb up over grass to the stream of Krokelva, which is followed to a southwest-facing gully (snow early in the season). The top of the snow gully opens onto a hanging valley which is crossed leftwards to Geitgaljen's northeast ridge. Follow this ridge, with some steep rocks, to the top.
FA. Prof.J.Norman Collie, G.Hastings, H.Priestman, H.Woolley, E.Hogrenning 14.8.1901

The information in this section is largely taken from Ed Webster's 1994 *Climbing in the Magic Islands*, and it is likely that much of that came directly from Per Prag's 1950 *Rock Climbs in Lofoten*. Interestingly Per Prag never actually visited the islands! Treat the information with care and let us know about any inaccuracies that you find, and send us improved descriptions.
These routes are all suited to big boots, woolly socks and large rucksacks. Sticky rubber not needed!

Trakta (980m)

Austnalletu

Trakta

(The Funnel) Trakta, also called Litlkorsnestinden, is reputed to be one of Norway's most difficult summits. There are actually two tops - Vestre Trakta, the main summit, and Østre Trakta the lower summit. The deep chasm between the two is called Djevelskar (the Devil's Gap). Fallen slabs have formed a bridge up to 8m thick across part of the gap. Base camp is usually set up near the farm at Korsneset at the entrance of Kjernadalen, the steep valley, southeast of the peak.

6 Nordvest ryggen . . . .

(Northwest Ridge) Walk up Kjernadalen to the remains of the Kjerna Glacier. Continue up vegetation and slabs to the glacier to the left where a gully runs up towards a gap in the northwest ridge. Climb a fairly direct route up the face. Two blocks situated under a wall afford an easy but airy traverse around to the right onto the north face. Next climb a chimney and continue up to the gap in the ridge. The ridge consists of several wide tilted slabs. Climb the left side of the ridge, facing the Kjerna Glacier, to the final pull up onto a sloping platform. Then comes the crucial section which is *"severe, delicate and exposed"*. The ridge narrows to about a half metre wide, but is relatively flat.

Time - 7 hours up, 4 hours down.
Descent - Reverse the route.
FA. Alf B.Bryn, Carl Wilhelm Rubenson, Ferdinand Schjelderup 3.8.1910. Several attempts were made on Trakta before the notable first ascent - yet another pearl in the long string of famous firsts done by Bryn, Rubenson and Schjelderup in 1910. It was an arduous endeavour taking many hours.

7 Vestpillaren . . . . 5+ A1

This long route has reasonable quality rock, but there is some vegetation. Approach up Kjernadalen to the pass between Vestre Trakta and Trolltindmuren, then go down a gully to the southwest, with one short abseil to reach the foot of the West Pillar. The route starts on the pillar's right-hand side below a chimney.

1) 5, 40m. Climb up a slab and into a right-slanting V-groove, then up a crack to the right of a roof. Traverse back left above the roof into a chimney. Belay above.

Vestpillaren continuied...
2) 5+, 40m. Climb up to a ledge, then move down and right across another ledge into a corner. At the top of the corner, angle right across the top of a slab, then climb the corner above, which is the hardest climbing on the route.
3) 3+, 40m. Traverse down and left, finally climbing up a chimney to a belay on the left.
4) 4, 40m. Climb another chimney on the left, traverse right on a ledge, then climb a corner up and right, then another chimney up and left to a belay ledge.
5) 5-, 40m. Traverse right, then climb a corner to a ledge, then another corner leads up to a belay.
6) 3, 20m. Step left, climb a corner, then up the right side of a slab to a belay.
7) 5- A1, 40m. Step right into a slightly right-slanting corner (*A1* - with 3 points of aid). Climb another corner above, move right into a chimney, then climb up and left to a belay.
8) 5-, 20m. Climb up a crack up a slab, then traverse easily up and right to the next belay.
9) 5, 40m. Step right, and climb diagonally right across a slab to a ramp. Then climb two narrow corners to a grassy ledge. Belay on the right-hand side.
10) 5-, 40m. Climb chimney cracks up a slab or face, then climb just to the right of a corner to a belay just left of another small corner.
11) 4-, 40m. Climb up this corner, move up right, then back left, up past ledges to the belay.
12) 20m. Walk right along a ledge and up to a belay.
13) 4, 40m. Step left, then back right, and climb two corners to the next belay.
14) 4+, 40m. Climb up and left across a face, walk left on a ledge, climb a corner up to the right, then step left over a slab to the belay.
15) 5-, 25m. Step left into a corner, then finish up and left up another corner.
From the top of the pillar, follow the ridge and scramble to the summit. Descend down the northwest ridge route.
FA. Arild Meyer, Johnny Lauritsen, Kjell Skog 7.1976. 9 hours of climbing, 20 hours tent to tent. It was so warm that the climbers sunbathed naked on the summit and waved hello to a passing plane flying low overhead.

The West
Henningsvær
Kalle
Kabelvåg
Svolvær
Trolltindan
Walking Peaks
Bouldering

Vestre Rulten (1035m) Austre Rulten (1062m)

Trehakkatinden

Eiterådalen

4

5

3

Rulten

Thought by many to be the finest summit in Lofoten, Rulten is not the tallest of the Trolltindan peaks, but it is perhaps the most beautiful. Its rocky summit is located in the remote centre of the peninsula. It is usually approached from the Raftsundet fjord, with climbers generally using either of the two idyllic, seaside farms of Reknes and Kveitvika as a base. Rulten's two summits - Vestre Rulten (1,035m) and Austre Rulten (1,062m), Lofoten's third highest summit - are separated by a spectacular deep-cut notch.

❶ Vestveggen (Vestre Rulten) . . . ☐
(West Face) From Reknes, climb up what is left of the Snøskar Glacier. Go up this and over the col at the glacier's west end, and continue west towards Austnesfjorden. Descend a short way down the col's west side, then make a hard traverse to the south, climbing across small ledges to the base of a long, wide gully leading up to the mountain's North Ridge. Climb the gully, avoiding a higher gully, which branches off to the left. There is a good mixture of climbing in this section (and there may be snow), a cave pitch featuring a jammed block, and some rock slabs. Traverse out of the snow gully as and when needed to keep to the easiest line, then from the gully's top, continue easily to the summit. 6 hours up, and 4 hours down.
FA. Prof J.Norman Collie, William Cecil Slingsby, William Slingsby 10.8.1903

❷ Nordryggen (Vestre Rulten) . . ☐ **4+**
(North Ridge) A hard direct line to the summit. The flat topped fore-peak on the mountain's north ridge is called Kristoffelstinden. Start at the pass at the western head of the Snøskar Glacier. There are seven pitches, plus some scrambling. From the pass, climb up an easy rope length with some loose rock (**3**). Continue up grass, then descend to a small saddle, before continuing to the left onto a big platform from where progress ahead looks tricky. Climb straight up (**3+**) then continue to another large platform. Climb up, finishing with a hard, 6m jamming crack which ends on the summit of Kristoffelstinden. Descent is possible from the col between Vestre Rulten and the Kristoffelstinden, by descending a loose gully that heads back east to the Snøskar Glacier.

Nordryggen continued...
Follow the upper north ridge (**3**) to the start of a smooth steep rock wall. Climb this directly (**5** *A1*), or avoid this section by traversing right onto the easier upper northwest wall. From here *"A pleasant climb (**3** and **4**), with moss and grass digging, leads to the top!"* Descend down the *Vestveggen* or *Sydrenna*.
FA. Two Dutch climbers, one by the name of van Mourik Broekman, made the first ascent of Kristoffelstinden on 30.7.1965. They returned later and climbed the North Ridge's upper section, finishing up the Northwest Wall. Arild Meyer and Jens Blix-Nilsen made the first complete ascent of the entire ridge, including pitch 6, on 22/23.5.1968

❸ Sydrenna (Vestre Rulten) . . ☐ **3**
(South Gully) The south gully is the easiest route up or down the peak. Climb to the west end of Eiterådalen, the valley immediately south of Rulten, but don't be tempted directly up the south ridge, because it ends in a vertical-walled chasm. Instead, climb to the col at the head of Eiterådalen, then diagonally up and right on grassy ledges, aiming for the gully in the upper part of Vestre Rulten's south face, close to the upper south ridge. About 125m below the summit, the final section becomes relatively easy. In mid-summer, there is plentiful loose rock. This is better done early in the season, when you can climb it mostly on snow.
FA. Lars Nordby, Martin Heggedal, Emil Olsen, Magnar Pettersen 7.1945

❹ Østryggen (Vestre Rulten) . . . . ☐
(East Ridge) This lengthy expedition reaches the summit from the notch between Rulten's two summits. Gain the notch by first climbing the *Østryggen* of Austre Rulten then make two abseils into the col, and follow the exposed upper east ridge which involves *"a lot of up and down climbing along a very long and solid ridge."* The descent was made by reascending the fixed abseil ropes back to the summit of Austre Rulten, and reversing the entire route!
FA. Magnar Pettersen, Wilhelm Höyer, Emil Olsen 7.1955. This was the first ever traverse of both of the summits. Magnar fondly remembers when his climbing partners put a large rock in his rucksack before they started the descent as payment for his doing a lot of the leading on the ascent when they had to carry his pack for him, plus their own!

5 **Østryggen (Austre Rulten)** . . 🔲

(East Ridge) The eastern summit of Rulten climbed by the east ridge is one of Lofoten's best and most historic mountaineering routes. A superb, varied, and lengthy route. From the farm at Reknes, climb up to a col just to the west of Lille Rulten or Trehakkatinden, the prominent, triple summited peak which forms the lower part of the mountain's east ridge. Climb up grassy slopes for a short way up the ridge until forced leftwards by slabs, moving left into a gully. At the top of the gully move northwest up the ridge, staying on top of (or slightly off) the ridge crest for some distance. Climb several short interesting rock pitches, with grass slopes, ledges, and a small cave. Cross a notch in the ridge, then climb a 40m V-groove up the ridge itself. A short steep pitch on good holds leads to another cave. Above this, climb carefully up a 100m gully to another large depression in the ridge. The final pinnacle is below the summit just beyond and is bypassed by a traverse south. A subsidiary ridge runs south from the pinnacle - cross the depression to its west side below the final pinnacle, descend 20m on steep grass slopes, then curve left up grassy rock for 80m and climb over the subsidiary ridge, well below its highest point - follow the easiest line through here. Now descend 100m down the west side of the subsidiary south ridge, heading diagonally right into a green gully and making for a long gully which may contain snow. Either go up the snow gully towards the final gap, or traverse cracks in the rock slabs above and to the east of the snow gully to a point 20m below the final gap. Cross the snow gully, then continue up mossy slopes between slabs on the east side of the main south ridge into an easy gully which leads to the last rock wall below the summit. This final wall is split by two chimney cracks about 10m apart. Climb the left-hand chimney to the top in two pitches, or for one last thrill, step right onto the exposed north wall into another chimney (**5-**) which leads to the top. Another easier finish avoids the chimneys altogether by descending the final couloir below the summit and finishes up the main south ridge.

Time - 8 to 9 hours up, 4 to 5 hours down.

FA. William Cecil Slingsby, Prof. J.Norman Collie, H.S.Mundahl, D.Northall-Laurie 17.8.1903

Austre Rulten (1062m)

Snøskar Glacier

Trehakkatinden

5

1
2

Reknes

The West

Henningsvær

Kalle

Kabelvåg

Svolvær

Trolltindan

Walking Peaks

Bouldering

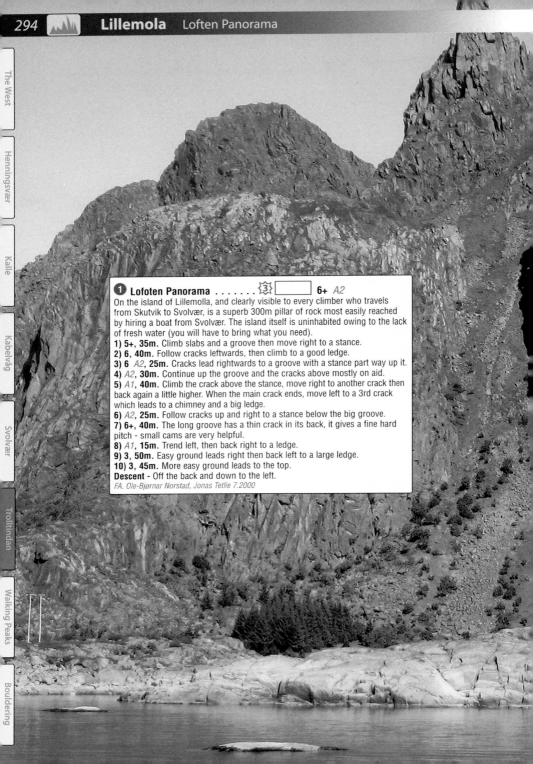

❶ **Lofoten Panorama** . . . . 〚 〛 **6+** *A2*

On the island of Lillemolla, and clearly visible to every climber who travels from Skutvik to Svolvær, is a superb 300m pillar of rock most easily reached by hiring a boat from Svolvær. The island itself is uninhabited owing to the lack of fresh water (you will have to bring what you need).

1) 5+, 35m. Climb slabs and a groove then move right to a stance.

2) 6, 40m. Follow cracks leftwards, then climb to a good ledge.

3) 6 *A2*, **25m.** Cracks lead rightwards to a groove with a stance part way up it.

4) A2, 30m. Continue up the groove and the cracks above mostly on aid.

5) A1, 40m. Climb the crack above the stance, move right to another crack then back again a little higher. When the main crack ends, move left to a 3rd crack which leads to a chimney and a big ledge.

6) A2, 25m. Follow cracks up and right to a stance below the big groove.

7) 6+, 40m. The long groove has a thin crack in its back, it gives a fine hard pitch - small cams are very helpful.

8) A1, 15m. Trend left, then back right to a ledge.

9) 3, 50m. Easy ground leads right then back left to a large ledge.

10) 3, 45m. More easy ground leads to the top.

Descent - Off the back and down to the left.

FA. Ole-Bjørnar Norstad, Jonas Tetlie 7.2000

The West

Henningsvær

Kalle

Kabelvåg

Svolvær

Trolltindan

Walking Peaks

Bouldering

Descent over ridge to gully

The West
Henningsvær
Kalle
Kabelvåg
Svolvær
Trolltindan
Walking Peaks
Bouldering

Walking Peaks

Blåtinden (621m)

The West

Henningsvær

Kalle

Kabelvåg

Svolvær

Trolltindan

Walking Peaks

Bouldering

Austvågøya has a fine collection of peaks forming the backbone of the island. Many of these are remote and quite difficult to reach, especially those in the north of the island, though quite a few make suitable objectives for walks. Although of generally modest heights, the ascents almost invariably start from sea-level. Here is a selection of the more popular summits close to Henningsvær and Svolvær.

Blåtinden (621m) and Fløya (590m) seen from the southwest.

Festvågtinden (541m)

Presten

P

N

Col

△ Festvågtinden (541m)

Gandalf

P

Heiavatnet

P

Festvåg

About 1km

Festvågtinden

The nearest peak to Henningsvær and a popular (if steep) half-day walk, giving good views of the cliffs in the area and the option of a dip in the lake of Heiavatnet. Park as for the Festvåg cliffs and walk past the old granite water reservoir before follow the trail up the back of the valley to a plateau with the small lake of Heiavatnet, the former Henningsvær water supply. Turn left and follow an easy rounded rock ridge, with a faint path, to the crest above, and then to the summit.
Descent - Reverse the route.
Time - About 1.5 hours to the summit.

The West | Henningsvær | Kalle | Kabelvåg | Svolvær | Trolltindan | Walking Peaks | Bouldering

Festvågtinden seen from Henningsvær.

Glåmtinden (419m)

See page 255 for a photo
of the northwest ridge

Glåmtinden
A popular and easy peak with great views.
The normal route is via the old road and
the north ridge. The east ridge, starting
from the causeway across Hopen, offers an
interesting alternative with the option of a
traverse of the peak.
Descent - Reverse the route.
Time - 1 to 1.5 hours to the summit.

From the
Hopen side

E10

Old road

Hopsvatnet

Hopspollen

P

Rørvikvatnet

N

Hopen

P

About 1km

Glåmtinden (419m)

The West
Henningsvær
Kalle
Kabelvåg
Svolvær
Trolltindan
Walking Peaks
Bouldering

The fine peak of Glåmtinden rising
above the inlet of Hopen.

Vågakallen (943m)

(816m)

Storpillaren

The West

Henningsvær

Kalle

Kabelvåg

Svolvær

Trolltindan

Walking Peaks

Bouldering

Vågakallen

With its omnipresence, towering over every-thing, Austvågøy's most beautiful mountain presents an impressive challenge when seen from any angle. An ascent of its inaccessible summit is an experience not to be forgotten - the summit panorama of sea, sky, the neighbouring peaks and islands is magnificent. The peak should not be attempted in poor weather as the route finding is difficult at the best of times and the main problems are encountered near the summit. Although the peak offers a great variety of technical routes the *Sydveggen*, the original route up the mountain, provides a non-technical way to the summit. Despite this, a rope could be useful for some parties, as the ridge traverse (known as Hustaket by the locals) is very exposed.

Sydveggen

(South Face) Start from the parking at the end of Djupfjorden and follow the path along the north shore. Just before the pine grove, branch right through a wet area and cross the stream connecting the two parts of Djupfjorden, just above where it begins to tumble down into the lower lake. A tricky-to-follow path leads up and across several granite slabs, heather and bogs, up into the upper part of Durmålsdalen. Boulder hop up the scree and grass at the back of the valley heading to the prominent col between Vågakallen and Kvanndalstinden (see photo on page 112). There may be large snow patches early in the season (May/June). From the col, descend diagonally down and left (facing out towards the sea) across grass slopes to the bottom of the left-hand of two gullies and follow this up onto the mountain's west ridge. Make an exciting traverse astride the top of the ridge, or friction traverse (very exposed) 5m lower on the south side, heading right towards the upper rocky summit - a rope is often used here for the timid. This is climbed by again moving right (vague tracks) into another loose, scree-filled gully (could be snow) which leads up onto the upper south face of the mountain. Above a good ledge (cairn) scramble up a series of grooves and over loose rock-covered ledges (exposed in places) to the top.

Descent - Reverse the route back to Djupfjorden.

Time - 5 to 7 hours round trip.

FA. Martin H.Ekroll, Angel Johannesen 1889. These two Norwegian mountaineering pioneers, both from the island of Skrova, climbed via the South Face, "ascending the mountain straight from their row boat".

Vågakallen (943m)

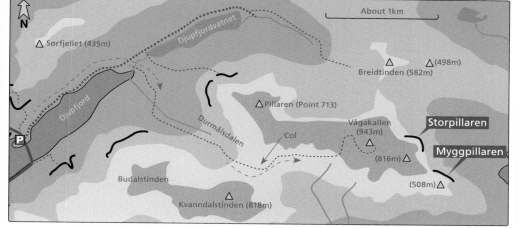

N

About 1km

Djupfjordvatnet

△ Sørfjellet (435m)

△ (498m)

Breidtinden (582m)

Djupfjord

△ Pillaren (Point 713)

Durmålsdalen

Col

Vågakallen (943m) △

Storpillaren

Myggpillaren

(816m) △

P

Budalstinden

(508m) △

△ Kvanndalstinden (818m)

The West

Henningsvær

Kalle

Kabelvåg

Svolvær

Trolltindan

Walking Peaks

Bouldering

Kongstinden (522m)

Løva (640m)

Løva and Kongstinden
(The Lion and *King's Peak)*. Two tops on the same ridge
- Kongstinden is the lower and easier summit. From
here it is possible to continue to the higher top of Løva,
the final section requires some exposed scrambling - a
rope might be useful for the timid. Trackside parking is
available on Kongsmarka, by the northeastern shore of
Kongsvatnet, by the hydro building. A rather indistinct
track starts by following the line of telegraph poles to
reach the ridge crest.
Descent - Reverse the route.
Time - 2 hour round trip for Kongstinden, about 3 hours
for the Løva round trip.

The West

Henningsvær

Kalle

Kabelvåg

Svolvær

Trolltindan

Walking Peaks

Bouldering

Blåtinden
△(621m)   The Frog

Løva (640m)
△ ----- △ Kongstinden (522m)

Fløya
△(590m)

E10

Svolværgeita

Svolvær

Stor-Kongsvatnet

P

Tjeldbergtinden
△(367m)

Tjeldbergvika

Kabelvåg

About 2km

N

Blåtinden (621m)

The West

Henningsvær

Kalle

Kabelvåg

Svolvær

Trolltinden

Walking Peaks

Bouldering

Blåtinden

This is the conspicuous pointed rocky peak to the northwest of Svolvær. Limited parking is available on Villaveien. Take the steep track that starts opposite Knutvikveien and follow it to a sharp right turn towards the peak from just before the small lake of Knutvatnet. Follow the track, then a path that heads towards the shallow col between Blåtinden and the small peak of Tuva further northwest. At the col, turn right and follow the exposed ridge out to the summit.

Descent - Reverse the route. It is also possible to follow the ridge eastwards to Fløya, with some sections of scrambling, and descend here for a great loop.

Time - 2 hours round trip.

Tuva (477m)

Knutvatnet

Blåtinden (621m)

The Frog

Fløya (590m)

Villaveien

Svolvær

Svolværgeita

E10

About 2km

N

Fløya (590m)

Geita

The West

Henningsvær

Kalle

Kabelvåg

Svolvær

Trolltindan

Walking Peaks

Fløya

This is the fine peak to the north of Svolvær and home to the famous feature of the Svolværgeita (page 274) leaning against its flanks. Park on Blåtindveien as for the Svolværgeita. The path is marked. Head through the boulderfield and follow the path up into the hanging valley above. Continue to the col at the head of the valley then turn right and follow the exposed ridge out to the summit. Do NOT try to get between the Geita and the summit (up or down) - there have been at least two fatalities here.

Descent - Reverse the route.

Time - 2 hours round trip.

The West

Henningsvær

Kalle

Kabelvåg

Svolvær

Trolltindan

Walking Peaks

Bouldering

Ali Kennedy on the Stem Bastensen boulders. Photo: Tim Wilkinson

Bouldering

The West

Henningsvær

Kalle

Kabelvåg

Svolvær

Trolltindan

Walking Peaks

Bouldering

Jonathan Lagoe attempting the 'Separate Reality' roof crack on the Presten Boulders. Photo: Andy Hyslop

The bouldering potential on Lofoten is massive and virtually limitless. So far development has concentrated on beach or roadside boulders and much of this is hard due to the ability level of the activists. This approach to bouldering is also connected to the way it is perceived - for many it is an easy day between big routes in the mountains, and the serious bouldering bug has yet to hit Lofoten. When it does some impressive problems will be climbed.

Local climber Sveinung Råheim documented the best of the current developed locations in a bouldering map in 2007 and he has kindly allowed us to use his information. The intention is to tell you the rough locations of the boulders with only a brief amount of information about what is found there, and a few grades and individual problems. This gives plenty to explore and, you can be sure of one thing, the scenery and views in all these areas will be magnificent.

LO Profile - Sveinung Råheim

Sveinung Råheim (1970) from Reinli in Valdres, has lived in Bodø the last 11 years and works as an environmental advisor.

My Lofoten: My first trip to Lofoten was in the winter of 1993. Heaps of codheads in the harbours, spring conditions in the mountains and a scary jump with big plastic boots on The Goat left lasting impressions. I keep going back, there are always new things to explore. The main reasons for my Lofoten passion are the rock quality, world class scenery and easy access to everything.

My climbs: A bit predictable maybe, but I must answer *Vestpillaren*. Another great moment was when we discovered the fantastic sea cliff bouldering at Bunessanda (in the west of Lofoten.) The bays on Yttersida make the Henningsvær area feel urban and should not be missed!

My story: On an ascent of *Vestpillaren* with Remi Bendiksen, another Bodø climber, we started out with light rain in the air, but the rock was dry. This lasted until a couple of pitches above the Storhylla. Then a southwest weather front struck us with full force. We topped out dripping wet after a couple of leader falls and lots of wet cracks and slippery slabs. By the time we came down, the weather cleared up and we could enjoy a couple of beers in the sunset.

Kvalvika

A beautiful set of boulders above a perfect beach. There is plenty of potential although a lot has been done and not documented on the set overlooking the small lake. There are a few more boulders a little further up the beach.
Approach - The walk across from the road takes around 1.5 hours.

Utakleiv

Roadside - Three good boulders in a beautiful location by the parking space on the old road.
Beach - One isolated big boulder plus some more further along the rocky shoreline with good problems.

About 1km

Utakleiv Beach

Utakleiv Roadside

Utakleiv

To E10

To E10

Kvalvika

Sørvalle

Kvalvika

Kvalvikvatnet

Litljordtinden
(758m)

Maltinden
(651m)

Krystad

About 2km

Eggum

Eggum

Unstad

Borge

Austvågøya

E10

Kabelvåg

E10

Vestvågøya

Flakstadøya

Leknes

Henningsvær Area

Kalle Area

Ramberg

Gravdal

Stamsund

Henningsvær

Stortind

Ballstad

Bodø
5 hours

Svolvær
1.5 hours

Moskenesøya

Heilt Rå-steinen

A great boulder 5 minutes from the road on the bend at the southern end of the Flakstapollen. Currently four problems and a project.

Sund

Bunestranda

This beautiful beach below Helvestinden is awkward to get to but well worth it once you get there. The bouldering consists of a few boulders on the beach, and some extraordinary seacliff bouldering on the far side of the headland on the west of the bay - Aussoden.
Approach - By ferry from Reine to Vindstad (see page 56) and then up the side of Bunesfjorden and over the col.

Stamprevtinden
(759m)

Kjerkfjorden

About 2km

Helvetestinden

Merraflestinden

Aussoden

Reine

Moskenes

Bunestranda

Storskiva
(848m)

Bunesfjorden

Kjerkfjorden

Bodø
4.5 hours

Vindstad

Rostad

Reine Ferry

About 10km

N

The West

Henningsvær

Kalle

Kabelvåg

Svolvær

Trolltindan

Walking Peaks

Bouldering

The West
Henningsvær
Kalle
Kabelvåg
Svolvær
Trolltindan
Walking Peaks
Bouldering

Ali Kennedy on the Stem Bastensen boulders.
Photo: Jamie Moss

Stem Bastensen

This area consists of several separate boulders situated about 1.3km west from the junction with the E10 and the Henningsvær road. It is easily recognised by the name 'Stem Bastensen' written in white paint on a large roadside boulder. There are a couple of boulders just north of the graffiti with roof and arete problems, right by the road, and with good landings. On the other side of the road on a boulder beach is a big boulder with a telegraph pole right behind it. Overall there are around 20 problems and plenty of potential.

Monster Boulder - A lone roadside boulder.

Presten Boulders

This popular area gives inspirational bouldering of all standards with plenty of easier face climbing and some awesome roof problems including the most hideous-looking thin-hand, roof crack east (and west!) of *Separate Reality*. It is situated south along the road from Presten, at a high point in the road, and on a bend.

Randalf

A fun wall with some good problems and the only documented bouldering in the book! Situated down towards the sea from the free camping spot.

The Randalf Boulders

❶	Fotball .		V0
❷	Left . . .		V1
❸	. . . . . .		V2
❹	SG		V6
❺	Metolius		V3
❻	. . . . . .		V2
❼	. . . . . .		V0+
❽	. . . . . .		V1
❾	Riss . . .		V0-

Skokkelvika
Two boulders by the road, excellent rock on the main boulder. 3 to 4 problems in total.

Fiskebøl

Laukvika

Laupstad

Sandsletta

Eggum

Eggum

Unstad

Borge

Trolltindan

Austvågøya

Svolvær

Utakleiv

E10

Vestvågøya

Svolvær

Kabelvåg

akstadøya

Leknes

Henningsvær

Kalle

Kabelvåg

Gravda

Stamsund

Henningsvær

Kalle Boulders
A small area but with some popular testpieces like *Midnightsun*. Passed on the approach to Paradiset.

Monster

About 1km

Nordfjellet △ (528m)

Hopen

Stem Bastensen

E10

Cornflakesveggen

Rørvika

Honnikornsvaet

816

Henningsvær Area

Kallebukta

Kalle Boulders

Sørfjellet (435m)

Maurpillaren

Djupfjord

Pianokrakken

Sjøsvaet

Paradiset Boulders

Paradiset

About 1km

P

Paradiset Boulders
An extensive and complex area with lots of easy and moderate problems, and a few hard ones. The rock is a bit sharp. Once developed with a full Font-style painted circuit (see page 211 for the story) but this is no longer followable.

Presten Boulders

Presten

Festvågtinden (541m)

The Presten Boulders

Gandalf

P

Helavatnet

Randalf

P

Festvåg

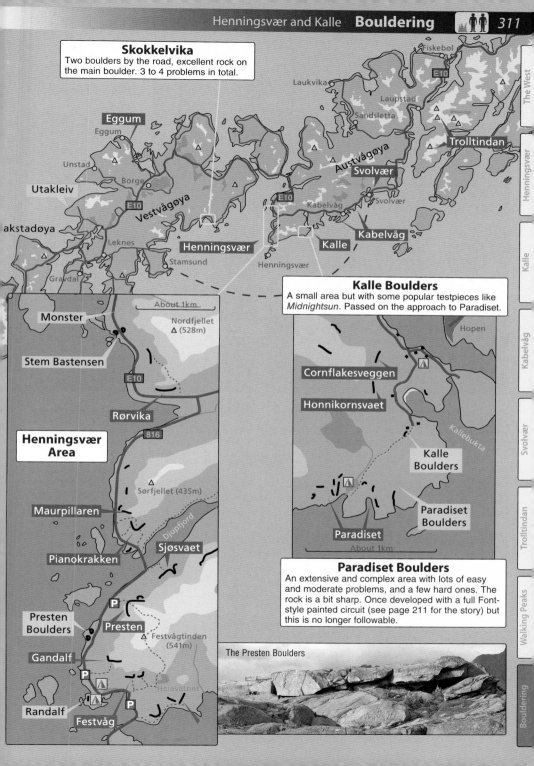

The West | Henningsvær | Kalle | Kabelvåg | Svolvær | Trolltindan | Walking Peaks | Bouldering

Early winter snows on Higravtinden and Geitgaljern.
Photo: Kjell Ove Storvik

The West

Henningsvær

Kalle

Kabelvåg

Svolvær

Trolltindan

Walking Peaks

Bouldering

There is a lot of rock in Lofoten; most of it is climbable in summer, but not all. There are loose gullies, broken ribs and ridges, slabs with water pouring down them, and so on. In winter all this turns in to fantastic winter climbing. The waterfalls and streaks freeze and what is unclimbable moss and turf in summer, turns into the best winter routes.

Despite this vast potential, not much has been done yet. This is for the same reason that there is a lot of unclimbed rock on Lofoten - there is so much to choose from and only a few local climbers.

For the winter climber who has a sense of exploration, and who is prepared to put in the effort, the rewards are huge. There are plenty of lines available with short approaches so you don't need skis, but bring them anyway, because if the climbing conditions are bad, due to heavy snowfall, the ski conditions will be perfect. The best time to come is when the sun and daylight is back and before it gets too warm - mid January until end of March is the season.

For pure water ice you will probably be better off going to Rjukan. On the other hand, if you want to climb mixed routes of ice, snow, rock, turf often with a nice summit thrown in (the Scottish way) while the sun sets in the Atlantic, surrounded by the sea - best try Lofoten.

At the end of your trip you will most likely have done a few new routes. Please inform the Nord Norsk Klatreskole (**post@nordnorskklatreskole.no**). There might even be a winter version of this book one day! Until then, you will find plenty of detailed information on winter climbing on Lofoten in the climbers' cafe in Henningsvær.

Lofoten Winter

313

The West

Henningsvær

Kalle

Kabelvåg

Svolvær

Trolltindan

Walking Peaks

Bouldering

Arild Meyer descending from Rulten.
Photo: Mathias Strømquist.

Bjørn Kirkehaug on the first ascent of *Cyclotron*, Vestre Rulten.
Photo: Mathias Strømquist

Winter Climbing Highlights

- In the 1930s, Arne Randers Heen made the first winter ascent of *Svolværgeita*.
- In March 1934, Arne Randers Heen and Julius Jacobsen made the first winter ascent of Vågakallen via *Austryggen*.
- In 1976, Arild Meyer and Kjell Skog made the first winter ascent of the northeast face of Vågakallen, climbing 14 pitches of varied winter terrain.
- In 1978, Arild Meyer, Kjell Skog and Kjell Ove Storvik made the first winter ascent of Vågakallen *Nordryggen*.
- In the winter of 1979, Arild Meyer and Kjell Ove Storvik made the first ascent of the gully in the northwest face of Vågakallen.
- In March 1979, Sjur Nesheim and Kjell Skog made the first winter ascent of the *Vestpillaren* of Presten.
- In November and December 1981, Sjur Nesheim and Yngvar Julin made the first ascent of *To krigere* on Presten.
- During the rest of the 1980s and the early 1990s, many easier lines were done, mainly in the eastern part of the islands.
- In February 1996, Odd-Roar Wiik and Magnar Osnes made the first winter ascent of *Storpillaren* on Vågakallen in 5 cold days.
- In March 2003, Guy Robertson and Pete Benson made the first ascent of the *Scottish Route* just left of *Storpillaren*, giving it the grade ED1.

During recent years several new routes have been done but few details are available, and most ascents feel like first ascents due to this dearth of information.

The West

Henningsvær

Kalle

Kabelvåg

Svolvær

Trolltindan

Walking Peaks

Bouldering

Lo-Profile - Mathias Strømquist

I was born in 1980 and come from Sweden. I work as an ambulance driver in Svolvær.

My Lofoten: I visited Lofoten Folkehøyskole nine years ago for the first time. I thought the place had so much to offer me, both the climbing (rock and alpine) and the environment, that I decided to move here.

My climbs: *Vestpillaren* on Presten is my favourite route. It is easy to get to, has fantastic climbing and is in a beautiful setting - I never get bored with it. One summer I climbed it twelve times!
Other favourites are *Storpillaren*, *Bare blåbær* and *Gelbe kante* at Paradiset. I think the best peaks on Lofoten are Higraftind and Rulten. My favourite first ascent was *Cyclotronen* on Vestre Rulten.

My story: The day before we were going to climb *Cyclotronen*, we had a discussion about the first pitch. Bjørn Kirkehaug and I though it would be steep ice, but Arild Meyer was quite sure it was only a small snow plod. "*Hardly needs crampons*", he said. The next day we were under the first pitch. We had ice climbing gear, and Arild, had his old Chounard Zero with its bamboo shaft. It was 60m of steep ice and slightly overhanging at the start. We turned back. There was also considerable avalanche danger, so we did not blame it all on the Zero. Next time around we succeeded, Arild now with his proper ice climbing gear.

The southwest face of Geitgaljen in the Trolltindan. Photo: Heike I Vester - Ocean Sounds

The West

Henningsvær

Kalle

Kabelvåg

Svolvær

Trolltindan

Walking Peaks

Bouldering

The West

Henningsvær

Kalle

Kabelvåg

Svolvær

Trolltindan

Walking Peaks

Bouldering

The West · Henningsvær · Kalle · Kabelvåg · Svolvær · Trolltindan · Walking Peaks · Bouldering

The West

Henningsvær

Kalle

Kåbelvåg

Svolvær

Trolltindan

Walking Peaks

Bouldering

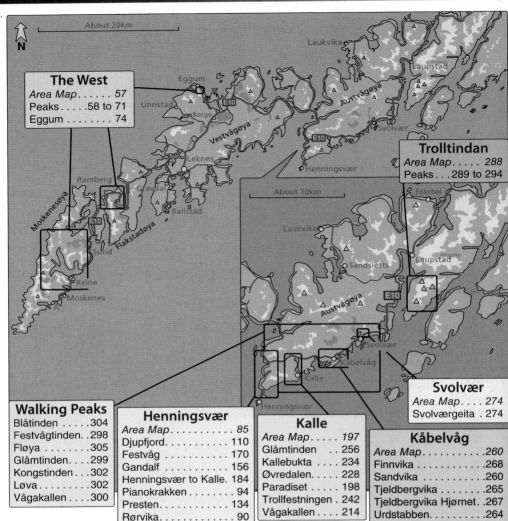

The West

Trolltindan

Svolvær

Walking Peaks

Henningsvær

Kalle

Kåbelvåg

Mountain Rescue
Dial 112